BACK IN THE SADDLE

BACK IN THE SADDLE

*Essays on Western Film
and Television Actors*

edited by
GARY A. YOGGY

FOREWORD BY
James Drury

INTRODUCTION BY
Archie P. McDonald

McFarland & Company, Inc., Publishers
Jefferson, North Carolina, and London

To the memory of my parents,
Albert and Ernestine Yoggy,
who first introduced me to the Western

British Library Cataloguing-in-Publication data are available

Library of Congress Cataloguing-in-Publication Data

Back in the saddle : essays on Western film and television actors /
  edited by Gary A. Yoggy ; foreword by James Drury ;
  introduction by Archie P. McDonald.
      p.   cm.
    Includes index.
    ISBN 0-7864-0566-X (sewn softcover : 50# alkaline paper) ∞
    1. Western films—History and criticism.   2. Motion picture
  actors and actresses—United States—Biography.   3. Westerns
  (Television programs)—History and criticism.   4. Television
  actors and actresses—United States—Biography.   I. Yoggy,
  Gary A.
  PN1995.9.W4B23   1998
  791.43'6278—dc21   98-22474
                                                              CIP

Manufactured in the United States of America

*McFarland & Company, Inc., Publishers
  Box 611, Jefferson, North Carolina 28640*

PREFACE

by Gary A. Yoggy

The Western, along with jazz, the musical comedy and the detective story, has been rightly classified as an indigenous American art form. Of these, the Western is the most deeply rooted in the mythology of American culture. It finds a basis in familiar folk tales and morality plays. Widely popular among all classes, the Western has helped to define and reflect the character and standards of the American people, as well as their hopes and fears.

The Western film in its many variations—silent, "B," adult, traditional, revisionist—presents the essential literary Western adapted for a performance medium thus enhancing the meaning and significance of the genre. Whether viewed in black and white or Technicolor, in a theatrical setting or on the home screen, the film Western portrays the evolution of the culture and character of the American people.

This book provides both an examination and celebration of many of the individuals who have contributed to the artistic success of that art form. Actors and actresses, stars as well as bit players, those whose fame came on the silver screen and some whose careers were built primarily on the television tube are featured here, selected in a process explained by Archie McDonald in the Introduction.

My involvement as editor came late in the development of this work, after Archie felt he could no longer commit the time necessary to complete the project. Much credit is due him for the countless hours he spent in recruiting the initial contributors, editing their final essays and selecting a publisher. Archie's original Introduction is included for its warm personal touches and insightful background information. It greatly enhances our anthology.

Archie and I would both like to express our gratitude to the excellent team of writers whose hard work has made this volume possible: Lane Roth and Tom W. Hoffer, William E. Tydeman III, R. Philip Loy, Gary Kramer, Raymond E. White, Michael K. Schoenecke, Sandy Schackel, Jacqueline K. Greb, Jim Collins and Richard Robertson.

We are all appreciative of the contribution of James Drury, star of television's *The Virginian* and a prominent movie actor. Mr. Drury's foreword offers a first person perspective of movie making, particularly of Westerns, that none of the writers or the editor can match. He was a participant while we were spectators.

I would like to thank my wife, Anna Jean, for keeping me inspired, focused and financially solvent!

I hope readers will find in these pages a continued fascination for that uniquely American art form, the Western.

CONTENTS

FOREWORD

by James Drury

In the old West if you wanted to get an idea of the lay of the land you headed your horse for higher ground. I suppose that when I was asked to write this foreword to *Back in the Saddle*, it was felt that I might have such a perspective. Having just read, with great enjoyment, Archie McDonald's *Shooting Stars*, and having seen a list of the authors and chapters for this new book, I can't wait to read it. Every chapter in the first book offered information and insight into the life and career of its subject that was brand-new to me and, I am sure, to the majority of the readers. *Back in the Saddle* should do the same.

James Drury

It will evoke a feeling of closeness and understanding with these men and women, each one of whom can bring forth in our minds, especially if we close our eyes lightly, memories as fresh and clear as the water from a mountain spring. Memories of great moments in time, relationships, heartbreak and anger and passion that we, as members of the audience, are sure we have lived through ourselves.

All the people who are pictured for us in both books had the ability to make us believe, not just at the moment we first saw their images flow across a motion picture screen, but for all our lives long, that we were there, we were in the saddle, we held the smoking Colt .45 in our hand or the girl in our arms, that the barbed wire was cutting into our flesh. That as Steve McQueen and Yul Brynner said in *The Magnificent Seven* "we have *no* enemies ... *alive!*"

As you look at the title of each chapter in *Back in the Saddle*, do yourself a favor: stop a moment, lean back, close your eyes and let Tom Mix, Steve McQueen, or Barbara Stanwyck and the rest gallop across your mind. Then do a *slow* zoom into an extreme close-up and as you do, watch their face change into yours and their passion spring from your heart.

Of course, this ability to implant themselves into our consciousness is not limited to actors and actresses who work in Western films, it is evident in the great performances we remember on the silver screen in all types of films from all periods of history.

It is part of the magic of film that while we can all remember great performances or parts of performances we have seen in the theatre, only film can put us, the viewer, into the picture.

I have been acting or trying to act, since the age of eight, and in all these years I have seen many magnificent performances on the stage. They are great and lasting memories for me but they are faded at the edges and in any case I was watching someone else perform a role I might someday play myself.

The great screen roles are seldom repeated, *The Virginian* being one notable exception, and if they are, a generation or more will pass between performances.

It is often said that film is a director's medium or an editor's medium and indeed it is, in that both professions have great control over the finished product. In my view, however, film is first, last, and always, an actor's medium. It is the place where the actor gets a chance to achieve that which is forever denied mortal man; immortality. The immortality only comes, however, for those actors who, like the subjects of the chapters in this book, make us believe them.

Spencer Tracy is supposed to have said in an interview that "Acting is a great profession if you don't get caught at it." Every time you, as a member of the audience, see something in a performance that somehow does not ring true, you have just seen someone get caught acting. It is an awful moment for the viewer. And, believe me, it is an awful moment for the actor or actress. Because they know, usually right away, but sooner or later, they know. There hasn't been an actor born yet who hasn't been caught at it and it gives us all nightmares.

Harley Granville Barker, the great British stage director and the man who originally staged many of the plays of George Bernard Shaw, wrote in *The Exemplary Theatre* that "acting is the creation of the illusion of reality." I've never seen a better definition. Actors and actresses use all their skills, which include everything they are and everything they know, to create this illusion. Of course, there are as many variations of this "reality" as screenwriters and playwrights can devise and a myriad of different approaches taken by the director and the actors and actresses in their creation.

Motion pictures as we know them are just a few years over one hundred years old. Most historians agree that the birth of world cinema took place in Paris, France, on December 28, 1895. Eight years later in 1903 the world saw the first close-up shot in a film. It was a six-gun fired at the audience at very close range in *The Great Train Robbery*, a Western. Since then, hundreds and hundreds of Western films have been shot in Hollywood and on location all over the world.

American filmmakers took to the genre naturally because the history of the West as they saw it was anybody's guess. They were free to invent it and re-invent it as they saw fit. Cinematically the backgrounds were and are, some of the most beautiful ever photographed and a screenwriter could let his imagination flow freely in constructing the conflict, the tension, and the subsequent drama that we all wanted to live again and again.

The Western film and the Western novel became the only truly American folklore. Since that brave beginning in 1895, at which admission was charged, motion pictures have been an "industry." At least, that is how its professionals have always thought of it. Live theater is looked at as more of an art form. Yet, more artistry and beauty have been seen on film than the stage has ever reached. Into this framework and against these backgrounds have come thousands of actors and actresses with all degrees of enthusiasm, willingness, and despair and every other emotion in between. Some have been superbly trained artists from the live stage, some have never seen a horse before, and some fall in between. Those who were able to put us in their places, make up believe that we were there, they are the people in *Shooting Stars* and *Back in the Saddle*.

Much has been said about the demise of the Western, but we must remember it is the most imitated form of motion picture in history. The Italians, the Japanese, the Germans, the South Americans, and for all we know, the Norwegians have made hundreds of Western films in their native languages that are never shown outside their own countries.

Shakespeare said almost four hundred years ago that we "Must hold the mirror up to nature," and I believe that that is why the Western is very much alive.

The concepts of the triumph of good over evil, man over nature, and order over chaos are deeply embedded in films that are made and released every year.

These contemporary films may not have a horse in sight but the idea that we can take control of our own lives and solve our problems is one that has always appealed to filmgoers and always will.

Television became saturated with Westerns in the 1950s and 1960s and when *Gunsmoke* left the air in 1975, everyone thought we would never see another one. *Lonesome Dove* had absolutely nothing in its story that we haven't all seen before in countless Westerns, but the way the story was written earned it the Pulitzer Prize. It also became one of the most popular mini-series in the history of television.

The amazing thing was that everyone loved it. Men and women, young and old. The emotions were real, the story touched our hearts, and the actors made us believe that we were there.

As for me, I search every day for a script that will give me goosebumps when I read it, because it may then give me goosebumps when I play it and then maybe, just maybe, give you goosebumps when you see it. It may be a Western but the chances are it will be a contemporary film that contains those elements the Western is responsible for defining.

The triumph of good over evil and the triumph of the human spirit create the feeling Joel McCrea told Randolph Scott he was looking for in *Ride the High Country* when he said "I want to enter my house justified." By showing us simple moments of human satisfaction like that the Western has had, in my view, more influence over American, and thus world, morality, beliefs, and behavior in this century than any other form of film.

It lives on.

INTRODUCTION

by Archie P. McDonald

"Back in the Saddle," the abbreviated title and opening line of Gene Autry's theme song, is borrowed with respect and affection to apply to this tribute and examination of Western actors. Seven of the essayists whose work is presented here participated in an earlier project titled *Shooting Stars: Heroes and Heroines of Western Film*, published in 1987 by Indiana University Press. They are joined in this collection by five other writers, plus James Drury, a star of television and movies.

"Back by popular demand," that old Hollywood boast, would be a wonderful tribute, and in a way it is true. Our first effort received reviews in approximately fifty newspapers, journals, newsletters, and annual publications that ranged from the Audie Murphy Fan Club Newsletter to *Zweihundert Jahre amerikanische Verfassung*, published in Heidelberg. Most accepted our offering for what we claimed it to be—a "tribute, study, and celebration of the ... heroes and heroines of the silver screen"—and a few even said some complimentary things for all to see. The one question pervasively raised, called a "quibble" by more than one, concerned actors *not* included. For example, why include Ken Maynard but not Tom Mix or Buck Jones? Why Gene Autry, but not Roy Rogers? There are two answers. One is that we did not have unlimited space, and the potential cast was too vast for a single volume; the other is that Ray Merlock wanted to write on Autry, not Rogers, and Ray White wanted to write on Maynard, not Mix or Jones. Surely, all of them qualified, and their exclusion reflected no intended slight.

But that is one of the justifications for the present book. We hope to fill in some of the inevitable gaps by providing essays on Western film actors not covered in our previous effort. As Abe Hoffman wrote in *The Californian*, "The reader comes away from [*Shooting Stars*] with two impressions: the astonishing variety of Western films and how easy it would be to create a second volume profiling those actors omitted from this one." Hoffman continued with a list of nominees, and three of the five appear in this book.

An equally important goal is to offer to Western movie buffs, including those who employ film in classrooms, a biographical profile and film analysis for persons and topics covered. Although there is no essay on John Wayne in this volume, his life and career offer an excellent example of how this can be done. In teaching a class entitled The Western Hero, I used many of Wayne's films to reinforce lectures. For example, *Stagecoach* (1939) offers an opportunity to examine both transportation and professions (career education) in the West. Consider how many professions were represented by the characters in this story: law enforcement, medicine, teamster, salesman, army officer, banker, gambler—and outlaw and saloon girl. The film prompted a lecture not just about stagecoaches, but one that discussed the development of the railroad, steamboats, wagons, and even the telegraph—remember that it was cut telegraph lines that revealed that the banker in *Stagecoach* was a thief. Similar use can be made of the films of most of the actors profiled in this book.

Such practical use of the study of Western film may be fortunate, but it is not the primary purpose of this book. The writer is of an older generation than most of the contributors and my fascination with Western film has less of an academic content, despite what the preceding paragraph might imply, than an interest in the values of these actors and their films and in the times in which most of them were produced. My introduction to them came in the 1940s when I attended a show each Saturday morning at the Jefferson Theatre in Beaumont, Texas. It was called the Organ Club because the Jefferson was one of those old vaudeville houses that had converted to showing films and it had a magnificent organ in the orchestra pit. Each Saturday a man named Al Sacker played that organ in accompaniment for teen-age (and younger) contestants in an amateur show. We were treated to cartoons, serials, short subjects, and previews seemingly without end, and finally to a feature film, invariably a Western.

Several things happened while the show was on the screen. The older kids "courted" (in the reserved language of the time), much popcorn and candy was consumed, and quite without being aware of it, we learned most of what many of us would ever know about the West. Of course most of it bore little resemblance to real history, for it reflected what Hollywood filmmakers knew of the West, or thought they knew of it, but it taught us just the same. Some of us survived that experience, and later attended colleges where we learned the facts. Our education came with a price: we forfeited a great deal of the romance of the West, our unquestioned patriotism, and our confidence that right made might. We were introduced to a world where in fact it was the other way around, a real world in which prejudice, confused national purpose, and the power of the mighty—whether right or "wrong"—usually prevailed. Of course it had to be that way, for we could not remain forever in the comfortable cocoon of the Organ Club, or whatever similar groups were called elsewhere.

Now, several decades later, it is fun—unvarnished fun—to view again those bravely innocent films, and see again the youthful figures, all now aged or deceased, who acted in them. They played their part in the development in the genre of the Western, which began as early as there was a West. John Smith began the theme with his exaggerated personal testimony of the colonization of Virginia. It continued in made-up heroes who glorified the work of the cowboy or the lumberjack. *The Virginian*, by Owen Wister, continued to celebrate the theme in literature, and it reached into the mass media of the twentieth century through the force of film, radio, and television.

Other than print, film did more than any other medium to give Westerns permanence. G. M. Anderson, better known as "Broncho Billy," was the first Western film hero, but he was followed by many more, including those profiled in this collection. I cannot explain why Westerns are no longer made, except to say that television glutted the market, or that they are expensive, or perhaps that the explicit sex and bad language so common in modern film is inappropriate to the Western. These are some of the suggestions made by Jim Collins in his essay in this book. He may be correct, and there may be other reasons. When I reflect on films I viewed during my youth, Westerns stand out both because they were abundant and because they made impressions of values that only a few seem to think are still valid. In an interview published in *Playboy*, John Wayne condemned the trend toward explicitness in films made in the 1970s, stating that such blatant realism was not for him; he preferred the romance of earlier films, and I think he said in his unequivocal fashion that romance and illusion were what had made them commercially, financially, and socially successful.

This is not to say that all films or even all Westerns must be static or sterile. The medium is too vital for that, and besides, the times do change. But I agree with former President Ronald Reagan's statement on a visit to Japan that citizens of that country should buy an American motion picture production company because *somebody* had to teach Americans how to make good, moral movies again. Still I don't feel like condemning modern movies. What I hope this book accomplishes is to remind those who read it that once there was a film genre that entertained and instilled values that can yet have meaning, and that provided role models and examples of courage, independence, love of country, and caring for others. Not all Westerns did that well, of course, and it can be done in other forms of film; sometimes Westerns did it, if at all, by showing just how mean or low down humanity can be. And towards the end of their heyday Westerns portrayed violence just for the sake of showing violence. True, the West could be a place of sudden danger, even death, as modern life has become because of poverty and the disease of substance abuse, among other causes. Perhaps we see so much real violence now that we long for the narcotic of the television situation comedy that puts our minds in idle, or the "message" movie that carries us away from the real problems we must face. Westerns used to do that, and perhaps did it better, for they rarely called upon us to judge our country, as do the recent films on Vietnam. There is also a place for those kinds of films; they serve a purpose that it is difficult to imagine a Western even attempting.

To explain the organization of this collection, the team of writers whose work is published in this book wrote independently. Writers were asked to *analyze* the body of the work of the individual on whom they wrote in the light of the times in which their actors worked and to evaluate them against their peers. Most simply could not suppress a degree of hero worship. Please also bear in mind that the writers selected actors whom they admired, and they have said so and why; that they have presented the biographical material as they have been able to learn it despite the efforts of some of the subjects to keep their private lives private; that they have analyzed film and television appearances, viewing many hours of both, mostly for enjoyment but calling it research; and that some have even looked for threads and meaning in the Western that provide a social statement for their times.

There will still be some who wonder why there is no essay on Henry Fonda or Kirk Douglas, and the answer is that no one could be found who wanted to write on these fine actors. We have attempted to tell the story of the actors who are included in a way that will inform, perhaps amuse, and with luck, remind those who examine these pages of the films and actors who taught them so much about the American West. Some of what we learned there was inaccurate, but we have historians who can straighten out the curves. These men and women entertained us.

We are pleased to have James Drury, star of the television series *The Virginian*, provide a foreword for this second volume of essays on Western actors. Mr. Drury has seen the varmint, as the old Westerners used to say, from the other side of the camera and he brings us a perspective none of the academics and film buffs could provide. Lane Roth and Tom W. Hoffer contributed the essay on "Broncho Billy" Anderson, and give us an insight into the birth of Western film through their story of this first Western film hero. William E. Tydeman III takes care of some of our omissions from *Shooting Stars* with his article on Tom Mix, as does R. Philip Loy with one on Buck Jones; both actors were significant in the development of the Western. Gary Kramer's essay on Tex Ritter reminds us that actors can be educated and demonstrates that they can be successful in several fields. Raymond E. White has written about the career of Leonard Slye, known to us more familiarly as Roy Rogers, king of the cowboys. Michael K. Schoenecke's essay reminds us of the many films we have enjoyed starring James Stewart. Sandra Schackel provides a story of a strong woman, Barbara Stanwyck, who held her own in what was essentially a male-dominated art form. Jacqueline K. Greb traces the treatment of Indians in film and laments the lack of using real Native Americans to portray themselves, and Jim Collins reminds us of all those familiar faces without names that made these films work. Richard Robertson examines the troubled life of Steve McQueen. And finally, Gary A. Yoggy concludes the volume with an essay on the quintessential television Westerner, James Arness. Each has reviewed the films and television episodes and provides us with a fresh and entertaining look at their subjects. We have not attempted to provide a complete history of Westerns. That has been done. Instead, we have concentrated on actors in Westerns, hoping to entertain as much as to inform.

The Westerns we mostly watch now are broadcast on independent television stations that fill Saturday formats with syndicated reruns of shows made two or three decades ago. Occasionally a late movie revives a classic, and God bless Ted Turner and other movie-channel proprietors who resurrect the oldies for us, although usually at times we already should have been asleep. Those of us who burn the candle for the old-time Western are happy to have the old Hell Box to remind us how James Arness looked in 1955, or to see life again in the image of John Wayne and Tex Ritter. With them, we are back in the saddle again.

G. M. "Broncho Billy" Anderson: The First Movie Cowboy Hero

by Lane Roth and Tom W. Hoffer

The durable Western genre, according to André Bazin, is "the American film par excellence...."[1] The distinct segments in the evolution of this genre were (1) the early identifiable screen personalities, and (2) the industrial mechanisms which made the proliferation of the Western film possible. This study is about the earliest screen "hero," G. M. "Broncho Billy" Anderson, his first Western series, and the fundamental traditions of the genre as these were popularized by the fledgling film medium. Anderson's contributions in the manufacture of a steady flow of product to theatres and his influence on Charlie Chaplin's early career are also explored.

Anderson as Hero

Western subjects like cowboys, Indians, and cattle roundups had proved their popularity in vignettes and reconstructions as early as the days of Kinetoscope and Mutoscope peep shows. The Edison Company's *The Great Train Robbery* (1903), depicting a train holdup, a chase on horseback and shootout, demonstrated to film producers the box office success of the narrative film and especially outdoor adventure stories.[2] The Edison Company's *Race for Millions* (1906) featured an early screen contest between an automobile and a train (the train won), and a climactic gun duel on a painted street set. Here was the confrontation between individuals representing the Manichaean forces of good and evil.

But, as William K. Everson observed,[3] the key ingredients for success of the Western were still missing. The films of the time suffered from inadequacies in length, location shooting, acting and physical action. Until 1907

This essay originally appeared in Journal of Film and Video *30, 1 (Winter, 1978), 5–13, and is here reprinted with permission.*

Westerns ran about one reel (ten to twelve minutes) and had little storyline or character development. Location shooting took place in the environs of the film studios which were located in New York, Philadelphia, and Chicago. Horsemanship and fisticuffs were restrained and acting was unrealistic. And there was as yet no identifiable hero on whom to focus.

In 1908, G. M. Anderson filmed a two-reel outdoor Western called *The Bandit Makes Good*, based on a story by Peter Kyne titled *Broncho Billy and the Baby*. *The Bandit Makes Good* was a story about a sheriff who captures a bank robber (Broncho Billy) but subsequently loses the retrieved bank money while gambling. Broncho Billy manages to hold up the gamblers and return the money to the sheriff, thus earning himself a pardon and an appointment as deputy. The *New York Times* reported that "the fan response was so great that Mr. Anderson started a series around the Robin Hood type of bandit."[4]

Anderson frequently used the name Broncho Billy in the film titles and continued to play the lead himself. Between the years 1908 and 1915 Anderson created over 375 Broncho Billy one- and two-reelers of which he was producer, director and star. George Fenin and William K. Everson acclaimed these films as "the first real 'series' Westerns, the first with an established star, and the films that really established Westerns as a genre."[5]

As Broncho Billy, Anderson established many traditions of the Western. Although he admitted he never really perfected his horsemanship or marksmanship, he recognized the appeals of the horse and the gun in the Western and exploited these motifs. In *Broncho Billy and the Greaser* (1914), he bid adieu to a woman by waving to her while he rode his horse seated backwards. While not adept himself at faster-paced scenes in the saddle, he realized the appeal of outdoor action and became one of the first Western stars to regularly employ a stunt man as a "double." He became adroit at rope-twirling and introduced this rodeo motif to film. Frank Manchel described Broncho Billy's Western wardrobe: "Broncho Billy's costume was almost always the same: a big Stetson hat, a dark wide-open shirt with a large white bandana, wide gloves, fancy corduroy chaps and boots, and two guns."[6] Frederick Elkin wrote, "Most of the Western heroes, following the old movie tradition, are serious, manly, rugged, grim, and have no romantic inclinations."[7]

This movie tradition started with Broncho Billy Anderson. Everson provided one perception of Broncho Billy as hero:

> A man who was rugged and a law unto himself, but also possessed the nobility and courage of the Arthurian knights.... His bulky frame, paw-like hands and rough-hewn face ... his clumsiness and lack of self-confidence in dealing with the ladies. The sheepish grin and the awkward fumbling with his hat when confronted by the heroine—a standard bit of business for every cowboy from Ken Maynard to John Wayne—was born in the Broncho Billy Westerns.[8]

Broncho Billy Anderson, the screen's first cowboy hero, in an early publicity photograph.

Anderson emphasized action in his films: "We never played our pictures for the physical. We played them for laughs or action."[9] But there seemed to be a particular and profound sense of ethics that permeated the hundreds of Broncho Billy films. The psychological appeal of the Hollywood Western, maintained Elkin, was that:

> The moral values are those of our Christian society. In the conflict of Good and Evil, the Good is invariably held up as right. On the side of Good are honesty, loyalty, sympathy for the oppressed, respect for just law, and, if it is occasioned in the story, love of children and respect for religion.[10]

As Fenin and Everson[11] and Joe Franklin[12] emphasized, Broncho Billy Anderson was the very first Western hero to create this precedent. Manchel defined his individualism and strong moral fiber: "Anderson presented the dramatic image of the heroic Westerner—a strong individualist who lived by his own laws, a tough man with saintly virtues."[13]

According to Bazin, "Those formal attributes by which one normally recognizes the western are simply signs or symbols of its profound reality, namely the myth."[14] Orrin E. Klapp outlined different types of mythical and legendary heroes from various cultures. One type, typified by the conquering hero, the clever hero, and the unpromising hero, emphasized individual success. The other type centered "about the idea of benefit or service to a group ... the act performed by the hero is of benefit to someone besides himself, involving even personal sacrifice or martyrdom."[15]

The Broncho Billy hero would appear to be typical of the second category. As the righter of wrongs and defender of justice and the weak, he benefited not himself but the community. Rescuing the damsel in distress availed Billy neither material gain nor feminine companionship, as he usually rode off as he came, alone. In addition to the role of Defender, Broncho Billy seemed to have been what Klapp calls the Benefactor, or kind-hearted hero. According to Edward Wagenknecht,

> Anderson was probably most popular in the films which exemplified the spirit of renunciation, like *Broncho Billy's Christmas Spirit*, where he sacrificed his horse for a destitute family. Frequently he gave up a girl, and then we might see him gazing in upon her happiness with his rival from the wrong side of a lighted window and trudging out into the night with his traps as sadly as Chaplin ever walked down the lonesome road.[16]

These references to Broncho Billy's saintly virtues, bravery, celibacy, renunciation and sacrifice conform to the Christian ideals of the hero. Moreover the tension inherent in the duality of the Christian cosmos, the vision of the material world as a battleground for the forces of good versus evil in continual combat for the possession of man's soul, is reflected in the "Broncho

Billy" Westerns. Broncho Billy was the embodiment of the dilemma of the antinomic pair: good vs. evil:

> [At first] Broncho Billy could be seen as a lawman one week and a die-hard villain the next…. But before long, this inconsistency came to Anderson's attention and his response was a combination of the two, pioneering the "good/bad man," which later proved to be Bill Hart's springboard to success.[17]

G. M. Anderson's establishing of the traditional Western genre can therefore be seen as a significant contribution not only to cinema but to modern mythology as well since the Western hero is the personification of many American as well as Christian ideals.

Anderson as Commercial Artist

Accidental beginning. The man who at once created and became the archetypal screen cowboy was a real dude named Max Aronson. His birthplace—Little Rock, Arkansas in 1882—was a few miles west of the Mississippi River, which could technically qualify him as a Westerner; the young Max, however, spent his childhood in the South and never learned to ride a horse or shoot a handgun. As a young man he worked as a travelling salesman and then moved to New York where he unsuccessfully tried vaudeville under the name Gilbert M. Aronson. Meanwhile he supported himself by modeling for illustrators, among them Howard Chandler Christy, and this led to his first association with the West: posing as a cowboy for a cover of the *Saturday Evening Post*.

His movie career began by accident.[18] Ezra Goodman recounted:

> One day, in 1902, he wandered into the Edison studio on Twenty-third Street to apply for a movie job—stage thespians shunned the "flickers" then—and was immediately hired by Edwin S. Porter as a leading man at fifty cents an hour. Anderson's first opus was entitled *The Messenger Boy's Mistake*. It dealt with a young fellow who quarreled with his sweetheart and attempted to mollify her with flowers and an enclosed card: "If you forgive me, wear these next time I call." The messenger delivered a pair of pajamas by mistake and when the swain arrived to call on his girl, her brothers gave him a sound drubbing.[19]

Aronson next appeared in Edwin S. Porter's *The Great Train Robbery* (1903). Joe Franklin explained:

> He got the job by claiming to be an expert horseman, but after mounting the horse from the wrong side, and later being thrown off, his deception was quite apparent and he was shifted to on-foot activity for the rest of the one-reel epic.[20]

A poster for one of Broncho Billy's Westerns.

G. M. Aronson played three roles in Porter's *The Great Train Robbery*: one of the bandits, one of the passengers who was held up and then shot in the back, and a brakeman. Since these scenes were all photographed in long shot, his triple role-playing was not noticeable.[21]

Six months later Aronson changed his name again to Gilbert M. Anderson. Anderson then left the Edison Company to work as a production assistant for a chief competitor, the Vitagraph Company. There he quickly worked his way up to $25 per week directing and acting in one-reelers. In 1905 he directed his first box office hit, *Raffles, the Amateur Cracksman*.

Essanay. The next year he began to work for the Selig Polyscope Company in Chicago, a competitor to Vitagraph and Edison. By 1907, according to Kalton C. Lahue, he took a Selig unit to Colorado to make a number of Westerns—films that both audiences and Selig failed to appreciate.[22] As a result, Anderson left Selig to establish a new motion picture company with George K. Spoor,

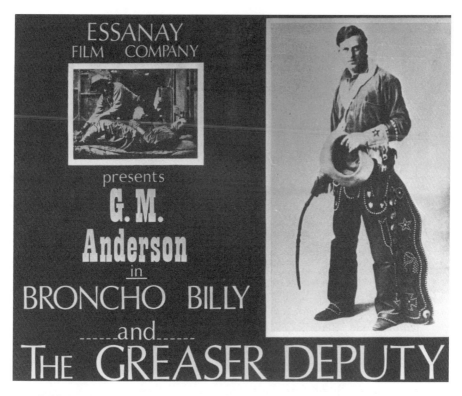

G. M. Anderson in a typical outfit and pose for a Broncho Billy poster.

then an exchange man, with film exchanges throughout Chicago, where his famous "Magniscope," a forerunner of the present-day Motion Picture cameras, was netting him a fortune. Mr. Anderson persuaded Mr. Spoor to enter the producing end of the business and volunteered to do the work if Mr. Spoor would furnish the money.[23]

Their new company, located in Chicago was called Essanay, an acronym for their surname initials "S" and "A." The Essanay trademark was an Indian head similar to that on a U.S. penny. In 1908, Anderson established another Essanay studio in Niles, California, when he also made *The Bandit Makes Good*. Considering his abortive attempt at playing a cowboy on horseback five years earlier, Anderson did not intend to act in this film, let alone star in a series of them. But, according to Lahue,

unable to find an actor in the wilds of central California who was willing to risk his professional career in such a venture, the desperate producer had no choice but to undertake the chore himself. And so G. M. Anderson became producer, director and actor.[24]

Early formula. Anderson successfully formularized the business aspects of the first Western series. According to Goodman[25] and *The New York Times*,[26] each Broncho Billy film was budgeted at eight hundred dollars and grossed as much as fifty thousand dollars. "Shooting from a skimpy script,"[27] Anderson churned out one Broncho Billy film a week. A 1909 article in *Moving Picture World*[28] described how Anderson shot a nineteen-scene movie on location to Colorado in only one day. Production costs were minimized by using natural lighting, allowing only a few minutes for actors' make-up, improvisations on dialog, and minimal, if any, rehearsal. The emphasis was on speed. The article commented on "Anderson's Gatling gun directions" and the shooting of "scene after scene without halt."

Anderson sometimes photographed his interior shots in the Chicago Essanay studio but used scenic locations in various places like Colorado, Las Vegas, Catalina Island, the Rockies, and California.

He maintained a low overhead in terms of talent and production costs not only by using himself as the main character but also with a small crew and more or less permanent cast. These included cameramen Jesse J. Robbins and Roland "Rollie" Totheroh, and actors Jack O'Brien (villain), Arthur Smith (character roles), and W. K. Russell, who was "property man and assistant hero and villain."[29]

Yet the Broncho Billy films, according to Lahue, had "solid production values," "elaborate and realistic" Western sets, and "were characterized by sharp photography and the excellent camera work."[30] Although "the dialogue subtitles [were] often overdone, in the manner of western pulp fiction,"[31] the authentic outdoor Western settings gave the series a unique appeal. In 1916, Ivan Gaddis wrote:

> It was due to "Broncho Billy" more than any one else that the ridiculous "stage cowboy" vanished from the screen and in its stead appeared the typical "puncher" of the plains. He was the first actor to pose his plays in the West itself, where real mountains and sagebrush lent the proper atmosphere instead of the canvas mountains and other artificial Western scenes enacted in Eastern studios.[32]

The prolific production rate of one or two reels each week mitigated against community and consistency of characterization.

> When you have to think up a story a week, it does not pay to be fussy about consistency, and Broncho Billy's admirers could never be quite sure which side of the law he was going to be on. In *Broncho Billy Reforms* (1913) he was an outlaw who refused to join his fellows in robbing a store kept by the local schoolteacher, and in *Why Broncho Billy Left Bear County* he not only reformed but got religion. In *Broncho Billy's Scheme* he was a medical man, but in *Broncho Billy's Mother* he was a "booze fighter" who shot up the town.... In *Broncho Billy's Conscience* he was even killed....[33]

Of course Broncho Billy was "revived" without explanation to appear in another story the very next week. It was the character, not the story, that unified the series of films.

Audience. And the character was popular. When G. M. Anderson visited New York City in late 1911, *Variety* stated "he started almost as great a riot on the streets and in the restaurants as [he] does in the movie pictures he is the leading figure of."[34] Wagenknecht recalled how Broncho Billy was loved by his contemporaries[35] and how he won fifth place in the first popularity contest conducted by *Motion Picture Story Magazine* in June 1912.[36] Manchel claims that Broncho Billy was "King of the Cowboys" from 1908 to 1915.[37]

Who comprised Broncho Billy's audiences? His popularity was at its height during the days when the primary exhibition outlet for motion pictures was the nickelodeon. With the later development of larger movie palaces and the concomitant demand for feature films, there was a sudden decline and termination of Anderson's career. While the exact composition of early film audiences will probably forever remain a mystery, Russell Merritt concluded that the audiences around 1912 expanded to include the "better educated workers."[38] Lahue attributes Broncho Billy's popularity to Anderson's being "correct in his estimation of the audiences."[39] Film historians have commented that Anderson did offer his movie-going public something special: the first identifiable screen cowboy hero. In 1912, *Variety* reported that "there are three famous picture actors, known to all who watch the sheets. Mr. Anderson is one," and that while he was in New York City, "men and women seemed to recognize his features immediately."[40] Key factors in Anderson's success were his lack of effective competition and his regular weekly bookings. In a sense he was saturating the market. Manchel noted: "No other cowboy character appeared so frequently at the local theatres."[41] The Broncho Billy films made Anderson a wealthy man.

Compared to his salary of fifty cents an hour at Edison a few years before, he was now earning an annual income of $125,000. He had discovered the formula for screen success: in his own words, "the maximum amount of entertainment for the minimum amount of price."[42]

The Chaplin Connection

Neither G. M. Anderson nor Essanay were involved exclusively with "Broncho Billy." Anderson acted in other vehicles[43] and Essanay produced a variety of films, including comedies.

> Calling itself "The House of Comedy Hits," Essanay, almost from its beginning in 1907, set the pace for popular comedies.... The Essanay product came to be known for its snappy, crisp action and good technical work.[44]

The first film Anderson made in California was a comedy short with cross-eyed ex-vaudevillian Ben Turpin.[45]

But Essanay's greatest comic was Charlie Chaplin. Through his representative Jesse Robbins, Anderson offered Chaplin a substantial salary increase and bonus if he would leave Sennett's Keystone studio. Chaplin accepted in 1915 and although the promised bonus was not promptly negotiated in full,[46] Anderson travelled to Los Angeles to personally escort his new acquisition to the main Essanay studio in Chicago, where Chaplin began working for $1250 a week, a considerable salary at that time. Essanay promptly publicized their new star:

> On January 23, 1915, Essanay announced in a display advertisement that they were "now offering exhibitors three of the greatest stars the photoplay world has ever seen—the 'A.B.C.' of drama and comedy—Mr. G. M. Anderson, Mr. Francis X. Bushman, and Mr. Charles Chaplin."[47]

Chaplin wrote, directed and starred in over a dozen one- and two-reelers for Essanay, all photographed by Roland H. Totheroh. Chaplin had left Chicago after *His New Job* to work in Niles, California, where Anderson made his Broncho Billy Westerns. Later Anderson rented a studio for Chaplin, at his request, in Los Angeles, Anderson and Chaplin each made a guest appearance in the other's film.[48]

Although Chaplin worked for Essanay for only about a year before moving to Mutual,[49] Essanay's publicity played an important role in popularizing Chaplin. Richard Schickel claimed that it was Essanay's "publicity blast that fixed Chaplin firmly in everyone's mind forever."[50]

Twilight of a Career

About the time that Chaplin left Essanay, Anderson's career coincidentally started to decline. Essanay was one of the founders in 1908 of the Motion Picture Patents Company that worked to bring stability and regulation to the motion picture industry by ending patent wars among its ten members.[51] This vertical consolidation represented a monopoly to various independent film exchanges (distributors) and exhibitors, who soon began lawsuits for alleged damages pursuant to the Sherman Anti-Trust Act. By 1913 the Motion Picture Patents Company and the General Film Company, which released Essanay's films, were found guilty of violations of the anti-trust law, and injunctions were obtained.[52] By 1916 Essanay's distributor could no longer compete with the independents.[53]

Meanwhile another major change occurring within the industry was the shift to feature films. The longer movies, five reels or more, were preferred because these enabled longer narratives in the larger theatres with greater seating capacity. Popular feature length Westerns appeared, such as *The Squawman* (1913) and *The Spoilers* (1914). Men who were soon to emerge as motion picture luminaries were attracted to the Western genre: D. W. Griffith, Thomas Ince, William S. Hart, Tom Mix, Cecil B. DeMille and John Ford. According to Lahue,

> [Anderson's partner] George K. Spoor opposed the investment necessary to produce features and G. M. Anderson was tired. Selling his half of Essanay, the actor-director-executive retired Broncho Billy to become an independent producer. Never again would he know the fame or financial security which Broncho Billy had brought.[54]

Anderson next abortively attempted a career as a Broadway theatre owner and producer,[55] and then returned to Westerns with some Broncho Billy shorts and features.[56] Joe Franklin summed up this phase of Anderson's career:

> Billy moved into feature Westerns too late, and as soon as he saw that he couldn't compete with Hart and Mix, he withdrew to concentrate on producing comedies again. He made a particularly fine series with Stan Laurel—which came to an end when Anderson, never too good a businessman, found that under his releasing arrangement with Louis B. Mayer, he couldn't make enough profit to make all the effort worthwhile....[57]

Not much is known about Anderson's activities after he retired in 1923. According to Ernest Corneau, "he had so completely drifted into obscurity that many people believed him to be dead"; but during the late 1940s, a renewed interest in the history of motion pictures caused a nationwide search for Anderson, leading to his "rediscovery" in 1948.[58] G. M. Anderson made his last screen appearance in a cameo role in Alex Gordon's 1965 release *The Bounty Hunters*. A Western film fan until the last, he died at the age of eighty-eight in the Motion Picture Country House rest home on January 20, 1971.

In 1957 the Motion Picture Academy of Arts and Sciences honored G. M. Anderson, "motion picture pioneer, for his contributions to the development of the motion pictures as entertainment."[59] Broncho Billy had left his brand on the movies as a medium of mass communication.

The authors gratefully acknowledge the assistance
of Gary Roth, who provided relevant data from
the Oral History Collection of Columbia University.

Notes

1. André Bazin, "The Western: Or the American Film Par Excellence," *What Is Cinema?*, II, trans. Hugh Gray (Berkeley: University of California Press, 1971), pp. 140–148.
2. The success of *The Great Train Robbery* was imitated by other filmmakers like

Sigmund Lubin, who replicated Edison's film practically shot for shot and released his version the next year (1904). Among the many copies of *The Great Train Robbery* was Edison's own spoof, *The Little Train Robbery*. Michael Parkinson and Clyde Jeavons noted that train robberies were still a fact of life in the first decade of the century, so the theme retained its popularity. See *A Pictorial History of Westerns* (London: Hamlyn, 1972), p. 12.

3. William K. Everson, *A Pictorial History of the Western Film* (New York: The Citadel Press, 1969), p. 16.

4. The *New York Times*, 21 January 1971, p. 38.

5. George N. Fenin and William K. Everson, *The Western: From Silents to the Seventies* (New York: Grossman Publishers, 1973), p. 54.

6. Frank Manchel, *Cameras West* (Englewood Cliffs, N.J.: Prentice-Hall, Inc., 1971), p. 9.

7. Frederick Elkin, "The Psychological Appeal of the Hollywood Western," *Journal of Educational Sociology* 24 (September 1950): 77.

8. Everson, pp. 18 and 20.

9. Quoted in Manchel, p. 10.

10. Elkin, p. 73.

11. Fenin and Everson, p. 53; Everson, p. 8.

12. Joe Franklin, *Classics of the Silent Screen* (New York: The Citadel Press, 1959), p. 120.

13. Manchel, pp. 9–10.

14. Bazin, p. 142.

15. Orrin E. Klapp, "The Folk Hero," *Journal of American Folklore* 62 (January–March 1949): 21.

16. Edward Wagenknecht, *The Movies in the Age of Innocence* (Norman, OK: The University of Oklahoma Press, 1962), pp. 50–51.

17. Kalton C. Lahue, *Winners of the West: The Sagebrush Heroes of the Silent Screen* (New York: A. S. Barnes and Company, 1970), p. 27. Hereafter cited as Lahue, *Winners*.

18. A conflicting account of Anderson's early screen career is reported in Ivan Gaddis, "The Origin of 'Broncho Billy,'" *Motion Picture Magazine* 11 (1916): 98–101. According to this version Anderson simultaneously broke into films and Westerns in Chicago appearing in *James Brothers*. Barney Pierson (Idaho Bill), of Hastings, Nebraska, "cowpuncher and promoter of Wild West shows," is here credited as "the man who discovered 'Broncho Billy'" and "who first gave him his lessons in horsemanship." The authenticity of this account is dubious for at least two reasons. First, the production company, director and Aronson's role in the film are not indicated. Second, the date of the production is given as "back in 1908 ... about the time the famous 'Great Train Robbery' film was enacted." Anderson could not have been working in West Orange, New Jersey, in *The Great Train Robbery* at the same time he was allegedly in Chicago making *James Brothers*. Moreover, by 1908 *The Great Train Robbery* was already five years old, Anderson had been in films for six years, and his Essanay Company was about a year old.

19. Ezra Goodman, *The Fifty-Year Decline and Fall of Hollywood* (New York: Simon and Schuster, 1961), pp. 341–342.

20. Franklin, p. 120. This is corroborated by Anderson's own account told to Columbia University's historians. See Interview with Mr. Gilbert M. ("Broncho Billy") Anderson (1959) in the Oral History Collection of Columbia University.

21. Anderson's multiple role playing in the film is cited in the *New York Times*, 21 January 1971, p. 38; and Goodman, p. 342.

22. Lahue, *Winners*, p. 25.

23. Roberta Courtlandt, "A Chat with G. M. Anderson ['Broncho Billy']," *Motion Picture Magazine* 8 (1915): 100–101; Fred J. Balshofer and Arthur C. Miller, *One Reel a Week* (Berkeley: University of California Press, 1967), p. 55.

24. Lahue, *Winners*, pp. 25–26.

25. Goodman, p. 343.

26. The *New York Times*, 21 January 1971, p. 38.

27. Manchel, p. 9.

28. *Moving Picture World* 5 (4 December 1909): 801–802. Reprinted in George C. Pratt, *Spellbound in Darkness: A History of the Silent Film* (Greenwich, CT: New York Graphic Society, 1973), pp. 127–130. Quotes from p. 129.

29. *Ibid.*, p. 127.

30. Lahue, *Winners*, p. 27.

31. Franklin, p. 120.

32. Ivan Gaddis, "The Origin of 'Broncho Billy,'" *Motion Picture Magazine* 11 (1916): 99.

33. Wagenknecht, p. 50.

34. "Broncho Billy a Riot," *Variety* 29 (3 January 1912): 6.

35. Wagenknecht, p. 50.

36. *Ibid.*, p. 62. The winners, in order, were: Maurice Costello, Delores Cassinelli, Mae Hotley, Francis X. Bushman and G. M. Anderson.

37. Manchel, p. 9.

38. Russell Merritt, "Nickelodeon Theaters: Building an Audience for the Movies," *AFI Report* 4 (May 1973): 7–8. See also: Garth S. Jowett, "The First Motion Picture Audiences," *Journal of Popular Film* 3 (Winter 1974): 39–54.

39. Lahue, *Winners*, p. 26.

40. "Broncho Billy a Riot," *Variety* 29 (3 January 1912): 6.

41. Manchel, p. 8.

42. Quoted in Goodman, p. 343.

43. Wagenknecht recalls Anderson's appearance as a prize fighter in *"Spike" Shannon's Last Fight* (1911), in a series of multiple reel "mystery players" (1914–1915), and in *The Good for Nothing* (1914), p. 49. According to a *Variety* review, in *The Good for Nothing*, Anderson plays a "bad boy of the family, a souse, gambler and finally ordered from home by his father, besides having his name erased from the partnership of his pop's brokerage concern." The libertine goes West where he saves an Indian stricken with smallpox from a lynching. Although Anderson summons a doctor at gunpoint, the Indian succumbs to the disease. Before dying, the Indian gives him a map of a gold claim. Anderson strikes it rich, returns home to rescue his parents from the poorhouse and reestablishes the family firm. This is not a Broncho Billy film, but it is thematically similar in that the West is the setting for a "bad guy's" reformation to "good guy." *See:* "The Good for Nothing," *Variety* 35 (12 June 1914): 21.

44. Kalton C. Lahue, *World of Laughter: The Motion Picture Comedy Short, 1910–1930* (Norman, OK: University of Oklahoma Press, 1966), p. 26.

45. The film was shot on location at Westlake Park, Los Angeles, and involved a simple gag with Turpin diving for a duck, only to have a real life policeman intercede and dive in after Turpin. Appropriately called *Ben Gets a Duck and Is Ducked*, the short was filmed by just three people: Turpin, Anderson and a cameraman.

46. According to Chaplin, Robbins offered him ten thousand dollars, but Anderson brought a check for only six hundred, promising that his partner Spoor would pay the difference when they arrived in Chicago. Apparently Anderson had acted completely on his own because Spoor, who did not know who Chaplin was, became frantic when he learned of the amount of money involved. Spoor balked and evaded Chaplin for a while until he became convinced of Chaplin's commercial value. *See:* Charles Chaplin, *My Autobiography* (New York: Simon and Schuster, 1964), pp. 160–161, 165–167. Fred J. Balshofer had offered Chaplin another contract but Anderson's offer was obviously better. *See:* Balshofer and Miller, p. 113.

47. Wagenknecht, p. 192.

48. Among Chaplin's films of the year 1915 was a two-reeler, *The Champion*, containing a "guest performance" by "Broncho Billy" Anderson, playing an enthusiastic ringside fan. Chaplin paid for Billy Anderson's contribution to *The Champion* by himself

appearing in a saloon sequence in *His Regeneration*. Chaplin is wearing his usual tramp outfit and the scene is a farce interpolated in the middle of a dramatic story about a thief's conversion. Totally unmotivated as an episode and brief though it is, it is funny and typical of Chaplin. As soon as he leaves the dance floor the main drama continues. Uno Asplund, *Chaplin's Films*, trans. Paul Britten Austin (Newton Abbot, Devon: David and Charles, Ltd., 1973), p. 164.

49. The image of Essanay that Chaplin provides in his *Autobiography* suggests a catchpenny company: "When I wanted to see my rushes, they ran the original negative to save the expense of a positive print. This horrified me. And when I demanded that they should make a positive print, they reacted as though I wanted to bankrupt them ... their last consideration was the making of good pictures," (p. 166). Chaplin says he preferred Anderson to his partner Spoor (p. 169), and that it was Spoor's failure to provide cash upfront that terminated negotiations for Chaplin's contract renewal with Essanay (p. 174).

50. Richard Schickel, *Movies: The History of an Art and an Institution* (New York: Basic Books, 1964), p. 66.

51. Essanay started as a competitor of Anderson's former employers, i.e., Edison, Vitagraph, and Selig. In the first decade of the twentieth century, the large companies and numerous smaller ones fought internecine business wars over ownership rights to patents and films. With the current copyright laws, there was much piracy, illegal duplication and subsequent litigation. The first attempt to stabilize and regulate the U.S. motion picture industry came from within the industry itself. The ten companies that comprised the Patents Company were: Biograph, Edison, Vitagraph, Essanay, Lubin, Selig, Kalem, Méliès, Kleine and Pathé. For a general discussion of this period, *see:* Gerald Mast, *A Short History of the Movies* (Indianapolis: Pegasus, Bobbs Merrill, 1971), pp. 57–58.

52. The *New York Times*, 22 January 1913, p. 9; 12 February 1913, p. 16; 24 December 1915, p. 7.

53. Lahue, *Winners*, p. 29.

54. *Ibid.*

55. With H. H. Frazee he bought the Longacre Theater on West 49th Street. He produced several plays but never became firmly established. The *New York Times*, 21 January 1971, p. 38.

56. Some Broncho Billy shorts were *Naked Hands* (1918) and *Shootin' Mad* (1919). One of the features was *The Son-of-a-Gun* (1919). These are some of the only surviving Broncho Billy films available for sale, through Blackhawk Films, Davenport, Iowa.

57. Franklin, p. 121.

58. Ernest N. Corneau, *The Hall of Fame of Western Film Stars* (North Quincy, MA: The Christopher Publishing House, 1969), p. 23.

59. Paul Michael, ed., *The American Movies* (New York: Garland Books, 1969), p. 361.

Tom Mix: King of the Hollywood Cowboys

by William E. Tydeman III

He rode into the 1920s, the age of broadcasting, with a manufactured past. His sense of style and personal flamboyance derived from the Wild West shows was the embodiment of the Jazz Age. He practically invented the cowboy culture of celebrity. Nearly sixty years after his death, the legend of Tom Mix, King of the Cowboys, lives on.

Tom Mix invented Tom Mix. One of the great stuntmen of Western films, Yakima Canutt, recalled Mix's storytelling ability:

> During the day a group of spectators came to the set to watch the filming. They circled around Tom and started asking him lots of questions.... That morning on the set, he entertained the crowd with several of the wild adventures he had had before entering motion pictures. He captured horse thieves and fought bands of outlaws single-handedly. To make some of his yarns a little more believable, he would turn to one of his cowboys and say "you remember, Tex, when the outlaw shot my horse out from under me."
>
> Tex, knowing who was buttering his bread, would answer with an awed, "Do I remember! Boy, that was a day I'll never forget."
>
> When the group left, I turned to Mix. "Tom, I said, you're a bit reckless with the truth, aren't you?"
>
> "What do you mean 'reckless'?" he retorted half-angrily. "They wanted to be entertained, so I took a few sequences from my pictures and turned them into reality." Then he calmed down a bit and added, "Look, Yak, when you're in show business, you've got to meet people and entertain them. As long as a lie don't hurt anyone, there's no harm done." Then he gave me his big winning smile. "They ate it up, didn't they?"[1] Storyteller, yarnspinner or "the goddamndest liar that ever lived."[2]

Tom Mix's life story was designed to resemble his movies.

The creation of the public Tom Mix began in 1910 with his first movie, *Ranch Life in the Southwest*, in which he was erroneously billed as a United States marshal. His publicity releases, right up to his death in 1940, contained a string of heroic adventures. According to various publicity accounts, Mix was born in El Paso, Texas, one-eighth Cherokee; his father was Captain Mix

Tom Mix with Tony, the Wonder Horse.

of the seventh cavalry; Tom was a sheriff, deputy United States marshal, and Texas Ranger; he attended Virginia Military Institute; he participated in the Spanish-American War; he saw provisional army service in the Philippines and in the Boxer Rebellion in China; he was in South Africa for the Boer War; and fought in the Mexican Revolution—all before 1910. Then Mix reached a point when his love of adventure waned and he decided to settle down. Later, his publicity releases put it this way: "He figured he had done his share of rough work in the settlement of the great southwest and he calculated (with considerable business acumen) that the public would be interested in seeing a real cowboy doing real stunts on the screen."[3] Tom Mix would transform himself from a hero adventurer into a heroic cowboy.

Mix's actual life contained just enough adventure to provide the basis for a self-created myth. He was born in Mix Run, Pennsylvania, in 1880. At the age of ten, he had a near conversion experience when Buffalo Bill's Wild West Show came to town. His interest in the West and extravagant spectacle began then. By the time the Spanish-American War began, he had used his exceptional athletic skills to master horseback riding and learn the rudiments of the lasso. He enlisted in the Navy but saw no action, for he was assigned the routine duty of guarding the Du Pont powder works in Delaware against sabotage, and was discharged in 1899. Mix reenlisted, perhaps in hope that his unit would see action, if the United States entered the Boer War. He married (the first in a series of ill-fated marriages) and went AWOL. Tom Mix was a deserter.

From 1901 to 1905, Mix lived a vagabond existence and worked in a variety of dead-end occupations—physical fitness instructor, drum major, bartender, and part-time ranch hand. Two events stand out: meeting and befriending Will Rogers, then a rodeo clown in a Wild West show, and joining Colonel Joe Miller's 101 Ranch as a ranch hand. By 1910, the year he entered the movies with the Selig Brothers, Mix had divorced his first two wives, married a third, Olive Stokes, and polished his riding and roping skills with the Wilderman Wild West Show in Amarillo, Texas. By the end of that year, he was again working at the Miller's ranch. One piece of the legend had substance—he did work as a deputy sheriff and night marshal in Dewey, Oklahoma. He allegedly legalized gambling and cracked down on demon rum. But Tom Mix's life had not yet taken on film qualities.

Mix's work on the Miller ranch, the impact on his life of Buffalo Bill's Wild West Show, and his subsequent rodeo and circus work created an amalgam that determined Mix's conception of the American Western film. His early films, made for the Selig Brothers from 1910 to 1917, are often dismissed by film historians. Yet these films revealed Mix as a comedian in the Will Rogers vein. Mix, for all his later promotion and publicity, revealed quite early, a capacity for not taking himself or the film medium too seriously. Film historian William Everson notes that in these early films, Mix developed

Tom Mix in fancy formal attire.

daredevil stunting "and a semi-comic folksy approach that emphasized the light-hearted camaraderie of ranch life and were close to the spirit of Will Rogers."[4] Mix and Rogers had met at the St. Louis World's Fair in 1904, when Mix was a drum major in the Oklahoma Cavalry Bank and Rogers worked as a clown for The Colonel Zack Mullhall Wild West Show. They became good friends and Rogers introduced Mix to Olive Stokes, who later became Mix's third wife.[5] Both Mix and Rogers shared a sense of the ridiculous that was part of the rodeo tradition.

The comic, the slapstick, the spectacle of high entertainment, the sense of decoration and display were all part of the Wild West show and rodeo tradition that Mix incorporated into his screen character. The exaggeration, the stories of great adventure, and faith in the gullibility of the audience combined to create the Mix public persona.

Overall, Mix worked in sixty-four films for the Selig Polyscope Company; it is generally conceded that in the course of making these early silents, Mix's talents improved. The films were mostly Westerns, but several were classified as adventure and comedy. Most were short, one- to two-reelers, used small casts, and were extremely profitable for their producers. A few of these films, such as *Sagebrush Tom, Mr. Haygood Producer*, and *Moving Picture Cowboy* (1914), are notably self-reflexive. They were comedies built around the Western film industry. These films featured backstage views of the sets and close-ups of the Selig script with notes to cameraman and crew.[6] In a comedy scene from *Sagebrush Tom*, Mix sees a poster for the Italian version of *Quo Vadis* and gets the bright idea to redo the famous fight scene, but this time with a bull in a western corral. This boyish sense of play, the "joi de vivre," were essential ingredients in Mix's evolving screen persona.

Mix's films for Selig were formulaic. A later Selig film, *Along the Border* (1916), is typical of the genre and illustrates how a Mix film often incorporated current issues. As one film review noted, "The story is particularly timely because of recent depredations of Mexican bandits along the U.S.-Mexican border. In the story, Grace, a rancher's daughter, and Tom Martin, are in love. Buck Miller is the disappointed rival in love. Buck swears to be revenged and plans with Delgado, a Mexican outlaw, to capture Grace and her father and hold them for ransom. Grace makes a sensational escape and tells Tom and his pals of the outlaws' actions. Tom and the boys rescue Grace's father and capture Delgado and his outlaw band. The action is hot and heavy and Tom gets his chance to perform many of his sensational and death-defying feats."[7]

It is easy to dismiss these films. They were amateurish and often lacked coherence; the camera work was primitive and the plots were usually an excuse for showcasing Mix's riding and stunting. But, they were action-filled and tremendously popular. To compare these films unfavorably to the films of Broncho Billy Anderson and William S. Hart misses the point. These were entertainments, moneymakers, in the same popular tradition as the Wild West shows and rodeos. In fact, these early Westerns made Tom Mix an international star. Film critic George Pratt reminds us that "the French rushed to deify Tom Mix.... In Paris, thousands crowded the many theaters showing Tom Mix films in 1914.... The Italians were not above trying their hand at Westerns.... Hungary and South Africa clamored for American Westerns. So did England.... The Queen of Romania ... was so enamored of American 'Wild West' features ... that she sometimes ordered them screened three and four times for her benefit."[8] In many countries the demand for Tom Mix was so great, the films were divided into several parts and shown over several days.

Before Hollywood dominated the film industry, Western towns, in the best booster spirit, advertised widely to lure Mix and other Western Film companies to their locales. Mix's Selig films were made in Missouri; Canon City, Colorado; and Arizona. Even Las Vegas, New Mexico, snagged Tom Mix. Advertisements from the Las Vegas Commercial Club appeared in the *New York Dramatic Mirror* "Las Vegas [will] Make You Famous and Us, Too—Let's Get Together; The Cameraman's Paradise. Good stuff to shoot—no

retakes and no static. Las Vegas will add years to the life of the director."[9] The heavy promotion and Mix's friendship with the leading town merchant, Ludwig Ilfeld, were enough to bring Mix to Las Vegas. He arrived in
Las Vegas in June 1916 and was welcomed with a parade and appointed deputy
sheriff.[10]

Mix took over a studio formerly occupied by Romaine Fielding, who was
also making pictures in New Mexico. The studio employed a number of extras,
including Leo Carillo, who later became famous in the Cisco Kid series. Las
Vegas, preparing for its Fourth-of-July gala and cowboy reunion, buzzed with
excitement. Mix used cowboys from the reunion in his first feature made in
Las Vegas, *Never Again*. Townspeople were invited to sit in their cars on Gal-
linas Street near the studio and watch the outdoor action. The Las Vegas *Optic*
declared, "Tom Mix is pleased with Las Vegas. He likes the people and the
spirit of cooperation."[11] Mix made at least six films in the Las Vegas area in
1915, including the *Rancher's Daughter* and the *Country Drugstore*. Thirteen
years later the millionaire star returned for a brief visit with old friends. Similar stories could be told about other location sites for Mix films. At the time,
they were signal events in the history of these locales and attest to Mix's ris-
ing status as a film star. Kevin Brownlow, who has written one of the most
perceptive accounts of Mix's career, adds, "These early Selig westerns, even
more than the pictures shot at Inceville, represent a fortunate historical accident, for they were photographed in the heart of the West when cattle ranch-
ing was more or less a thriving concern and when the custom and character
of the old days was still very much in evidence.... The foreground may have
been hokum but the background was pure documentary."[12]

Clearly, Mix, who directed, wrote, and produced many of these films,
had an interest in the grandeur and vastness of the American West. Many of
these films were made in national parks, especially the Grand Canyon and
Yosemite, but this interest was always ancillary to the camera's central purpose—photographing Tom Mix. The backgrounds were mundane to the cowboy star, and most of the action was filmed against blank backgrounds to
obliterate competing landscape and focus all attention on Mix.[13] Moreover,
Mix never intended these films, and certainly not his Westerns made with Fox
in the 1920s, to be recreations of the actual West. The prevailing spirit was a
sense of fun and boyish enthusiasm. Mix's stunts were highly entertaining.
Still, these Selig features foreshadow the conception of the Western that Mix
would exemplify later in the 1920s. There is none of the traditional tension
between frontier and civilized society. Mix's cowboy hero, with his spirit and
love of life, exhibits none of the traits of the doomed hero; Mix's West is the
West of technology and change whose frontier and civilization blend to create adventurous opportunities.

Opposite: **Tom Mix in an early publicity still.**

During the Selig period, Mix played a cowboy hero who never drank, swore, or engaged in unnecessary violence. Rather than a gunfighter, he was a skilled cowhand who used his rodeo-style roping and stunting skills to invent ingenious ways to capture badmen. He never played outlaws, and his considerable ego never permitted him to play the dude. Nor was he a cowboy Valentino.[14] There was, however, romance in the Selig films; Mix would, upon occasion, actually kiss the heroine, after he had saved her from distress and won her heart. But this image would be sharpened and refined when Mix left the financially troubled Selig Studio and went to work for William Fox.

While it is by no means clear if this was Fox's or Mix's handiwork, before the 1920s began, Mix's cowboy image soon underwent a transformation. He had always projected a wholesome image, and he was proud that his movies were proper family entertainment. Now, the Fox Studios made a more concerted appeal to the juvenile audience. No more tender embraces of leading ladies; Mix may have won her heart, but he now only held her hand. Action was also stepped up and the love scenes were left to the imagination. As film authority, Frank Manchel, observes, "Since Hart's films had avoided stunt work and fancy tricks, the Fox star went out of his way to include spectacular riding sequences and superb rope-twirling episodes in his adventures, even when they added little to the story. He reasoned that his movies were made mostly for youngsters, who preferred lots of action to a logical tale. Then too, he felt his audiences were bored, as he was, with realistic films. They came to the movies for escape and entertainment, not for accuracy."[15]

Tom Mix's stuntwork in his Fox films was spectacular. Perhaps no other cowboy hero has ever matched Mix's unique combination of athleticism, inventiveness, and artistry in stunting. He took chances and risked injury in amazing displays of raw physical courage. Stunts helped make Tom Mix the King of Cowboys.

Mix was an outstanding athlete. During his scholastic days he played baseball and football, raced bicycles, and was a superb boxer, often sparring, perhaps more for publicity than anything else, with Jack Dempsey. He kept in excellent physical condition, watched his diet, and long before it was fashionable, worked out regularly. Mix's great box office appeal related directly to his beguiling physicality—the strong, powerful body, his size (he was reputed to be over six feet tall), and strength.

Thus, the invention of Tom Mix rested on his physical capabilities. Mix's studio built the myth that his powerful hero did all his own stunts—and it seems plausible that if given a choice, he would have. Stuntman Harry Parry said that "even at the height of his career Mix loathed the idea of a double. But the studio insisted on it. They'd take him down the road to show him

Opposite: **Tom Mix astride Tony in a photo used to promote his appearances with the Sells-Floto Circus.**

something and while they were doing that, I'd do the stunt. He'd come back, raise hell and fire me."[16] Jack Montgomery, another famous stuntman, recalled a story that typifies Mix's attitude about his stunts. In 1920, Montgomery was to double for Mix but a barroom brawl caused an angry discussion between the director and Mix. The director insisted it was simply too risky for the star to leap from a collapsing stairway into the center of the saloon.

> "Why take a chance on crippling yourself in an accident that could tie up production for weeks and cost a fortune? Why not let a stunt man do it for you?" was the director's reasonable argument. Mix, however, was proud of his hard-won reputation for personal bravery, and stubbornly refused to consider changing the filming tradition that had built his legend. But finally, after considerable haggling, the director won him over, possibly by reminding him that there was more at stake than his screen image—namely, a large slice of the production profits, which might go a-glimmering for nothing more serious than a broken ankle. Whatever the star's real reason for agreeing to the change, it prompted the director to cast about immediately for someone on the set who resembled Mix enough to serve as a double.[17]

Throughout his career, Mix remained very sensitive about his stunting. His publicity releases insisted he had never used a double. In an autobiographical article entitled "Roping a Million," he claimed to have made more than 370 pictures and never used a double. As a result, he also claimed to have over 150 stitches and thirty-three broken bones.[18] Even normally cautious historians, such as William Everson and George Fenin, resort to hyperbole when they describe Mix's injuries: "His body was literally a mass of scars while shattered bones were held together with surgical wire."[19] Mix's stunts did involve risk and injury. There is reliable evidence to suggest that not all his broken bones and gunshot wounds were a publicist's fabrication.[20]

The importance of these injuries lies not in the number of broken bones but in Mix's conquest of injury and pain. Mix distrusted doctors, and like the rodeo cowboy, he often refused medical treatment. There is even a story that while suffering from a toothache, he tried to pull his tooth with a pair of pliers. In the rodeo tradition, pain was flaunted and injuries worn as a badge of pride. Thus, stunts and the resulting injuries demonstrated not only physical courage but mastery over pain and the physical limitations of the body. In an interview in 1931, at the age of fifty-one, Mix reported that he had never felt better in his life, that he felt like a man of thirty.[21] The mastery of injury and pain provides a somatic link in Mix's cowboy image and his heroic status.

The rodeo tradition and the Wild West show were also the origins of the fancy clothing that defined the Mix image and promoted his celebrity status. When film executive Allan Dwan was asked about Tom Mix, he claimed, "to explain Tom Mix you have to go back to Buffalo Bill. He set up the picture for the world. He said 'That's the West—tight white pants, a sharp coat, guns all over the place, and underneath fancy white embroidered materials with diamonds down the side of the pants.' It was all a case of dressing up. It's like any style that people pick up—Beau Brummel swept through Europe with his clothes. Most rodeo cowboys were professional guys, and their clothes were practical. But when they went out on parade they had the damnedest-looking outfits on."[22] Mix's costume practically became a uniform and his garish and flamboyant designs became his trademark. The *New York Times* review of *The Lucky Horseshoe* (1925) noted, "after seeing Tom Mix in his gorgeous apparel as Don Juan in the dream chapters ... one would not be the least surprised to hear that he had bought one of the minor European kingdoms so as to be able to wear the clothes that go with the job."[23] Mordaunt Hall, the film reviewer for the *New York Times*, referred to Mix as "that C. B. DeMille of Cowboys, ... who two hundred years hence may be the inspiration for books and fashions...."[24] By the mid–1920s, his costumed image was established and soon became the most visible aspect of the Mix legend.

It is difficult to date exactly the introduction of these gaudy, impractical outfits. Yakima Canutt noted that he always "dressed a bit fancy" for the rodeos and especially in the parades. He later claimed that Mix liked the design of one of his shirts and had his tailor make several patterns from it.[25] The Mix costume—Stetson hat in black or white, embroidered shirts, fancy belt buckle, gloves, tight pants with accent lines, and hand-tooled boots clearly derive from the rodeo and the Wild West shows. For example, Buck Taylor, the first cowboy hero with Buffalo Bill's Wild West Show, was photographed wearing large hats, embroidered jackets, large belt buckle, and fancy chaps. In 1887, the publication of Prentice Ingraham's *Buck Taylor: King of the Cowboys* promoted the popular entertainer as the epitome of cowboy culture and later provided a moniker used by the Mix publicists.[26] Regardless of these origins, Mix's fantastically embroidered costume (his off-screen outfits were even more extreme) became part of the Hollywood cowboy image. Mix added gloves, reputably because of his soft hands,[27] and the Hollywood Cowboy costume was complete. It remained for later stars, such as Gene Autry and Roy Rogers, to make the rhinestone cowboy the standard entertainment image.

Mix's cowboy image of costumed elegance, daredevil adventure, and physical prowess were showcased in the silent Western films made for William Fox Productions. Between 1918 and 1928, Mix appeared in seventy-eight films, including several non–Westerns. Most were formulaic with melodramatic plots that lacked any particular distinction. But, judged by the standards of the time, they were good Westerns and a few, such as *Rough Riding Romance* (1920) and *Tumbling River* (1927), were excellent. Several are notable for their great stuntwork. *Skyhigh* (1922), one of the few Mix films to survive, has thrilling action scenes filmed on the rims and precipices of the Grand Canyon. Mix played Grant Newburg, an immigration officer intent on breaking up the illegal smuggling of Chinese laborers. The alpine and canyon-top thrills include beautiful photography by Ben Cline and snappy direction by Lynn Reynolds. Mix rescues his daughter (Eva Novak) and brings the criminals to justice. William Everson suggested that the film, "which might have been subtitled 'Stunting in the Grand Canyon,' is about as typical a Mix film as it is possible to find, and is as thrilling and exhilarating now as in 1922."[28] *The Great Train Robbery* (1926), shot on location in Colorado, is pure action. It was magnificently filmed by Mix's favorite cameraman, Dan Clark. The plot, based on a novel by Paul Leicester Ford, is replete with exciting action on a fast-moving train. Mix, in the role of a railroad detective, arrives from Texas to bring the outlaws to justice. Posing as an outlaw himself, Mix not only subdues the gang but wins the heart of the daughter of the railroad company president.[29] In *Rainbow Trail* (1925), Mix's great athletic and stunting ability are displayed continuously. In a dazzling series of incidents, he halts an Indian wagon train attack, saves an Indian maiden from unwanted attention, rescues another woman from a forced marriage, and finally saves his uncle from an Indian attack. Mix was at the height of his career in these films, and *Rainbow Trail* contains some of the greatest stunt work ever filmed.[30]

Several other notable films featuring Mix appeared during the Fox period. Critics praised *Rough Riding Romance* (1920), *Just Tony* (1922), and the *Lone Star Ranger* (1923). *Just Tony*, featuring Mix's horse, was a favorite of Dan Clark, Mix's long-time photographer. It deserves mention not only because of its action but for its remarkable animal photography. It was in the same genre as William S. Hart's *Pinto Ben* and *Narrow Trail*—tributes to Hart's horse, Fritz. Tony was a very intelligent animal and an important part of Mix's celebrity image.[31] The beautiful, white-stockinged chestnut could perform great feats. Tony pulled his master from blazing fires, leapt great chasms, untied his master's hands, and understood human speech. In *Just Tony*, the horse is the star. He is the leader of a herd of outlaw desert horses, and seeks revenge against those who have mistreated him. Based on this all too-human premise, Tony, nonetheless, exhibits a wide range of human emotions. In the climax, he rescues Mix and the heroine because Tom previously had saved the horse from a beating.

Just Tony, with its themes of animal rage and affection, also demonstrates a dichotomy in Mix's silent era films—the wild and the tame. As previously mentioned, Mix was not purist in depicting the West. His West was safe and modern, where the Wild West of the past was an anachronism; in Mix's West, technology and modernity were triumphant. In fact, Mix's subjugation of renegades, outlaws, and runaways often depends on the automobile or the airplane. In one of the few extant Mix film scripts of the silent era, *Silver Valley*, the camera pans the town of Standing Rock, Nevada. The script calls for a wide shot of main street. It reads, "Establish character and atmosphere of typical Western mining town in the mountains. Mountain lake nearby surrounded by high peaks. Stage drives on from around the bend and comes down street. The stage is an old stagecoach body mounted on a dilapidated auto chassis."[32] In the exciting climax to *Silver Valley*, Mix rescues Sheila (Dorothy Dwan), a female reporter who has come West for local color, from an exploding volcano by dropping a rope and pulling her to the safety of an airplane. In these films, the juxtaposition of the Wild West and the tamer, more modern West is never one of persistent tension. The wild frontier functions only instrumentally to provide the excitement and an excuse for action. The automobile and the airplane, symbolizing the rescue and triumph of the technological West, invigorate the action and provide new plot lines. Perhaps just as importantly, these plots would later serve as inspiration for Hollywood cowboys, such as Gene Autry and Roy Rogers, in the 1930s and 1940s.

Mix made his last pictures for Fox in 1928. He apparently argued with the studio over his extravagant production costs, and Fox may have felt that at the age of forty-eight Mix's days as a cowboy star were over. Mix signed on with Joseph Kennedy's Film Booking Office (F.B.O.) and made six more silents. The critics all noted these films were cheaply done and poorly filmed. A review of *Outlaw* (1929) practically shouted, "Not so hot, Mr. Mix, not so hot. The saddle girths are slipping under the 'King of the Cowboys.' He'll do well to lay low, till he gets some new gags under his high hat. Here's the same old thing, only worse, without enough sparks, color or action to keep an eight-year-old happy. Another flop like this and the kids will shout a lusty 'applesauce.'"[33] Reviews of the other five films were equally negative.

The Depression only made things worse. Indeed, Mix lost more than a million dollars, his Hollywood mansion, and his Arizona ranch. He withdrew from films and went on the road with Sells-Floto Circus. Here Mix was in the center ring—still the star attraction. But, the 1930s were a difficult time for the aging cowboy hero. He suffered a series of mishaps, including a smashed shoulder, ruptured appendix, a broken leg, and there were also unconfirmed reports of a shooting. The Internal Revenue Service sued him for back taxes. All those bone-wearing stunts and one-night performance shows for the circus exacted a toll. Many in the film industry felt that his career was finished. Mix, however, was still resilient.

In 1932, despite all these mishaps, the King of the Cowboys returned to film. Carl Laemmle, of Universal Studios, was willing to risk talking Westerns and he cast Mix in nine talkies for Universal within a year.

Much of the discussion of Mix's films in the sound era center on his acting talents and the suitability of his voice for talking pictures. But this debate misses the larger point: Mix's athletic plots were ideally suited to the silent era; silents were the perfect vehicle for the spectacle and parade of action. Clearly, the irresistible allure of the Mix film was his physical genius, his body in motion. Mix's films not only moved, they were the fastest moving. With his blazing riding and spectacular stunting, Mix represented pure action

Tom Mix showing off the remarkable physique that enabled him to perform many of his own stunts.

adventure. Silent films could focus attention on the visible body, on action uncomplicated by sound. The subtitles provided a limited verbal message that was subsumed by the motion and physical form of the actor. In silent film, the body and gesture defined character—and no Western film star of the silent era possessed the bodily presence of Tom Mix.

The sound era changed this emphasis on action. The Western formula was revitalized to include music and song that could capture the attention of the audience. This produced the singing cowboys, and more character development, less action. Feelings were no longer conveyed by gesture or motion but by words. At age fifty-two, Tom Mix's genius was out of place in the new Westerns.

Mix's sound Westerns were a different breed from his F.O.B. disasters. Mix was reunited with his old cameraman, Dan Clark, who had not worked with him at F.O.B. because of contractual limitations. Mix was given control over the pictures, large budgets of $100,000 to $150,000, and a weekly salary of $10,000. He could pick his stories and his cast. Six features a year were scheduled.[34]

Mix made nine sound films. *Destry Rides Again* (1932), his first Universal film, is the most outstanding of the group, but the entire collection was of high quality. With the possible exception of Ken Maynard's films for Universal, they were not only the best budgeted and most lavishly produced, they were among the best series of the decade. Only *Hidden Gold* (1932) seemed sub-par.[35] Mix retired from films on Christmas Day in 1932 when the filming for his last Universal release, *Rustler's Roundup*, was completed. He had injured his leg seriously only a few months before when Tony, the Wonder Horse, now twenty-three years old, stumbled on an embankment and rolled over on Mix. After retiring from pictures, Mix returned to where he began, the circus. He was back in the limelight in 1934 with the Sam D. Hill Circus. In 1934, Mix bought the circus at a cost of $400,000 and traveled the country. Tom Mix, ever the showman, traveled over 10,000 miles a year for the next three years, playing 216 stands in 1935, 217 in 1936, and 195 in 1937. Mix was on the road again in 1938, but the circus did not survive the season.

Mix remained in the limelight. The showman extraordinaire toured England in the 1938-39 season, but there were disturbing reports that he drank heavily. Allan Dwan observed that:

> Tom Mix was a likeable kind of guy. Not a jolly fellow, and he didn't mix with everyone. He was reticent. But underneath he was a philosopher. He recognized that he was in a phony business—show business—and he gave it the works.
>
> In the theater, he'd spin ropes with his patent leather boots that wouldn't have stood one minute of the real work around a ranch. He hated it as much as anybody did, but he did it because it was profitable. He got a fortune for it, built himself an estate and was a very unhappy man in general.[36]

Still dreaming of pictures and the limelight, Mix paid a visit to Twentieth Century–Fox Studios. Lefty Hough recalled the visit.

> He was a little seedy, with the boots, the hat, the white suit and everything. He said to me, "I want to see Jack Ford or Sol Wurtzel [the studio manager] to find out what I can do in the picture business." He had lost a million dollars in the circus, and there was no money left. Ford was shooting *The Grapes of Wrath* but he took him to lunch. He told him, "this picture business has passed you by a long time ago." He got the same thing from Wurtzel. What the hell could they use him for? He came to my office and we sat there and talked a while and I could see he was quite depressed. "Lefty," he said, "I don't know what I'm going to do."[37]

On October 12, 1940, Tom Mix drove to Phoenix, Arizona, for a personal appearance. He failed to see a crew of highway workers, swerved, and the car went over the side of a hill; he was pinned beneath the car. A metal suitcase was believed to have struck him on the back of the neck, killing him instantly. According to legend, his white suit was unwrinkled, and he died wearing his boots and a diamond-studded belt buckle. He had $6,000 in cash and $1,500 in traveler's checks. Supposedly the suitcase that killed him was filled with twenty-dollar gold pieces.[38]

The King of the Cowboys was dead, but the legend lives on. The Ralston Purina Company, which began the Tom Mix Radio Show in 1933, continued to broadcast to Mix's youthful admirers until 1950. In the 1940s a series of Tom Mix comics (later Tom Mix Commando Comics) kept the legend alive. *The Miracle Rider*, part of the Mascot Series filmed in 1935, brought Mix to a newer generation of youngsters. Today, Mix's once youthful audiences are now an elderly generation with vivid recollections of the cowboy king.

Myths, of course, live on. The myth of Tom Mix, replete with dreams of wealth and ostentation, creates evanescent images for another generation to appropriate. Two recent novels, *Tom Mix Died for Your Sins* and *Tom Mix and Pancho Villa*, suggest this generation's sobering insight: "Fiction may be the appropriate and final form for understanding the truth about Tom Mix."[39] Blake Edwards' film, *Sunset* (1988), fictionalizes the life of Tom Mix and Wyatt Earp in a highly unrealistic Hollywood plot. His closing epitaph pays homage to the Mix silent era legend with these words, "And that's the way it really happened. Give or take a lie or two."[40] As the Bandera Kid says in *Tom Mix Died for Your Sins*, "Tom never kilt nobody 'cept the feller he once was. Some say he never kilt that feller neither, he just sort of rearranged him."[41]

Notes

1. Yakima Canutt, *Stuntman* (New York: Walker, 1979), p. 59.
2. Quoted in James Horowitz, *They Went Thataway* (New York: E. P. Dutton, 1976), p. 67.

3. From the Sells-Floto Circus Program for 1931. Quoted in Paul Mix, *The Life and Legend of Tom Mix* (New York: A. S. Barnes, 1972), p. 166. The entire text appears on pp. 164–170.

4. William Everson, *American Silent Film* (New York: Oxford University Press, 1978), p. 243.

5. *Mix, The Life and Legend of Tom Mix*, pp. 43–44. Tom Mix later copied Rogers' famous steer in the stands routine while Rogers did satires on Tom Mix and the Western in his later films.

6. George Fenin and William K. Everson, *The Western: From Silents to the Seventies* (New York: Grossman, 1973), p. 112.

7. Quoted in *Mix, The Life and Legend of Tom Mix*, pp. 85, 87.

8. George Pratt, Notes on an Early Phase of Western Films (1907–1914) Part II "The Posse Is Still Ridin' Like Mad," *Image* (September 1958), p. 153.

9. Quoted in "The Posse Is Still Ridin' Like Mad," p. 153.

10. Lynn I. Perrigo, *The Original Las Vegas*. 3 vols. Unpublished Typescript. Special Collections Department, University of New Mexico General Library, Albuquerque, NM, pp. 455–456.

11. Quoted in *The Original Las Vegas*, p. 456.

12. Kevin Brownlow, *The War, the West and the Wilderness* (New York: Knopf, 1979), p. 307.

13. *The War, the West and the Wilderness*, p. 307.

14. *The War, the West and the Wilderness*, p. 307.

15. Frank Manchel, *Camera's West* (Englewood Cliffs: Prentice Hall, 1971), p. 64.

16. Brownlow, *The War, the West and the Wilderness*, p. 307.

17. Diana Serra Cary, *The Hollywood Posse* (Boston: Houghton Mifflin, 1975), p. 17.

18. *Mix, the Life and Times of Tom Mix*, p. 64.

19. Fenin and Everson, *The Western*, p. 121.

20. The task, however, is complicated. In 1932, *Motion Picture Classic* ran a story on Mix's injuries. Twenty-six injuries were mentioned, including a hole through the pelvis garnered in his shoot-out with the Short Brothers. *Motion Picture Classic* noted that scars from the twenty-two knife wounds, the dynamite explosion, and buckshot wounds could not be shown. All the injuries were carefully plotted on a skeleton wearing a Stetson!

21. Fenin and Everson, *The Western*, p. 121.

22. Brownlow, *The War, the West and the Wilderness*, p. 309.

23. *New York Times* (August 18, 1925), n.p.

24. *New York Times* (December 2, 1925), n.p.

25. Canutt, *Stunt Man*, p. 68.

26. Photographs of Taylor are reprinted in William W. Savage Jr.'s, *Cowboy Life: Reconstructuring an American Myth* (Norman: University of Oklahoma, 1975), pp. 20–21.

27. Fenin and Everson, *The West and the Wilderness*, pp. 184–185.

28. George Mitchell and William K. Everson, "Tom Mix," *Films in Review 8* (October 1957), p. 394.

29. Dan Clark told Mitchell and Everson that during his years with Mix, he set cameras up on every conceivable part of locomotive—and on every kind of vehicle, including the cage of an aerial cable.

30. Fenin and Everson, *The Western*, p. 118.

31. Mix had acquired Tony from a friend, Pat Chrisman, in 1914. In all, Mix worked with four horses in his career, Old Blue, Tony, Tony, Jr., and Tony II.

32. "Tony Gets His Man," Filmscript, scene 11, n.p. DeGolyer Library, Southern Methodist University, Dallas, Texas. This film was later retitled, "Silver Valley."

33. Mix, *The Life and Legend of Tom Mix*, pp. 109–110.

34. Jon Tuska, "Destry Rides Again," *Views and Reviews 3* (December 1971), p. 43.

35. "Destry Rides Again," p. 44.

36. Quoted in Brownlow, *The War, the West and the Wilderness*, p. 309.

37. Mix, *The Life and Legend of Tom Mix*, p. 151.

38. John Nicholas, *Tom Mix Riding Up to Glory* (Oklahoma City: Persimmon Hill, 1980), is only the most recent of a long line of works stirred by boyhood memories of Mix.

39. Daryl Ponicsan, *Tom Mix Died for Your Sins* (New York: Delacorte, 1957). Clifford Irving, *Tom Mix and Pancho Villa* (New York: St. Martin's, 1982).

40. *Sunset* (Tri-Star, 1988).

41. Ponicsan, *Tom Mix Died for Your Sins*, p. 30.

BUCK JONES:
AN OLD-TIME COWBOY

by R. Philip Loy

Few of the men who made B Westerns were native to the Trans-Mississippi West. Even fewer of those whose film careers were primarily in small budget Westerns had been working cowboys. Since most Hollywood moguls thought it necessary that their movie cowboys appear to be authentic Westerners the studios created fictional biographies for those who were not. According to Hollywood lore, cowboy movie stars were expert ranchers, charged up San Juan Hill with the Rough Riders, chased Geronimo, and performed other heroic feats. Of course, little of these claims was true, but over the years fact and fiction merged until they became difficult to separate. As a result, the truth about the early years of many of the cowboy actors is elusive, shrouded in layers of Hollywood myth. Charles Frederick Gebhart, better known to 1920s and 1930s movie audiences as Buck Jones, is a good example.

Much of Buck Jones' early life remains a mystery. Fortunately we can dismiss most of his Hollywood legend. According to his fictional Hollywood biography, Jones grew up in Oklahoma Territory where he became an expert rider. Later, Jones supposedly ranched in Montana and served with the famed air ace Eddie Rickenbacker in France during World War I. All of that is false.

Buck Jones was born Charles Frederick Gebhart in Vincennes, Indiana, on December 12, 1891, although some accounts cite 1887 as the year of his birth. The confusion is easily explained. In 1907, young Gebhart wanted to join the Army, but he was not old enough to enlist. Either his mother or grandmother falsified his year of birth so he could enlist.[1] Jones used December 12, 1891, as his date of birth when he applied for a marriage license. There can be little doubt that that is the accurate date. Little is known about Jones' early life. His father, Frederick, may have been an insurance agent, but Odille Jones, Jones' wife, remembers that her father-in-law worked for the railroad and moved around a great deal. That agrees with what is known about Jones' early years. Within a month of Buck Jones' birth, the Vincennes newspaper reported that Frederick Gebhart was moving his family to Muncie, Indiana, to operate a dry goods store.[2] There is no evidence that the Gebharts ever lived in Muncie. It is more likely they left Vincennes for Indianapolis where Jones spent many of his early years. He attended school there and returned to Indianapolis in 1910 between Army enlistments.

Jones' parents divorced while he was still young. Jones remained with his father, who soon remarried a woman named India Cooper. Robert Stevens, director of the Lewis Historical Society of Vincennes University, found that Buck, his father, stepmother, and stepbrother were living in South Bend, Indiana, when the census of 1900 was taken.[3] Jones may also have returned to Vincennes during some of those early years. Stevens discovered a local historian who believed Jones became familiar with horses while hanging around a livery stable in Vincennes. Jones, it seems was adept at handling difficult animals.[4]

In January 1907, Jones enlisted in the United States Army—supposedly Troop G., Sixth United States Cavalry—at Columbus Barracks, Ohio. Stevens' efforts to obtain Jones' military records have failed; it is indisputable, however, that Jones served in the cavalry. Jones patrolled along the United States–Mexico border, then saw action in the Philippines at the time of the Moro uprising. He was wounded severely in the leg, and according to his wife the wound left a large scar.[5]

After recovering from his wound, Jones left the cavalry and returned to Indianapolis. Buck Rainey, Jones' best known biographer, writes that Jones worked for Henry Stillman at the Marmon Motor Company. He probably worked in the garage and drove a delivery truck. During that time Jones may also have done some test driving for Marmon at the Indianapolis Motor Speedway.[6]

Robert Laycock, the speedway historian, believes that there is no way to verify Jones' testing at the track.[7] According to Laycock, a series of short races were held during the summer of 1910. Between racing dates, the numerous motor car companies located in Indianapolis used the track for testing. Marmon, an automotive pioneer with a deep interest in automobile racing, did a great deal of testing at the track during 1910 and 1911. It is likely that an adventurous young man such as Buck Jones would have been drawn to the infant sport of motor racing.

In October 1910, Jones reenlisted in the cavalry and remained in the service until 1913. He switched from the cavalry to the recently formed Army Air Corps, but apparently became disillusioned and dissatisfied when his hopes of becoming a pilot were dashed.[8]

In October 1913, Jones was mustered out of the Army in Texas. He was a long way from Indianapolis and without a job, but fate intervened. The Miller 101 Wild West Show, then appearing in Galveston, advertised for workers. Jones applied and got a job. Two life-changing events soon followed. Jones first worked as a wrangler who handled stock but soon became a bronco buster and trick rider with the Miller 101 Show. In 1914, Jones met Odille Osborne, a young rider who joined the Miller 101 Show at Madison Square Garden. She was not much more than thirteen years old at the time, but Jones fell in love with her and their courtship began.

Odille left the Miller 101 Wild West Show to join the Julia Allen Show while Jones went with the Miller 101 Wild West Show on a tour of England. Jones, however, could not forget the young, pretty Odille Osborne. When the Miller 101 Wild West Show returned to the United States, Jones left it to join the Julia Allen Show. Buck Jones and Odille Osborne were married by justice of the peace Emmett E. Everett on August 11, 1915, on horseback in center ring while the Julia Allen Show played in Lima, Ohio.[9] It was a solid marriage which lasted until Jones' tragic death in November 1942. The couple had one daughter, Maxine.

During the next three years Buck and Odille Jones appeared with several circuses and wild west shows, including the Gollmar Brothers Wild West Show and the prestigious Ringling Brothers Circus. For part of 1916, the couple barnstormed on their own. They performed riding and other equestrian tricks in small towns and then passed the hat, living on whatever they collected.[10] Prior to the wild west shows and circuses, the couple had spent part of 1915 in Chicago where Jones helped to break and train horses destined for use by the European Allied Powers in the early years of World War I.[11] Contrary to Hollywood lore, Jones did not serve in the Great War.

While with the Ringling Brothers Circus in California in 1917, Jones learned that Odille was pregnant. Jones thought it was imperative to find steady employment in a job that did not require a vagabond existence. They rented a house in Los Angeles and Buck went job hunting. Like many wild-west-show and circus cowboys, Jones found work as a stuntman and extra in the rapidly expanding movie industry. During 1917 and 1918, he worked at Universal Studio and at Edendale on films starring William S. Hart.

In 1919, Jones began to work for the Fox studio. He stunted and doubled for both of that studio's major cowboy stars, William Farnum and Tom Mix. Farnum and Mix enjoyed great popularity in both two-reelers and feature-length films so Jones had a steady job.

Jones impressed studio executives sufficiently for them to place him under contract at $100 per week in October 1919.[12] In 1920, Fox released Jones' first Western, *The Last Straw*. During the next eight years he made over sixty films, nearly all Westerns, for Fox. Early in the 1920s he changed his name from Charles Frederick Gebhart to Charles (Buck) Jones. He also became a Mason.

Jones joined the Henry S. Orme Lodge No. 458 of Los Angeles in January 1924. The lodge no longer exists, but in 1924 a number of the Orme Lodge brothers were members of the motion picture community. Lambert Hillyer and Scott Dunlap, both of whom directed several of Jones' silent Westerns, were lodge brothers. Dunlap, in particular, became a good friend. The association between Dunlap and Jones which began at Fox Studio and the Orme Masonic Lodge in the 1920s would continue to grow up to the night Jones was fatally burned in the famous Coconut Grove Nightclub fire. Other lodge brothers included were Roy Steward, Richard Dix, and Raymond Hatton, all of whom were well known within the Western movie genre.[13]

Jones' Masonic connection was important to his career. For example, in 1941 Jones' old friend and fellow Mason, Scott Dunlap, then a producer at Monogram Pictures, developed a new B Western series called *The Rough Riders*. Jones became a partner in the endeavor and starred in the series with Tim McCoy, another popular cowboy-hero of the 1930s. Raymond Hatton, an Orme Lodge brother, supported Jones and McCoy as the third Rough Rider.

Few of Jones' silent films are extant but they were successful. *Variety* for the most part disdained Westerns, but gave Jones' efforts high marks for action and entertainment. Their reviews of Jones' films do not contain the caustic comments so characteristic of *Variety* reviews of other Westerns. By 1928 Jones was in the midst of a highly successful career. He was a well-known member of the Western Big Four: Tom Mix, Hoot Gibson, Ken Maynard and Jones. Then disaster struck.

In 1928 Jones quit Fox in a dispute over vacation pay. He ventured into the independent market with a feature film, *The Big Hop* (1928). In the film Jones plays a cowboy turned aviator who enters the Honolulu air race. When his partner is drugged and cannot pilot the airplane, Jones takes his place. Engine failure forces him to crash in the Pacific Ocean. Rescued by a passing ship, Jones returns to his ranch to catch the villains who drugged his partner and to win the heroine. Audiences preferred Jones on horseback rather than in an airplane, so *The Big Hop* was unsuccessful and lost money.

Out of work in 1929, Jones then formed his own combination circus–wild west show, the Buck Jones Wild West and Round Up Days, from the sizable savings he had amassed during his years at Fox. Jones' wild west show had an arena seating several thousand people, 102 performers, a payroll of 267 people, and 27 acts.[14] During May, June, and July of 1929, the show played locations in California, Nevada, Utah, Colorado, Missouri, and Illinois. It closed at Danville, Illinois, on July 12, 1929.[15] The reasons for the show's failure are uncertain. Some accounts suggest it was bankrupt; audiences had not produced enough income to meet the payroll. Other accounts lay the blame on a corrupt business manager. Whatever the case, Jones lost $250,000 in the venture, and he was broke.

Buck and Odille Jones, determined to start over and honor their debts, returned to Los Angeles. Jones apparently made arrangements to pay back wages to employees at ten percent per month until they were fully paid. That led to lawsuits. The *Los Angeles Times*, March 12, 1930, reported that Jones

Buck Jones in a typical action still.

was sued by several employees for back pay.[16] Jones eventually honored all of his financial commitments that resulted from the wild west show's failure.

Back in Los Angeles, Jones faced several problems. He was broke, but committed to pay off his debts. What he did best was to make Western movies, but unfortunately for Jones, the coming of sound had dealt a temporary set-back to Westerns. Most producers believed that Westerns—filmed mostly out-doors—could not utilize sound equipment. Producers also thought that the smaller theaters, the primary outlets for the Western film market, could not afford to convert to sound. Neither assumption proved to be true, and by 1930, well-known studios and the independents were once again making West-erns.

In this changed atmosphere, Sol Lesser, an independent producer, pro-posed to Buck Jones that he star in a series of independently produced West-erns to be released by Columbia. Jones agreed to make eight pictures for Lesser for $300 per week.[17] The Lesser pictures were made cheaply, but they proved to be popular with the public.

After eight pictures, Columbia took over production of the series. Jones' salary was increased to $500 per week and his films' budgets were raised to $25,000.[18] Columbia now had both Tim McCoy and Buck Jones, two of the 1930s most popular cowboy-heroes, under contract.

In 1934, Columbia loaned Jones to Universal so he could make one serial per year for that studio. Soon Universal officials convinced Jones to sign a contract with them. From 1934 to 1937, he made films for Universal Pictures. His salary increased to $1,000 per week and each film was budgeted at $65,000, a large sum in the 1930s for a B Western.[19] More significant, Jones assumed control of his films. They were now Buck Jones Productions dis-tributed by Universal Pictures. Jones' Universal Westerns are some of the best films of his entire career.

In 1937, Universal Studio changed management in an attempt to shake the financial effects of the Depression. The new executives offered to renew Jones' contract, but at the salary he had been receiving. Jones declined the offer and left Universal Pictures. Monroe Shaff signed Jones to a contract to make six pictures to be distributed by Columbia.[20] When Columbia refused Shaff's overtures to finance any future Jones Westerns, they were discontin-ued. Out of work again, Jones' career was in decline.

In 1940, Jones played a supporting role in the Universal Pictures serial *Riders of Death Valley*, and he made a serial version of *White Eagle*, a film he made at Columbia in 1932. Jones' career had so declined that he appeared as a corrupt sheriff in the Republic production *Wagons Westward* (1940).

Just when Jones' film career seemed to be finished, his old friend and fellow Mason Scott Dunlap came to the rescue. Dunlap proposed a new West-ern series, *The Rough Riders*. Trem Carr, president of Monogram Pictures, approved the project, so Dunlap talked with Jones about starring in the films. Jon Tuska stated in *Filming of the West* that each man—Jones, Dunlap and Carr—put up equal capital to form the Great Western Picture Company. Profits were to be divided between the new company and Monogram on a thirty-five/sixty-five percent basis until Monogram's production costs were covered, and then the Great Western Picture Company and Monogram would divide the profits equally.[21]

Based on that arrangement, Buck Jones, Tim McCoy, and Raymond Hatton made eight Rough Riders Westerns in 1941 and 1942. Each picture was budgeted at $80,000.[22] While Jones and McCoy were co-stars, it soon became obvious that the films featured Buck Jones. McCoy became dissatisfied with the arrangement and entered military service in 1942. Rex Bell replaced him, and one last Rough Riders Western, *Dawn on the Great Divide* (1942), was produced. After that, Dunlap and Monogram made plans for a new series to star a more mature Buck Jones with Raymond Hatton as his sidekick. In the meantime, Jones, accompanied by Scott Dunlap, went on a bond-selling, promotional tour.

The tour concluded on Saturday, November 28, 1942, in Boston, Massachusetts. That day Jones visited a children's hospital, appeared at a rally of the Buck Jones Rangers in the Boston Garden, and attended part of the Boston College–Holy Cross football game at Fenway Park. By then he was tired, and he suffered from a cold. Good business practices, however, required him to attend a cocktail party given in his honor by Herman Rifkin, district manager of Monogram Pictures. After that Jones intended to return to the hotel and go to bed. Against his better judgment, however, he agreed to be the guest of honor at a dinner party hosted by one of the movie executives at Boston's famed Cocoanut Grove Nightclub.[23]

Jones and his party arrived at the crowded nightclub around 9:30 P.M. and were seated in the Terrace, across the dance floor from the band. Edward Keyes, author of *The Coconut Grove*, writes that around 10:15 P.M. Mickey Alpert, the band leader and master of ceremonies, started across the dance floor to greet Jones.[24] Somebody screamed "fire" and chaos ensued.

Tuska claims that Jones was dancing near the revolving doors at the entrance to the club and escaped. Unable to locate Dunlap, however, Jones went back into the burning building and was overcome by the smoke and flames.[25] Odille Osborne insisted on much the same thing. She wrote Buck Rainey that Jones helped several people to escape before he was overcome by smoke.[26]

Keyes' more recent research raises serious questions about those accounts. It is doubtful that Jones was dancing, and in fact, the dance floor was some distance from the front revolving doors. Besides, a large, overflowing crowd milled in the foyer, separating people on the dance floor from the revolving doors. During the panic, the revolving doors jammed. Not more than a handful of people escaped through those doors. If Jones had gotten out he could not have re-entered the building.

Jones was found near the Terrace with most of the Monogram party. His face and neck were burned, and he suffered the same severe pulmonary damage that claimed so many other lives. Buck Jones died on November 30, 1942,

Buck Jones astride his famous horse Silver.

at Massachusetts General Hospital. His ashes were spread over the Pacific Ocean he loved.

Buck Jones' film career falls into two distinct parts. His silent Westerns ended with *Branded Sombrero* in 1928. After that film Jones left Fox Studio, failed miserably with his own production, *The Big Hop*, and went further into debt when his wild west show folded. In 1930 he returned to motion pictures and continued to make Westerns until his death in 1942.

Jones' silent films are difficult to evaluate because so few prints remain. In 1918 and 1919, he had appeared with Franklyn Farnum in a series of two-reel films produced by Colonel Selig at Canyon Pictures. A few of these short films remain, but no more than a single Western from Jones' years at Fox is extant. On the other hand, nearly all of the sixty-six sound Westerns and six serials in which Jones starred are available.

Most of the eight Westerns Jones made for Sol Lesser, as well as his nineteen films produced by Columbia, were traditional Western fare. Standard conventions, plots, and iconography had developed slowly during the silent era, shaping the genre into a predictable format. Jones' Columbia efforts seldom challenged those standards. He frequently appeared as a sheriff, occasionally as a bumbling cowpoke who stumbled onto trouble, or even rarer, imitating William S. Hart, Jones might open the film as a badman. After a few celluloid feet, however, happenstance or misunderstanding drove Jones to the side of law and order. By the film's conclusion he had become one of those heroes.

Jones' pictures were action-filled. Western fans expected exciting chase scenes, daring rescues, fistfights, and dangerous stunts. Buck Jones' Columbia Westerns included all of those elements. They were fast-paced, action-filled, standard B Western movies.

Jones' films were better than most B Westerns because of Columbia's production values. Better scripts, sharp photography, good acting, and intelligent editing distinguish these films from those made by the independent producers and smaller studios such as Monogram and Mascot. Compare, for example, the Westerns Jones made for Columbia in 1933 and 1934 with the Monogram Lone Star productions in which John Wayne starred. Wayne's films are primitive when compared to Jones' efforts.

Still most of Jones' Columbia Westerns are similar to the dozens of B Westerns starring Tom Tyler, Bob Steele, Tim McCoy, Ken Maynard, and John Wayne. There is an element in Jones' Westerns, however, which makes one pause. One senses that Jones was willing to test the contours of the genre, to probe its outer boundaries. Jones, far more than any other B Western cowboy star, was willing to push out those boundaries a little.

Several of Jones' Columbia productions are examples of how his films differed from normal B Westerns. Jones portrayed the legendary Mexican bandit Juaquin Muretta in *The Avenger* (1931). William K. Everson liked the film so much he described it as a quality B Western with adult appeal.[27] One of Jones' most unusual films, *South of the Rio Grande* (1932), had a complete Mexican setting in which he played Carlos, a Mexican policeman. *Forbidden Trail* (1932) featured Jones as a practical joker, a cowboy always in trouble and constantly on the verge of being fired. Jones' films, then, had variety. The settings and plots varied, and he portrayed diverse character types. For one who grew up with the predictable repetition of singing cowboys, Jones' Westerns are delightfully different.

Two of Jones' Columbia films, *Ridin' for Justice* (1931) and *Desert Vengeance* (1931), stand out as particularly entertaining, off-beat Westerns which challenged conventional morality. In *Ridin' for Justice*, Jones is the favorite of dance-hall girls on whom he spends his money freely. He portrays a hard-working, although not too dependable cowboy whose practical jokes and fighting continually irritate his boss. Jones' image in *Ridin' for Justice* contradicts conventional expectations that the cowboy hero works hard, takes life seriously, and never consorts with dance-hall girls.

When Jones ignores the sheriff's deputy who tries to arrest him for carrying firearms in defiance of a town ordinance, the sheriff attempts to arrest Jones. Fleeing the posse, Jones inadvertently hides in the sheriff's house. He discovers the sheriff's wife is a young woman trapped in an abusive marriage to an older man. Defying 1930s conventional morality, Jones escorts the married woman to a masquerade dance, and he encourages her to divorce her husband.

In *Desert Vengeance*, Jones plays an outlaw who is swindled out of a large sum of money by a male-female confidence team. The male fakes death, and when Jones consoles the woman who pretends to be the deceased's sister, she expresses her love for Jones. When Jones discovers that the male is not dead and that he has been swindled, he kidnaps the two and forces them to accompany him to a deserted hideout. They live there as his slaves. By the film's end, after a violent shootout with a rival outlaw gang which left all of Jones' men dead, Jones mellows and rides away with the girl, now destined to be his wife. Throughout the film, however, Jones' character acts in stark contrast to the image cultivated by most B Western cowboy stars.

Another Jones Western, *White Eagle* (1932), stretched the B Western genre by raising a social issue, the romance between a white female and an Indian male. Jones plays a Bannock Indian living in the white world as a Pony Express rider. When Barbara Weeks, his boss' sister, comes West, a romance builds between her and Jones. Jason Robards, Sr., her brother, is warned about the relationship, but he replies, "White Eagle understands."

White renegades stir up trouble and the Indians fight back, but Jones tells Weeks he will not fight with the Indians. Weeks is so pleased she hugs Jones. Her brother sees her embrace and explodes in anger. Robards tells Jones, "I treated you like a white man, but you forgot you are an Indian." In true B Western fashion, all ends well when Jones learns that he is really a white man who had been kidnapped while a small baby by the Bannocks. Nevertheless, miscegenation fears overwhelm the film. They permeate nearly every theme and subplot. *White Eagle* stands apart from the rest of B Westerns, few of which touched on socially sensitive issues.

Buck Jones left Columbia for Universal Pictures in 1934. Not only was his salary increased, Universal also gave him responsibility for producing his own films. At least initially, Universal underwrote the films with an ample budget of $65,000 per picture. By the late 1930s Republic Studio invested even more in Gene Autry features as Autry's popularity grew, and Paramount eventually budgeted Hopalong Cassidy movies at over $125,000 per picture. Autry and Cassidy films were, however, unusual. Most B Westerns in the 1930s had budgets well under $30,000 per picture.

Jones' early Universal entries reflect the larger budgets. They are entertaining films with good scripts and adult appeal. Three of them are particularly noteworthy. *When a Man Sees Red* (1934) continued the trend of humor-laden, romantic Westerns that Jones had begun at Columbia. Peggy

Campbell plays a conceited Easterner who inherits her uncle's ranch. Determined to fire Jones, who plays the ranch foreman, and all the rest of the cowboys, she discovers her uncle had appointed Jones her guardian. There is little standard Western action in the film; instead there is a great deal of comedy and romance as Jones struggles to win Campbell's affection. *When a Man Sees Red* has so little action and so much romance, one suspects young boys walked out of the matinee shaking their heads in disappointment, wondering what their hero had done to them.

Stone of Silver Creek (1935), was even more startling. Jones played T. William Stone, owner of a gambling house–saloon. The film was a notable departure from B Westerns because it was unusual for a cowboy star to be associated with a saloon, thought by many to be an immoral business. *Stone of Silver Creek* was slow-moving by traditional standards, with no action until the very end. And once again romance was a primary theme.

The Ivory-Handled Guns (1935) had a great deal of action. It was full of hard riding sequences, excellent stunting, and tricks by Jones' famous horse, Silver. The film also had a main-street gunfight. But even this film, with all of its traditional B Western characteristics, demonstrated that Jones was willing to go beyond accepted conventions.

In the film, Jones' father had been crippled by a bullet from one of two ivory-handled pistols. Walter Miller, playing the Wolverine Kid, son of the man who shot Jones' father, carries one of the two pistols; Jones carries the other. During the climactic conclusion, Miller escapes a trap laid by Jones and returns to the ranch, determined to kill both Jones and his father. Jones crashes through a ranch window and both men grapple on the floor until Miller's ivory-handled gun discharges. Miller slumps dead, but Jones appears dead as well. Even though he moves slightly, the film ends with viewers in suspense. Was Jones killed? Was he like his father before him crippled by a bullet from the ivory-handled gun? Few other B Westerns end with the hero in such an uncertain predicament. The film defies an important convention; the cowboy-hero always triumphed over evil and escaped unharmed.

Diversity characterized Jones' Universal productions even more than his Columbia Westerns. The three films just discussed featured less action and more adult appeal than most B Westerns. But Jones also appeared in straightforward, typical B Westerns. *The Crimson Trail* (1935), *Border Brigands* (1935), *The Throwback* (1935), and *For the Service* (1936) stressed action and were much like B Westerns in which other cowboy stars appeared.

Whether the films stressed romance and comedy or action, most of the Universal–Buck Jones Productions of 1934–36 were edited crisply. They seldom lasted longer than 65 minutes and, usually were only about 60 minutes long. A lot of action was packed into them. In such films as *The Ivory-Handled Guns*, probably too much story and action were included, but few of them dragged. Good editing kept the plot unfolding at a fast pace.

With *Empty Saddles*, his last release of 1936, Jones' Universal Productions declined in quality. Films such as *Empty Saddles*, *Sandflow* (1937), *Left Handed Law* (1937) and *Sudden Bill Dorn* (1937) were slow-paced, confusing films. Plots and story lines were difficult to follow. Continuity depended less on action and more on dialogue to tie all the strands together. *Sandflow*, for example, remains confusing even after several viewings. It is so slow-moving, boring in fact, that the film is difficult to watch. The last few Buck Jones productions are disappointing. They have little action and are slow-paced to the point of being dull.

Sudden Bill Dorn, as dull and confusing as *Sandflow*, was the last Buck Jones Universal Production. The new studio management would not meet Jones' increased salary demands. It is just as well because the series was in noticeable decline. Jones' great strength was that he dared to be different. Unlike most other B Westerns, his earlier pictures were not dull repetitions of one another. In 1937, however, that strength became a weakness. His last few Universal films were strange, even bizarre. It is unlikely audiences would have continued to patronize them as they had other Buck Jones Westerns.

There are a few notable creative departures in the history of American B Western movies. Harry Sherman's screen adaptation of Clarence E. Milford's Hopalong Cassidy character and Nate Levine's gamble on Gene Autry as a singing cowboy are the two most prominent departures. Scott Dunlap and Trem Carr of Monogram Pictures also deserve recognition for their creation of the Rough Riders, an entertaining departure from the B Western norm.

Certainly Buck Jones and Tim McCoy, the main stars of the series, had little to lose. Both careers were in decline. By 1941 many thought they were finished as cowboy stars, chased off the studio lots by a host of singing cowboys. Raymond Hatton, the third Rough Rider, always had been a supporting actor. He had appeared in the late 1930s as Roy Rogers' sidekick and then as one of the Three Mesquiteers in that popular Republic series. Surprisingly, Jones, McCoy, and Hatton blended well together as the Rough Riders. The result was one of the best B Western series to appear on the screen.

Jones, McCoy, and Hatton made eight Rough Riders pictures. All of them were standard B type films. Each employed standard conventions and had fast-paced action. Unlike earlier Jones Westerns at Columbia and Universal, there was little variety in the Monogram series. After viewing one of them it is easy to anticipate the rest.

The idea behind the series was deceptively simple, Jones, McCoy, and Hatton play former United States marshals who come out of retirement each picture to capture the outlaws. Each film opened with a stirring rendition of the song, "The Rough Riders Ride Again," and each closed with the men riding off in different directions: Jones back to his Arizona ranch; McCoy back to his Wyoming retirement; and Hatton back to his bride in Texas. For nearly all of each picture the men worked independently, then at the climax the three pooled their efforts to capture the outlaws. In print the format appears pedestrian, but on the screen all the elements blend into entertaining B Westerns.

If the Rough Riders series did nothing else, it rescued Jones' film career. After two years of inactivity, Jones returned as the obvious star of the Rough Riders. When McCoy left the series to resume his military career, Rex Bell replaced him and one last Rough Riders film, *Dawn on the Great Divide* (1942), was produced. It was not up to the standards of the previous eight films so the series was scrapped. Dunlap, however, planned to star Jones in a new series of Westerns with Raymond Hatton as his sidekick, but the films never materialized. Jones was killed and Scott Dunlap was critically injured in the Cocoanut Grove fire before the new series could take shape.

Buck Jones was one of the most popular, perhaps the most popular, cowboy star of the 1930s. The Buck Jones fan club had over 3,000,000 members. Jones received up to 50,000 requests per year for autographed pictures. In 1936, the *Motion Picture Herald* asked film exhibitors to list those cowboy movie stars whose films attracted the greatest audiences. Buck Jones led the list. Yet even he could not stem the Autry and Cassidy craze which swept the Western film market; in 1937 and 1938 Jones dropped to third behind Gene Autry and William Boyd. Even though Jones made no films in 1939, he still finished eighth on the *Motion Picture Herald* list, one spot higher than John Wayne.[28]

Buck Rainey believes that Buck Jones, "...was probably the most loved and respected of all screen cowboys...."[29] Don Miller, author of the *Hollywood Corral*, agrees with Rainey. Miller writes, "There was about Buck Jones a mystique, an intriguing quality far apart from the rest of the cowboy performers."[30]

What qualities did Jones possess which merit such acclaim? Why do many people remember Buck Jones with such warm affection over a half century after his death? Popularity is not easily defined or explained. It is a soft concept dependent more on impression than on data. Data such as the *Motion Picture Herald*'s list point to popularity but do not define it. Jones was popular in two senses of the word. His movies were liked and regarded with favor by most persons; hence viewers paid to see them. Jones' movies were also popular as that word is used in "popular culture." Jones' films fit the prevailing tastes and values of the majority of Americans living in the turbulent decade before World War II. They reflected majoritarian values and norms. Several factors account for Jones' two-fold popularity.

Jones did not assume he would be popular. He worked at being accepted by the public and he had a deep respect for his profession. At no time did he assume that Westerns were merely a way to make money, and of no particular importance. In fact, Don Miller contends, "...the feeling persists that the respect for and devotion to his milieu and his craft ran deepest in Jones."[31] He could ensure that respect and care at Universal Studio because he had control over the production of his films. As one of the partners in the Great Western Picture Company, Jones also had a great deal of impact on the Rough Riders Westerns. Miller believes that Jones had a strong voice in his Columbia Westerns as well.[32]

Whether or not one likes B Westerns, Jones' films deserve respect. They featured competent acting, interesting story lines, and most had a lot of action. Jones was a leader in his craft, a craft he took seriously. William K. Everson agrees, and says of Jones' movies that he "...gave them such care and variety of plot that none of them had an assembly line look to them."[33] Everson overstates; some of Jones' films do have an assembly line look, but it is obvious that Jones' efforts were superior to most B Westerns of the time. Audiences responded to that quality and patronized the films. His efforts were appreciated and his films regarded with favor. They were popular.

If the movies were popular, so was the star. Buck Jones has been called a man's man. He possessed those qualities that audiences of the 1930s expected in a man. He was good looking with a broad-chested physique. Most of his films contained at least one expertly performed fight sequence. It was not unusual for Jones to have his shirt torn away to show his physique during the course of the fight. Jones, of course, seldom instigated the fight, but he was always more than able to take care of himself. As a man's man, Jones was always kind to children and firm, but polite, with women.

Jones also seemed comfortable outdoors. Viewers did not have to stretch their imaginations to picture Jones sleeping under the stars or cooking his meals over an open fire. He did not have to learn to ride a horse when he became a cowboy actor; Jones was an expert horseman. He sat his famous white horse, Silver, with ease and rode with grace and style, even at full gallop. Jones wore his gun with the self-confidence of one familiar with firearms, and he dressed in a Western-like but simple costume, not the printed, gaudy shirts and pants typical of the singing cowboys. Jones was popular because he was believable and because he conformed to popular perceptions of the Westerner. About a year before he died, Jones described himself as "an old-time cowboy."[34] That is the image he projected on the screen.

Jones was popular because he modeled those traits and characteristics pre–World War II Americans expected from their heroes and leaders. He personified the Westerner who was a strong moral force in American life, an embodiment of Manifest Destiny. The myth of America is that it is a new promised land, given to a people chosen by God to create a new, moral force in world history. According to the myth, Americans fought Indians and Mexicans and suffered through drought and blizzard to tame an inhospitable land. Buck Jones personified that myth at a time when it was taken seriously by many Americans.

By projecting a moral image on the screen, by working for justice, and by usually riding off with the pretty girl, Jones assured viewers that moral behavior was rewarded. His films also reminded Americans that each person had a duty, a job to perform, and that moral character required never shirking that duty even when afraid or when facing great odds.

Buck Jones was popular because his films expressed and supported those values. In most respects Jones' films seem quaint, naive, and exist in a later period because they do express those values. Contemporary viewers are not so sure those values are appropriate. Anyone who wants to understand the values and norms of the 1930s, however, and to see a good expression of them within popular culture, can learn them from Buck Jones' Westerns.

To his self-ascribed description as "an old-time cowboy," Jones added, "...the sort that kids used to want to grow up to be like."[35] The story is told of a young boy who fell out a fifth story window and broke nearly every bone in his body. He bit his lip and bravely said, "Buck Jones wouldn't cry and I am not going to cry either."[38] Jones was so touched that when the little boy was mending, he flew to New York to visit him. In 1973, Buck's daughter Maxine spoke not only for herself and the little boy who would not cry, but for millions of others and adults when Buck Jones was admitted to the National Cowboy Hall of Fame's Hall of Great Western Performers. Accepting the award Maxine said, "He was my dad, but he was my hero too."[37]

Notes

1. Buck Rainey, in *The Life and Films of Buck Jones: The Silent Years* (Waynesville, 1988), p. 17, wrote that Buck Jones' mother helped him deceive the Army. But in a letter to Robert R. Stevens, April 19, 1983, Edward Keyes wrote that Jones' daughter, Maxine, believes her father's grandmother helped him enlist.

2. *The Vincennes Western Sun*, June 19, 1892.

3. Letter from Robert R. Stevens to Dominick Marafioti, National Chief of Buck Jones Rangers of America, August 27, 1984.

4. Rainey, *The Life and Films of Buck Jones: The Silent Years*, p. 15.

5. Rainey, *Life*, p. 18.

6. Rainey, *Life*, p. 18.

7. Telephone conversation between Philip Loy and Robert A. Laycock, January 11, 1989.

8. Rainey, *Life*, p. 18.

9. *The Lima News*, August 12, 1915.

10. Rainey, *Life*, p. 22.

11. Rainey, *Life*, p. 22.

12. Rainey, *Life*, p. 27.

13. *Henry S. Orme Trestle Board*, June 1924, p. 5.

14. Fred D. Pfening, "Buck Jones Wild West and Round Up Days," *Bandwagon* (November-December, 1965), p. 26.

15. Pfening, *Bandwagon*, pp. 27–28.

16. *The Los Angeles Times*, March 12, 1930.

17. Jon Tuska, *Filming of the West* (New York, 1976), p. 223.

18. Tuska, *Filming*, p. 226.

19. Tuska, *Filming*, p. 281.

20. Tuska, *Filming*, p. 408.

21. Tuska, *Filming*, p. 410.

22. Tuska, *Filming*, p. 411.

23. Edward Keyes, *The Cocoanut Grove* (New York, 1984), pp. 22–23.

24. Keyes, *Cocoanut*, p. 24.

25. Tuska, *Filming*, pp. 415–16.

26. Buck Rainey, *The Saga of Buck Jones* (Nashville, 1975), p. 87.

27. William K. Everson, *A Pictorial History of the Western Film* (Secaucus, NJ, 1969), p. 131.

28. Phil Hardy, *The Western* (New York, 1983), p. 366.

29. Buck Rainey, *Saddle Aces of the Cinema* (San Diego and New York, 1980), p. 150.

30. Don Miller, *Hollywood Corral* (New York, 1976), pp. 31–32.

31. Miller, *Corral*, p. 32.

32. Miller, *Corral*, p. 32.

33. Everson, *Pictorial*, p. 130.

34. The *New York Times*, December 1, 1942, p. 100.

35. *Times*, p. 100.

36. Rainey, *Saga*, p. 91.

37. Robert Cotton, "Buck Jones: Hero in Films, Hero in LIfe," *Persimmon Hill*, Volume 8, No. 2 (Spring, 1978), p. 23.

TEX RITTER: AMERICA'S MOST BELOVED COWBOY

by Gary Kramer

Those who achieved stardom in B Westerns became so closely identified with the genre that it was nearly impossible for them to move successfully to other facets of film or entertainment. Thus, William Boyd *became* Hopalong Cassidy. Wild Bill Elliott was forced to spend the last years of his career doing Viceroy cigarette commercials on television and the only work Allen "Rocky" Lane could get was as the television voice of "Mr. Ed." Even Gene Autry and Roy Rogers are remembered primarily as B movie cowboys. There were, however, two notable exceptions: John Wayne made the transition to major motion picture star, and Tex Ritter used Western films to launch a thirty-year career as one of the country's top country-western singers.

Woodward Maurice Ritter was born January 12, 1905, in Murvaul, in Panola County in Eastern Texas about forty miles from the Louisiana border. He was raised on land settled by his great-grandfather, Frank Ritter, when the territory still belonged to Mexico. "Woody," as he was called by his family, was the youngest of six children of James Everett and Elizabeth Matthews Ritter. The Ritter family worked a 400-acre farm, raising cotton, corn, peanuts, hogs, and cattle. Ritter had little interest, however, in becoming a farmer and avoided farm chores when he could. Instead, he enjoyed politics, law, and especially music. He developed an interest in politics because it was often a topic of discussion in the Ritter home. Several members of the Ritter and Matthews families had been elected to state and county offices and his father was regarded as an influential figure in local politics although he did not personally seek office. Ritter's fascination with law resulted from the family's frequent trips to Carthage, the county seat of Panola County. Since Ritter's grandfather held the office of county clerk, his parents would leave him at the courthouse while they went shopping. He frequently wandered into courtrooms to watch the local attorneys plead their cases and soon decided that he, too, wanted to become a lawyer. Music was also an important part of Ritter's early life. The Ritter family liked to sing and regularly invited friends and relatives to their home for song festivals. It was on such an occasion that Ritter's two older brothers, who were both good singers, asked their mother to please make Woody sit down and stop singing because he was off-key. Each summer the local citizens of Murvaul hired itinerant music teachers to conduct singing schools for their children. Ritter looked forward to these sessions with much anticipation and used the opportunities to improve his singing talents.

When Ritter was fifteen years old, his family moved to Nederland, Texas. He attended South Park High School, located in nearby Beaumont, where he was involved in dramatics, served on the debating team, and also played basketball and football. He pursued his interest in music by joining the Loveless Theriot Barbershop Quartet and also singing at the First United Methodist Church. He also became interested in collecting and singing Western ballads.[1]

After graduation from high school, Ritter enrolled at the University of Texas in Austin in the fall of 1922. He studied pre-law, majoring in government, political science, and economics. Much of his time, however, was devoted to music. Ritter sang in a campus quartet and took courses in music history, guitar, trumpet, and voice. He also joined the glee club and in 1925 became the organization's president. The glee club traveled extensively in the United States and Mexico and the trips prevented Ritter from passing a physics class due to missed lab assignments. Ritter's refusal to abandon music probably kept him from achieving his objective of becoming a lawyer. Whenever it became necessary to choose between music and something else, Ritter could never bring himself to give up music. Although he had enough credits to graduate, Ritter lacked courses in math and physics that were required for a degree.

While at the University of Texas, Ritter met three men who influenced his life and encouraged him to pursue his interest in singing traditional Western ballads. They were Professor J. Frank Dobie, regarded as a foremost authority on Southwestern folklore; John A. Lomax, a well-known collector of American folk ballads; and Oscar J. Fox, composer of cowboy songs and director of the glee club.[2]

During the summer of 1928, Ritter was given an opportunity to sing authentic Western ballads on a thirty-minute, Saturday-morning radio program on station KPRC in Houston. He received no pay for doing the program, but in later years was credited as being the first singer of Western songs on radio.[3]

When the J. & Lee Schubert traveling company performed "Maryland, My Maryland" at the Hancock Opera House in Austin during the fall of 1928, Ritter attended all the performances by sneaking into the balcony via the fire escape. He soon became acquainted with members of the cast, and, when the show left town, Ritter joined the troupe as a member of the male chorus. The show worked its way back to New York City and then folded.[4]

After his arrival in New York, Ritter experienced hard times. He spent several months singing cowboy songs at private parties and doing occasional radio commercials. In reminiscing about his first months in New York, Ritter said, "When I went to New York, I had a whole suitcase full of books and I found a little place in the Village that sold second hand books, and I would go down there and sell one of my books for 75 cents and eat a sandwich that day. For Thanksgiving I woke up with ten cents to my name so I went down to a restaurant and ordered ten cents worth of french fries and poured ketchup all over them. This Greek that ran the joint gave me hell for using so much ketchup."[5]

Ritter eventually landed a job singing in the men's chorus of the Broadway production of Hammerstein and Romberg's *The New Moon*. After an extensive run on Broadway, the show went on the road. Ritter traveled to Chicago and enrolled at Northwestern University, hoping to complete his law degree. However, when *The New Moon* touring company reached the Midwest, Ritter rejoined the case. For a while Ritter attended classes and commuted each night to nearby cities to appear in the play. Ritter decided to go with the show when it left for Indianapolis, dropping out of school to continue his career as an entertainer.[6]

A few months later Ritter returned to New York, where he auditioned for a part in *Green Grow the Lilacs*, a Western stageplay by Lynn Riggs, which was revived several years later as *Oklahoma*. Ritter was chosen to sing four songs as well as understudy Franchot Tone in the leading role. The play's managers began to bill Ritter as "Tex" when they heard him addressed in that manner by members of the cast. To bring authenticity to the show, several real cowboys appearing in a rodeo at Madison Square Garden were hired for the cast. Among them were Hank Worden and Everett Cheatham, with whom Ritter soon developed a strong friendship. The play opened in Boston on December 8, 1930, and then moved to Philadelphia, Washington, and Baltimore before returning to New York for a successful eight-week run on Broadway. Ritter, Cheatham, and Worden shared a New York apartment located only two blocks from the theater and continued to room together when the show went back on the road.[7]

Ritter's work in *Green Grow the Lilacs* helped him to break into New York radio where he appeared on station WOR in a popular show called *Lone Star Rangers*. He also obtained character parts on several other programs, such as *Bobbie Benson*, *Gang Busters*, and *ENO Crime Clues*. Ritter gradually established a reputation as an East Coast radio personality through such programs as *Tex Ritter's Campfire* and *WHN Barn Dance*. In 1933 Ritter began a three-year engagement as a regular cast member of *Cowboy Tom's Roundup*, a popular daily children's program which was broadcast by WINS.[8]

Events occurred on the West Coast that changed the direction of Ritter's career. Financial problems which plagued the movie industry had curtailed Western film production in the early 1930s. Hoping to broaden the appeal of

Western movies, Nat Levine, of Mascot Pictures, hired Gene Autry, WLS radio personality, to make a series of musical Westerns. The Autry films became an immediate success. Edward F. Finney, an experienced film publicist who had worked for Metro, Pathé, and United Artists, foresaw an emerging trend for Westerns with music. When he was offered a position as director of advertising and publicity at the newly organized Grand National Pictures, Finney accepted the job with the understanding that he would be able to produce his own series of musical Westerns to be financed and distributed by the new film company.

Finney was familiar with Ritter's work on radio and in plays. He learned from a friend in Pennsylvania that Ritter usually could be found on weekends at the Bar H Dude Ranch near Wallpack Center in northern New Jersey. Finney registered as a guest at the dude ranch for three successive weekends and closely observed the young Texan until he was certain Ritter was the right choice for the projected film series. Finney invited Ritter to his office and asked him if he would be interested in making Western movies. Ritter quickly accepted the offer. Following a successful screen test, Finney placed Ritter under a personal five-year contract which paid him $2,400 for each picture.[9]

Grand National announced that eight Tex Ritter films would be released during the 1936-1937 film season. Ritter left immediately for the West Coast to begin filming *Song of the Gringo* (1936). Despite appearing a little too serious and uneasy before the camera, Ritter's initial performance was surprisingly good considering he had no previous film experience. He looked and sounded like a real cowboy and handled action sequences in an authentic and believable manner.

Edward Finney had hired several veteran filmmakers who were experienced with the production of budget Westerns to work on the Tex Ritter series. Lindsley Parsons, Robert Tansey, and director Robert North Bradbury hit on the right formula for Ritter's second film, *Headin' for the Rio Grande* (1936). The result was a good, action-packed Western which nicely showcased Ritter's talents as an actor and singer.

Budget restraints were partially responsible for the varying quality of Ritter's next few films, but the seasons ended on a high note with *Mystery of the Hooded Horsemen* (1937). Elements of mystery, hooded, serial-like villains, good production values, and excellent camerawork were combined to make it one of Ritter's best Grand National films.

The Ritter films were well received by the public. He was voted the sixth top money maker among Western film stars in the *Motion Picture Herald*'s annual poll of exhibitors in 1937. This was a significant achievement for an unknown Western actor whose films were being released by a new film studio still struggling to establish itself in the motion picture industry.

Despite the success of his films, Grand National tightened the budgets and only four Tex Ritter films were released in 1937-1938. Ritter's popularity at the box office was adversely affected and he dropped to ninth place in the *Motion Picture Herald*'s poll of exhibitors. Edward Finney became increasingly concerned about Grand National's financial instability and successfully sued the studio for release from his contract. Finney then signed an agreement to have Monogram Pictures take over financing and distribution of the Tex Ritter films. Budgets were increased by Monogram and the pictures also received better distribution. Production for the 1938-1939 season was increased once again to eight films. The Monogram releases resembled the Grand National films in many respects. Horace Murphy and Snub Pollard remained as Tex's sidekicks for three films. After Pollard was dropped from the series, Murphy remained for three additional releases. Karl Hackett and Charles King continued to be the principal villains in several of the early Monogram releases. One of the season's better films was *The Man from Texas* (1939). It was not a typical Tex Ritter film, more closely resembling the Jack Randall pictures that were simultaneously being released by Monogram. Ritter appeared for the first time without a sidekick and the film contained little music. *Variety*, often critical of Ritter's films, said, "Monogram's Western star in his best film to date. Trim and full of action, is paced and cut to a nicety. Well chosen exteriors, first-rate camera work and sound recording create a clear-cut and sparkling impression. Other definite assets to the production are Ritter's riding and baritone booming of two new songs. Ritter carries the picture with an excellent performance."[10] The move to Monogram helped Ritter to climb to seventh place in the *Motion Picture Herald*'s poll of Western film stars.

Edward Finney produced eight more Ritter films for Monogram release in 1939-1940. A veteran character actor, Nelson McDowell, was tried as Ritter's sidekick for two films. He was believable, but not very funny. *Roll, Wagons, Roll* (1939) got the season off to a good start. The film, about Ritter's attempt to lead covered wagons to Oregon, contained excellent action sequences and was shot on location with beautiful scenery. Unfortunately, these positive aspects were minimized due to the insertion of stock footage which was poorly matched to the action scenes in the film. Midway through the season, Arkansas Slim Andrews, who was more hillbilly than cowboy, became Tex Ritter's sidekick. Andrews was a tall lanky fellow with a handlebar mustache who galloped along behind Ritter on a mule named Josephine. Andrews was an asset to the Ritter films and there was a good rapport between Tex and Slim. A film audience could almost guess, at times, what Tex was thinking as he casually observed with unspoken amusement the screen antics of his rustic sidekick. In reviewing *The Golden Trail* (1940), *Variety* said, "From audience reaction to the Ritter gallopers in the hinterlands, it appears Slim Andrews should be turned loose for more of his tent rep learned musical didoes. Evidently the guy is being held in check, for no apparent reason."[11]

Andrews continued to be Ritter's sidekick for the remainder of the Monogram series and then made personal appearances with Tex for nearly ten years.

Only four Tex Ritter films were produced by Finney for the 1940-1941 season. *Take Me Back to Oklahoma* (1940) belied the fact that the series was coming to an end. It was one of Ritter's best films, had a longer running time at sixty-six minutes than any previous Ritter film, and effectively included Bob Wills and the Texas Playboys in the cast. Ritter's next two films, *Rolling Home to Texas* (1940) and *Ridin' the Cherokee Trail* (1941), were acceptable, but Finney and his production crew expended a minimal amount of money and effort on *Pioneers* (1941). It was obviously made only to fill the production quota for the season. Stock footage was used extensively and the overall result was extremely poor. It was by far the weakest Ritter film produced by Finney. Due to the reduced number of releases and inconsistent quality of the films it was no surprise that Ritter dropped to tenth place in the *Motion Picture Herald*'s exhibitor poll for 1941.

In early 1938 a contract dispute had developed between Gene Autry and Republic Pictures. When Autry refused to report for work, Ritter was offered a contract by a Republic representative. Ritter rejected the offer because Republic declined to also hire Edward Finney as a producer. Republic then signed Leonard Slye of the Sons of the Pioneers and changed his name to Roy Rogers. Rogers capitalized on the opportunity that Ritter rejected and eventually became Republic's top Western star.[12] Although Ritter's loyalty to his producer was admirable, it was not a wise career decision and he may have regretted it later.

Dorothy Fay Southworth was the daughter of a prominent physician who had served as president of the Arizona State Medical Society. She obtained her education at the University of London, University Hall at Oxford, the University of Southern California and the Caroline Leonetti School. One of her close friends, a Hollywood agent, helped get her into movies. Her first film was a Buck Jones Western. Ritter's friend, Hank Worden, was in the cast, and he introduced Dorothy to Tex during a break in the shooting schedule. Although their relationship developed slowly, they continued to see each other and Dorothy eventually co-starred in several of Ritter's films. Tex and Dorothy were married in 1941 in her hometown, Prescott, Arizona. Their wedding was attended by a number of Western film stars, including Buck Jones, Tim McCoy, Big Boy Williams, Raymond Hatton, Bob Baker, and Dick Foran.[13]

During the filming of the Grand National and Monogram pictures, Ritter had used four or five rented studio horses, all billed as "White Flash." In 1941 Ritter began an extensive search for a white horse to become the permanent "White Flash." He eventually located a suitable two-year-old animal which he purchased from Jerome Eddy of Chino Valley, Arizona. After having the horse trained by Glenn Randall, Ritter used him in the rest of his star-

Tex Ritter strumming his trusty guitar.

ring films and during personal appearance tours. White Flash's farewell appearance came during Ritter's successful tour of Europe in 1952.[14]

Tex Ritter and Edward Finney dissolved their partnership in 1941 after a five-year relationship. Ritter signed with Columbia Pictures for more money and an opportunity to appear in bigger budgeted films. Columbia was producing two popular Western series already, one with Charles Starrett and another with Wild Bill Elliott. In addition to signing Ritter, Columbia also hired Russell Hayden, who had been supporting William Boyd in the Hopa-long Cassidy films at Paramount. Columbia decided to co-star Ritter in the Elliott series and Hayden was assigned to work in the Starrett films.

In retrospect, it was probably a mistake for Ritter to leave Monogram. His career suffered because of the transition from solo star to co-starring roles. The scriptwriters developed stories to accommodate two stars, often resulting in Ritter's being cast in roles much different than the ones he had played in his Grand National and Monogram films. Although it gave Ritter an opportunity to be a more versatile actor, he was best as the traditional Western hero that he had portrayed in his earlier films.

It may have seemed like a good idea to cast two well-known Western stars in the same films, but a reviewer for *Variety* was quick to observe the disadvantage to such a format. Writing about *King of Dodge City* (1941), the first Elliott-Ritter film, he said, "In endeavoring to split footage and impor-tance of the two Westerners equally, scripter Gerald Gereghty hit a stonewall and Ritter suffers by comparison in the acting line against the better perfor-mance of Elliott."[15] Actually the scripts gave Elliott a definite advantage, espe-cially the six films in which he was cast as Wild Bill Hickok. Elliott already was identified with the character, having portrayed Hickok in a fifteen-chap-ter serial and several feature films. In these films Hickok had a reputation for his lightning fast draw and the mention of his name brought fear to lawless elements of the West. He was, however, level-headed, slow to lose his tem-per, and proclaimed himself to be a "peaceable man." The part was played to near perfection by Elliott. Ritter, on the other hand, was often required to por-tray a character who was hot-headed and impetuous. The miscasting of Elliott as a mountie in *North of the Rockies* (1942) and as Joaquin Murietta in *Vengeance of the West* (1942) did serve to balance the scales somewhat with respect to which actor received the better roles.

Neither Elliott nor Ritter was satisfied with the co-starring arrangement, and after eight pictures Elliott left Columbia to sign a contract with Repub-lic Pictures. Columbia decided to produce a second series of B Westerns again in 1942-1943 which would augment their popular Charles Starrett films. The studio elected not to continue the co-starring format initiated a year earlier, but it was Hayden and not Ritter that Columbia retained to star in the second series.

Ritter had little difficulty in obtaining a new film contract with Univer-sal Pictures. Universal's Westerns were generally better than those made by Columbia. However, once again Ritter was required to share top billing with Johnny Mack Brown, who was beginning his fourth year with Universal. Executives at Universal, even more than their counterparts at Columbia had done a year earlier, chose to emphasize their reigning star at Ritter's expense. Despite equal billing, it was clearly Brown's series and the scripts often cast Ritter in a less than favorable manner. In *Little Joe, the Wrangler* (1942), Ritter is a local sheriff under pressure to resign because he is unable to capture a gang of outlaws who have been robbing local miners. Naturally, Brown helps get the situation under control. In *Tenting Tonight on the Old Campground* (1943), instead of riding White Flash, Ritter makes his initial appearance as a passenger in a wagon, wearing a suit and tie. When Brown, instead of Ritter, is placed in charge of building a new road for the stageline, Tex refuses to help and spends his time at the local saloon which was opened by the villains to distract the stageline workers. Ritter even makes some unfair accusations to the heroine about Brown having been responsible for her brother's death. Such unheroic behavior certainly did not enhance Ritter's image as a Western hero. The Jimmy Wakely Trio had been signed by Universal to furnish much of the music for the pictures and at least one song in each film was provided by Fuzzy Knight, the studio's resident B Western sidekick.

The Brown-Ritter series, however, was popular with exhibitors and fans, and only the Westerns of Roy Rogers and Hopalong Cassidy ranked ahead of the Universal series in the *Motion Picture Herald*'s poll in 1943.

Ritter finally received the opportunity to star in quality B Westerns when Johnny Mack Brown left Universal in 1943. Ritter's first film, *Arizona Trail* (1943), was completed without difficulty, but before he could start work on his next film, an unfortunate accident occurred. While working in his barn, Ritter fell from the hayloft and seriously injured his leg. Universal decided not to hold up production and hurriedly signed Russell Hayden, who was still making films for Columbia, to fill in for the injured Ritter. Recognizing that Universal was in a difficult situation, Hayden's agent insisted on a two-picture contract and the studio's executives agreed. When Ritter returned for *Marshal of Gunsmoke* (1944), he was once again faced with the familiar situation of having a co-star. The Ritter-Hayden combination worked well, but after the film was completed, Hayden returned to Columbia to resume his own series and Ritter remained to star in *Oklahoma Raiders* (1944). Because of the strong production values and good scripts, the three Westerns Ritter made for Universal in 1943-1944 were among his best films. However, Ritter was released by Universal just as his film career seemed on the verge of reaching new heights. Financial problems primarily accounted for the studio's decision to promote a relatively unknown contract player, Rod Cameron, to star in their B Westerns.

To continue his film career, Ritter had to return to a less prominent studio. Producer's Releasing Corporation had been making low-budget Westerns since 1940, but their finances were limited and their product was seen only in second-rate movie houses. Ritter replaced James Newill in the *Texas Rangers* series which PRC had considered sufficiently successful to continue for a third season. Dave O'Brien and Guy Wilkerson, who comprised the other two-thirds of the original trio, were retained to co-star with Ritter. The

A wide, friendly smile typified photographs of Tex Ritter.

eight films produced for the season in 1944-1945 were not of the same quality as Ritter's previous films. It was not so much the limited production values as the inferior scripts that hindered these films. When PRC chose not to continue the series for another season, the decision brought Ritter's career as a Western film star to a close. However, by this time Ritter had become established as one of the country's top country-western recording artists.

Johnny Mercer organized Capital Records in June 1942. He signed Ritter as the company's first country-western artist. Ritter's earlier recordings had been moderately successful. He had received $100 for recording four songs in 1933 for the American Record Corporation. He also had recorded for Decca between 1935 and 1939, but after four years his contract was dropped. Surprisingly, Ritter did not record at all during the peak of his film career between 1939 and 1942. His first Capital release, "Jingle, Jangle, Jingle," was a success, and was soon followed by additional hits. By January 20, 1945, Ritter had the top three songs in the country, "I'm Wastin' My Tears on You," "There's a New Moon Over My Shoulder," and "Jealous Heart," according to *Billboard Magazine*'s list of most played "folk" records. This was the first time a recording artists had taken the top three spots at one time on a billboard chart. Ritter had two more number-one recordings the following year with "You Two Timed Me One Time Too Often" and "You Will Have to Pay (for All Your Yesterdays)." These were followed by several more top-ten recordings. *Billboard Magazine* has described the 1940s through the early 1950s as a "Golden Age for Tex Ritter."[16]

Ritter became known as Hollywood's most traveled entertainer during the 1940s as he crisscrossed the country in a battered 1940 station wagon playing one-night stands. He was on the road for as long as sixteen weeks at a time and would do as many as eight shows a day. He once played ninety towns in ninety days.[17] It was also during this time that Ritter was first billed as "America's Most Beloved Cowboy." Ritter's road show, which toured under various names and eventually became known as "Tex Ritter's Western Revue," regularly consisted of more than a dozen performers and included Ritter's horse, White Flash, and a trained chimpanzee.[18]

During the early 1950s it became increasingly difficult for Ritter to sustain the success he had enjoyed as a recording artist during the previous decade. He would have returned to films if he had received offers to do so. He lamented the fact that he was not in a position to produce his own films as Gene Autry was doing. Then two events occurred which helped to revitalize his career.[19]

In 1952 Stanley Kramer made *High Noon* with Gary Cooper and Grace Kelly. The film had long periods of silence with no dialogue. Instead of using a conventional musical soundtrack, Dimitri Tiomkin, a Russian composer, and his friend, Ned Washington, wrote a recurring title song. Film editor Elmo Williams, who previously had worked for Capital Records, recommended Tex Ritter to sing the vocal. Following an audition at Tiomkin's home, Ritter was offered $1,000 to do the song. The movie and the song were successes with the public and with the critics. On March 19, 1953, the film received four Academy Awards for best picture, best male actor, best music, and best song, and Ritter performed the song at the Motion Picture Academy's presentation ceremonies which were televised nationally for the first time.

Tiomkin wanted to release "High Noon" on record, but Capital was not interested in having Ritter do it. When Capital executives heard that Tiomkin had persuaded Columbia Records to let Frankie Laine record the song, they quickly arranged a recording session for Ritter. Capital was able to get Ritter's recording on the market a week ahead of Laine's version of "High Noon." A serious setback occurred, however, when Capital realized that a critical drum accompaniment had been omitted from the soundtrack and their initial releases had to be recalled. As a result of Capital's mistake and Columbia's superior promotional campaign, the Frankie Laine version of "High Noon" appeared first in the tradepaper charts, making it appear that Columbia and Laine had the original release. Both recordings sold well, but the initial advantage gained by Columbia allowed Laine's recording to become a million seller while Ritter's rendition fell just short of 800,000 in sales.[20]

The classic theme from *High Noon* started a trend in the use of musical narration in Western films. Ritter sang soundtrack scores for three additional pictures, *The Marshal's Daughter*, *Wichita*, and *Trooper Hook*, using the *High Noon* format, but none of them approached the success of *High Noon*.[21]

In 1952 William Wagnom, a prominent California promoter, persuaded radio station KFI in Los Angeles to do a Saturday night program to Chicago's *National Barn Dance* and Nashville's *Grand Ole Opry*. Wagnom called the show *Town Hall Party*. He hired most of the well-known country-western entertainers on the West Coast. When the show's popularity increased, it was picked up by the NBC radio network and a two-hour segment was televised by KTTV in Los Angeles. The expanded radio and television coverage increased the show's popularity even more and it became necessary to start a Friday night broadcast to accommodate the large crowds who waited to attend the "live" broadcasts. Wagnom needed a top name entertainer to headline the show and attract better sponsorship, so he hired Tex Ritter. The tremendous popularity of the program on the West Coast during the 1950s and his continuing success as a recording artist allowed Ritter to enhance his growing reputation as a country-western entertainer.

By the late 1950s, however, interest in country music had declined on the West Coast. *Town Hall Party*'s popularity dwindled and eventually the show was canceled. Ritter's songs were listed less frequently on the trade magazine charts and he felt he needed another successful record to boost his career. He achieved this objective by recording "Hillbilly Heaven," written by Eddie Dean and Hal Southern. Ritter resisted recording the song for nearly five years because he thought the term "hillbilly" was demeaning to country music artists. Dean and Southern gave him permission to change the lyrics, but Tex was unable to come up with anything more suitable so he recorded the song as originally written. Capital Records came up with a gimmick of having Ritter substitute the names of local DJs for one of the country music stars mentioned in the song and these individualized promotional copies were distributed to the local radio stations. The DJs naturally played the song to boost their own egos and the additional exposure helped the song to become a hit.

Ritter was extremely popular among his fellow performers. This was due, in part, to his active participation in furthering and strengthening the spread of country and western music.[22] As early as 1942, Ritter was quoted as saying that America was on the threshold of a great national appreciation of folk music.[23] Ritter was involved with the Country Music Association and was viewed as their roving ambassador, spreading goodwill and speaking on behalf of country music at every opportunity. He was, at least informally, the voice of the industry.[24]

In October 1963, Ritter was elected to the first of two terms as president of the Country Music Association (CMA). While serving as president, he was instrumental in the development of the Country Music Hall of Fame Museum and Library, located in Nashville, Tennessee. He later turned down a third term as president of CMA, but he did agree to serve as executive vice-president.

Because he was held in such high esteem by the country music industry, it was not surprising that on November 6, 1964, Ritter was inducted into the Country Music Hall of Fame, joining Jimmie Rodgers, Hank Williams, Fred Rose, and Roy Acuff. The announcement was made at Nashville Loew's Theatre during the premiere of *Your Cheatin' Heart*, a film based on the life and career of Hank Williams.[25] The fact that Ritter was president of CMA made it more difficult to conceal from him the fact that he was being chosen as the newest inductee into the Hall of Fame. However, association officials were successful in convincing him that the award would be presented to Ernest Tubb and when the announcement was made, Ritter was surprised.

Nashville radio station WSM offered Ritter a lifetime contract in 1965 to become a regular member of the cast of the Grand Ole Opry and co-host of a popular radio program. Ritter would have to leave his home of thirty years in California and move to Nashville while his wife remained on the West Coast until their two sons, Tom and John, completed college. Ritter signed the contract and on June 12, 1965, made his first appearance as a member of the Grand Ole Opry. Nine days later he joined Grant Turner as co-host of WSM's all-night radio program, *Opry Star Spotlight*. Ralph Emery later replaced Turner as Ritter's co-host. Ritter's contract allowed him to continue his personal appearance tours and required that he do the radio program only when not on the road.

Early in his career Ritter did not allow his political beliefs to enter into his professional performances. Over a period of time, this changed. By 1968, *Billboard Magazine* noted that Ritter made his political views known at every opportunity. Ritter also began to take an active part in Republican Party politics and he campaigned for Howard Baker, George Murphy, John Tower, Barry Goldwater, and Ronald Reagan.[26] Ritter, who was a personal friend of Richard Nixon, became part of a group called "Celebrities for Nixon" during the presidential campaign of 1968 and he even wrote a Nixon campaign song. When Ritter was touring in Germany, a special flight was arranged by Nixon to pick up Ritter and his wife so he could entertain at a rally in Knoxville, Tennessee, that was attended by nearly 25,000 persons.[27]

In 1970 Ritter ran in the Tennessee Republican primary as a candidate for the United States Senate against William Brock, heir to the Chattanooga candy manufacturing fortune. The Republican Party in Tennessee was split into two factions, one headed by Senator Howard Baker and the other by William Brock. Although Baker officially remained neutral, his supporters encouraged Ritter to seek the office. Ritter's campaign theme emphasized that he was "plowing the middle ground" between three-term Democratic incumbent Albert Gore on the left and William Brock on the right. Ritter claimed he had a better chance than Brock to defeat Gore in the general election.[28] Ritter fought an uphill battle from the start. Brock, a multi-millionaire who had served eight years in the House of Representatives, was an experienced campaigner and had the official backing of the Republican Party. The Country Music fraternity rallied behind Ritter. Roy Acuff, Johnny Cash, Chet Atkins, and Archie Campbell were all involved in Ritter's campaign, and more than sixty well-known country acts performed at campaign rallies throughout the state. Ritter sang at several of the rallies. Some people thought it inappropriate that a candidate for the United States Senate would strap on a guitar and sing country songs. Ritter did so against his own better judgment. "We had determined not to sing," he said later, "but people would say, 'Tex, looks like you'd sing one song anyway.' So I just finally said, 'Well, maybe one or two, that's all.'" He did not want the people who had come to see the Tex Ritter they remembered from movies to feel cheated.[29]

When the ballots were counted, Brock won easily with seventy-five percent of the vote. Ritter felt that the major factor which contributed to his defeat was the lack of money needed to run a statewide campaign. He had attempted to campaign by touring the state, and he could not match Brock's effective television campaign. Brock, who was intelligent enough not to run against a Grand Ole Opry star in Tennessee, shrewdly campaigned against Gore and not against Ritter.[30] Ritter took the defeat in stride. "I rather enjoyed the campaigning," he said, "and I'm not the kind of person who regrets many things, disappointments are going to happen to you. I've faced them before and I don't let them worry me too much. I did what I could do, and, as the fellow says, about all a mule can do is just keep working the harness."[31]

In 1971 Ritter recorded "The Battle Hymn of Lt. Calley" but Capital Records officials canceled distribution of the recording for political reasons. Somewhat annoyed by the decision, Ritter complained that he had been singing the song while on tour and telling audiences the record would be released and then upon returning to Nashville he learned the record was not going to be released. Ritter said he really could not see where the song was that objectionable and in view of the permissiveness of current motion pictures, magazine articles, and musical lyrics, he did not think the song was afoul of good taste. "It was a good record," Ritter said. "Drop over some night and we'll play it."[32]

In 1972 Ritter received the Country Music Association's award presented annually to the person who has done the most to promote country music. Ritter was cited as a cornerstone of the country music industry and called the greatest ambassador country music ever had.[33]

Ritter was considered for what would have been the best film role of his career, but was never offered the part. When his son, John, auditioned for *The Last Picture Show*, he was asked if his father might be interested in the role that eventually went to Ben Johnson. For a time producer Peter Bogdonavich considered casting both Ritters in the film.[34] It was a role for which Johnson won an Academy Award and Ritter said later he would have very much enjoyed doing it.

In 1973 the country music industry wished to express appreciation to President Richard Nixon for his support of country music. An album was produced that contained excerpts from Nixon's speeches interspersed with country songs. Ritter had been the catalyst for the project and he did the narration on the album, titled "Thank You, Mr. President." Because of Nixon's Watergate difficulties there was some reluctance about presenting the album, but Ritter encouraged his associates to carry out the presentation ceremony.

"We would have preferred the seas to be calm," Ritter said. "We started working on this before Watergate, but we decided to go ahead with it anyway. The stormy seas have nothing to do with our gift to the president." So on December 14, 1973, Ritter and several members of the Country Music Association went to Washington, D.C., and presented the album to President Nixon.[35]

Six days later Ritter recorded "The Americans," based on an editorial by a Canadian journalist. It was a staunchly pro–American recitation done to the background of patriotic music. Because of his patriotism, Tex was excited about doing the recording.[36]

After spending the Christmas holidays in 1973 with his family, Ritter returned to work. On Saturday, December 28, he appeared on the Grand Ole Opry and performed "The Americans," receiving a standing ovation. The producers of *W.W. and the Dixie Dance Kings*, a film being shot in Nashville starring Burt Reynolds, attended the show and were so impressed by the occasion that they visited Ritter backstage and offered him a role in the film. Ritter accepted and was advised that a script would be mailed immediately.[37]

Ritter performed a New Year's Eve show near Denver, Colorado, then flew back to Nashville for a brief rest prior to a three-day engagement at a dinner theater in Philadelphia that was to begin January 3, 1974. Ritter learned on January 2 that one of his band members, Lamar (Jack) Watkins, was in the Nashville jail on a non-support charge. Ritter and his son, Tom, drove to the jail about 5:30 P.M. to arrange bail for Watkins. After taking a brief tour of the facility, Ritter seemed to be in good spirits and joked with the officers. Ritter was sitting in a chair in the sheriff's office while Watkins was being processed for release when he suddenly grabbed his chest and slumped forward. Police administered oxygen and rushed him to Baptist Hospital where he died at 7:00 P.M. in the emergency room. The cause of death was a massive heart attack.[38]

In his book, *Singing Cowboys*, author David Rothel described Tex Ritter as "a movie singing cowboy who never seemed to find his proper niche on the screen."[39] But Ritter did find a niche for himself in B Westerns. More than anyone else, he was able to transcend the gap between action star and singing cowboy, thus attaining the goal which filmmakers had sought to achieve when they first introduced "singing cowboys" to motion picture audiences. Edward Finney stated that "As to Tex Ritter's place in Western films, I think he brought an authenticity to his characterizations, and a brand of singing that typified the cowboy ... unlike any other star, and his interpretation was more real than any other...."[40] It is necessary to look beyond the ten years that Tex Ritter spent in Hollywood making Western movies to understand his importance as a Western film personality. A versatile performer, Ritter's career as an entertainer spanned more than forty years. The fact that he became a giant in the field of country music after leaving films allowed the public to also remember him as a movie cowboy long after he quit making films. Ritter's stature and reputation continued to grow over the years until he became not only a living legend but also, as he had been billed for so many years, "America's Most Beloved Cowboy."

Notes

1. Johnny Bond, *The Tex Ritter Story* (New York: Chappell & Co., Inc., 1976), p. 14; Texas Jim Cooper, "This Was a Man," *The Tex Ritter Story*, July 8, 1978, p. 6.
2. Bond, *The Tex Ritter Story*, p. 15.
3. *Billboard Magazine*, December 7, 1968, p. 43.
4. Bond, *The Tex Ritter Story*, p. 17.
5. Jack Hurst, "Out in the Boondocks, Ritter Tracks a Fox," *Nashville Tennessean Magazine*, May 31, 1979, p. 4.
6. Bond, *The Tex Ritter Story*, p. 21.
7. Bond, *The Tex Ritter Story*, pp. 27–28.
8. Bond, *The Tex Ritter Story*, pp. 39, 43–44; Texas Jim Cooper, "Tex Ritter," *Films in Review* (April 1970), pp. 205–206.
9. Jon Tuska, "Oklahoma Raiders," *Views & Review*, Vol. 5, Issue 4 (Summer 1974), pp. 2–5; Bob Pontes, "Interview with Ed Finney," *Favorite Westerns*, No. 19 (Fall 1984), pp. 73–74.
10. *Variety*, August 2, 1939.
11. *Variety*, September 25, 1940.
12. Bond, *The Tex Ritter Story*, pp. 55–56; Texas Jim Cooper, "Tex Ritter—A Real-Life Hero," *Under Western Skies*, No. 3, (July 1978), pp. 13–14.
13. *Billboard Magazine*, December 7, 1968, p. 44; *Memphis Commercial Appeal*, August 2, 1973, p. 32.
14. Cooper, "This Was a Man," p. 10.
15. *Variety*, August 13, 1941.
16. *Billboard Magazine*, December 7, 1968, p. 46.
17. Cooper, "This Was a Man," p. 16.
18. *Billboard Magazine*, December 7, 1968, p. 43.
19. Bond, *The Tex Ritter Story*, p. 142.
20. Bond, *The Tex Ritter Story*, pp. 147–48; Cooper, "This Was a Man," p. 19.
21. Bond, *The Tex Ritter Story*, p. 157.
22. Carolyn Hollaran, "Tex Ritter in Memoriam," *Country Song Roundup* (June 1974), p. 13.
23. Cooper, "This Was a Man," p. 17.
24. Texas Jim Cooper, "Tex Ritter in the Twilight Years," *John Edwards Memorial Foundation Quarterly*, Vol. 13, No. 46, (Summer 1977), p. 79.
25. *Billboard*, December 7, 1968, p. 44.
26. Cooper, "Tex Ritter in the Twilight Years," p. 82.
27. *The Gringo*, January 1969, p. 7.
28. *The Nashville Tennessean*, July 28, 1970, p. 8.
29. *Detroit Free Press*, January 31, 1974, p. 1.
30. *The Nashville Tennessean*, January 18, 1970, p. 14.
31. *The Nashville Tennessean*, August 14, 1970, p. 21.
32. *The Nashville Tennessean*, April 7, 1971.
33. *Billboard Magazine*, October 28, 1972; *Cashbox Magazine*, November 4, 1972.
34. Cooper, "Tex Ritter—A Real-Life Hero," p. 29.
35. *The Nashville Tennessean*, January 3, 1974; Cooper, "Tex Ritter in the Twilight Years," p. 86.
36. *The Nashville Banner*, Thursday, January 3, 1974, p. 8.

37. Cooper, "Tex Ritter—A Real-Life Hero," p. 29.

38. *The Nashville Tennessean*, January 3, 1974, pp. 1, 4.

39. David Rothel, *The Singing Cowboys* (South Brunswick and New York: A.S. Barnes and Company, 1978), p. 15.

40. Cooper, "Tex Ritter—A Real-Life Hero," p. 18.

ROY ROGERS:
AN AMERICAN ICON

by Raymond E. White

Roy Rogers stands as one of the most significant figures in twentieth-century American culture. Through his long and varied entertainment career in radio, recording, films, television, and public appearances he has become an icon representing basic American values and symbolizing the cowboy, America's most cherished folk hero. His identity with twentieth-century Americans is so strong that the mere mention of his name, or that of his horse, "Trigger," or his wife, Dale Evans, evokes an immediate positive response. Roy Rogers' warm, friendly, and open personality binds him to a public that feels he is "just plain folks." As one fan stated, "He makes you feel like he's one of us."[1] In maintaining this common touch Roy Rogers possesses a strong sense of self and a humble democratic nature, factors that in themselves might explain his continuing popularity and influence in American culture.

Roy Rogers, born Leonard Franklin Slye in Cincinnati, Ohio, on November 5, 1911, has roots deep in Midwestern America. The third of four children born to Andrew and Mattie Slye, Leonard Slye grew up with his three sisters, Mary, Cleda, and Kathleen, on a houseboat docked at Portsmouth, Ohio, and on a farm near Duck Run, Ohio. His parents and his childhood experiences shaped and molded the talents and the personal character that became evident in his later public life. Both his mother and father were determined, hard-working people who instilled these values in their son and gave him a curiosity about life and a compassion for living things. Moreover, they introduced him to a world of music that he mastered and used to launch his professional entertainment career in the early 1930s. Perhaps most important is the fact that this strong, secure family environment gave Leonard Slye a confidence and self-esteem that permitted him to succeed and at the same time remain in touch with his Midwestern roots.[2]

Hard work in those boyhood days shaped Slye's character. Andrew and Mattie Slye required that their children share in the work responsibilities of the family. These duties were necessitated in part by the fact that Mattie was impaired physically from infantile paralysis. When the Slyes moved from Portsmouth to the Duck Run farm in 1919, the chores increased as the family constructed a house, cleared land, built fences, plowed fields, and tended stock. Unfortunately the farm failed to support the family, and Andy Slye returned to Portsmouth during the week to work in a shoe factory, placing additional responsibility on young Leonard to run the farm. Slye's extra income failed to make ends meet, however, prompting Leonard to hire out as a farm hand to plow the neighbors' fields. The habit of work that Leonard Slye developed in his youthful days in Ohio set a pattern for his future.

Although the Slyes worked hard they also found time for relaxation. Music was especially important to them, and Leonard Slye began playing stringed instruments at an early age. He learned from his parents. Andrew Slye was a self-taught guitarist and mandolin player who had performed on a showboat and with his four brothers at square dances throughout Ohio. Mattie Slye also played stringed instruments and loved to sing. The whole family regularly performed at neighborhood square dances with Leonard Slye becoming an accomplished caller by his tenth birthday. He also used his voice for yodeling, a skill that he perfected as he responded to his mother when she called him and his sisters in from play. The parental instruction, practice, and family experiences at public performances provided Leonard Slye with important musical skills that helped him when he began to perform professionally in California in the early 1930s.

The perfection that Slye sought to achieve in his music was transferred to other endeavors as well. As a youngster he became an expert marksman with rifle, bow and arrow, and slingshot, skills that often put food on the family table. He especially impressed relatives and friends with his expertise in both making and using slingshots. On one occasion his marksmanship protected a barrel of dried beans stored in the Slyes' cellar. According to his mother, Leonard loved beans and became infuriated when a colony of mice began digging into the barrel and carrying off the winter stores. Leonard made a strong slingshot, descended to the cellar before nightfall, and drew a bead on the mouse-hole in the bean barrel. Sitting there in the darkness and using the beans as ammunition he let fly with a shot whenever he heard the slightest sound. The following morning the family found that he had killed fourteen of the plundering mice in the pitch blackness of the cellar. As an adult he increased his proficiency with firearms and used his marksmanship not only for hunting and skeet shooting but also in his public performances as an entertainer.[3]

Leonard Slye's drive for perfection in marksmanship also revealed itself in his care and training of animals. In Ohio he possessed all sorts of pets, both domestic and wild, and had a knack for cultivating their trust. He named and trained four wild skunks to answer to his call and taught a groundhog to sit quietly while he practiced on his clarinet. A pet rooster often sat on his shoulder, and when his father brought home a black mare called Babe, Leonard immediately began to train the horse to do tricks. As a 4-H club member Leonard raised a pig, carefully regulating its diet and grooming it until he entered it in the Scioto County Fair where it won a blue ribbon. Slye's determination and patience in perfecting his talents and skills were important internal qualities that he used throughout his life to achieve the excellence that brought him success.[4]

The Slye family's economic situation prompted Leonard to drop out of high school and go to work with his father in a Cincinnati shoe factory. By this time his sisters, Mary and Cleda, were married, so Mattie, Leonard, and Kathleen moved into a small duplex that Andy Slye rented in Cincinnati. Leonard tried to combine the factory job with night school, but the physical strain proved too much, and eventually he quit his classes. The monotony and confinement of the factory demoralized both Andy and Leonard Slye to the extent that they decided to make a change in the family's life. They quit their jobs in the shoe factory and used their small savings to travel to California to visit Mary. After a four-month visit the family returned to Ohio, but restlessness overcame Leonard, and when the opportunity presented itself in the spring of 1931 he returned to California and within a short time his parents followed.

The Slye family's decision to move to California was an integral part of larger national developments. Like thousands of Midwesterners working to maintain themselves against the hard times of the Depression, they came to believe that greater opportunities existed for them in the Far West. They quickly discovered, however, that the Golden State had its own economic problems. Leonard and Andy Slye did find jobs, first driving gravel trucks and then as migrant workers picking fruit. They experienced from the bottom the worst economic and human disaster that the nation had ever faced.

While living in the migrant camps, Leonard realized how important music was to him, and he determined to pursue it professionally. After working in the evenings, usually around a campfire, he and his father would bring out their musical instruments. Other campers gathered to listen and often to join in with their own voices, harmonicas, fiddles, and guitars. The pure enjoyment that Leonard felt in performing, plus the positive reactions of his fellow migrant campers, convinced him that he wanted to become a full-time musician. When his father found work in a Los Angeles shoe factory, Leonard Slye refused to follow him. Instead he began to concentrate his efforts on a professional music career.[5]

The determination and hard work that Leonard showed as a youth in Ohio revealed themselves as he worked to perfect his musical skills and find work as a musician. First, he and his cousin Stanley Slye performed at beach parties and lodge gatherings for whatever money they could get by passing a hat. Then an appearance on an amateur talent radio show won Slye a job with the Rocky Mountaineers, a Western musical group that performed on radio and for local parties in the Long Beach area. While working with the

Mountaineers Slye met Bob Nolan and Tim Spencer, two musicians who later joined him to form the Sons of the Pioneers.

It was also while performing with the Rocky Mountaineers that romance entered Slye's life. In 1933 he met Lucile Ascolese, and after a short courtship the couple married. Undue pressure existed on the marriage from the start, resulting primarily from the time Slye spent practicing and performing. The pressure prompted one separation and ultimately an amicable divorce after fifteen months of marriage.[6]

It was also during this marriage that the Sons of the Pioneers came into existence, but before the trio organized Nolan left the Mountaineers for a more steady job as a golf caddy. When the Mountaineers broke up Slye and Spencer performed briefly with the International Cowboys and eventually with the O-Bar-O Cowboys, even making a tour with this group through the Southwestern states of Arizona, New Mexico, and Texas. Returning to California broke and somewhat discouraged, the group dispersed and Slye joined Jack and His Texas Outlaws and Spencer found work with the Safeway grocery chain.

Despite discouragement and the odds against success, Leonard Slye remained determined to form a successful Western musical group. Having confidence in the talents and skills of his two friends, Bob Nolan and Tim Spencer, he persuaded them to quit their jobs and try once more to put together a Western trio. Spending eight to twelve hours a day practicing, the three musicians perfected their instrumentation, their breathing, and their phrasing to the point that the close harmony they achieved represented one voice. Indeed, with their coordination, tone control, and precision, they originated trio yodeling and developed it to a degree of excellence and perfection that was unique among Western musical groups. The superb songs that Nolan and Spencer composed added to the group's originality. The hard work paid off. After six or eight weeks of practice the trio landed a job on the Los Angeles radio station KFWB performing with Jack and His Texas Outlaws. Billing themselves as the Pioneer Trio, they were an immediate success and soon got their own radio show and jobs as staff musicians for other programs. An announcer, thinking the trio too young to be pioneers, one day introduced them as the Sons of the Pioneers, a name they readily adopted. Within a year Hugh Farr, a talented Texas fiddler, joined the Pioneers and shortly thereafter his brother Karl, an experienced guitarist, was added, making the original Sons of the Pioneers complete. Slye played guitar and sang, usually alternating solos with Bob Nolan. He demonstrated his superb skills as a yodeler on several songs, particularly "Hadie Brown" and "The Swiss Yodel." Slye's single mindedness and determination brought these talented individuals together and his leadership provided the clay that molded them into one of the most successful Western singing groups of the 1930s and 1940s.[7]

The exposure of their unusual style and sound on radio earned the

Pioneers recording opportunities and then small roles in movie shorts and Western feature films. In 1934 the Pioneers began a six-month project of recording more than 280 songs for Standard Radio Transcriptions, and in 1935 they obtained a recording contract with Decca records. Their roles in the Hollywood feature *The Old Homestead* (1935) initiated a series of film appearances with such stars as El Brendel, Joan Davis, Bing Crosby, Larry Gray, Mary Carlisle, Jo Stafford, Phil Regan, Dick Foran, Gene Autry, and Charles Starrett. The roles with Foran, Autry, and Starrett were in Western features, and by 1936 the Pioneers had a contract with Columbia Pictures to appear in more of Starrett's films. Within two years the Sons of the Pioneers established themselves as talented and successful entertainers who had a bright future.

Another part of that future was Slye's marriage to Arlene Wilkins of Roswell, New Mexico, in 1936. The couple had met a few years before when Slye toured the Southwest with the O-Bar-O Cowboys. The match proved more successful than Slye's first marriage, perhaps because he was not faced with the same economic and professional uncertainties and pressures. At least it began at a time when Slye's professional career appeared to be on the upturn.[8]

At this point Slye decided he wanted to be more than a member of a Western singing group with secondary roles in cowboy movies. He wanted to be a Western movie star. As music changed the whole nature of Western films, and the singing cowboy altered the role of the traditional action hero, Slye determined to become a Western film star. At the newly formed Republic Studios, Gene Autry had established the persona of the singing Western cowboy that other Hollywood film factories copied. Autry's model was the one that Slye also chose to emulate, and in 1937 he auditioned with Universal pictures for the role of a singing cowboy. Unfortunately he lost out to Bob Baker, but a second opportunity came later in the same year when Autry had contract problems with Republic Studios and threatened to strike. Republic's officials looked around for a replacement and decided on Slye, whom they first used in supporting roles and billed as Dick Weston. Within a year Autry did walk out, and Republic quickly changed Dick Weston's name to Roy Rogers and gave him top billing in *Under Western Stars* (1938), a film originally scheduled for Autry. The hard work, determination, and persistence paid off for Slye. Within eight short years he rose from an unknown migrant worker to a star in a Hollywood Western.[9]

Slye felt comfortable with his new name, Roy Rogers, and eventually adopted it legally. It was original and creative and had an alliterative ring to it that possessed public appeal. Supposedly Republic officials discussed several names before deciding on one that combined that of humorist Will Rogers and the term "roy," meaning king. Within a year from the adoption of his new name and the release of *Under Western Stars*, Roy Rogers achieved national

Roy Rogers (courtesy of Ray White, Department of History, Ball State University, Muncie Indiana).

prominence and became a box office leader, ranking third behind Autry and William Boyd in the *Motion Picture Herald*'s poll of top money-making Western stars. Within another four years Roy Rogers jumped to the top spot on the money-maker poll, and from 1943 until 1954 he retained that position and won the title "King of the Cowboys." It was in his movie roles that Roy Rogers established himself as a national cultural figure, and while he added to his fame with recordings, radio, television, and personal appearances, the public identified him primarily as a Western film hero.[10]

The films that established Roy Rogers as a Western movie star numbered eighty-three and were released by Republic Studios between 1938 and 1951. In these films Roy Rogers epitomized the stereotypical American film cowboy with his role of a rugged but pure Western hero who struggled with an assortment of frontier villains. On the other hand, he possessed a style and charisma that was uniquely his own, one that combined his boyish good looks and gentle self-effacing manner with a soft wholesome sex appeal. Roy Rogers' female fans, both juvenile and adult, found a special physical attraction in Rogers that was unmatched by most other Western screen heroes. Moreover, women comprised a large segment of Roy Rogers' fan clubs and many presided over the regional and national organizations.[11] Male fans identified with his good looks, his quiet, unassuming confidence, and the considerable physical skills he demonstrated with his fists and his horsemanship. His youthful, boyish appearance did not detract from the Western hero he portrayed in every film. Indeed, his remarkable screen presence, his natural and easygoing acting style, and Republic's careful attention to his appearance made Roy Rogers an immediate national film celebrity. While the early Rogers Westerns were not as glitzy as those of Gene Autry, they nevertheless were solid features with good stories, skillful direction, and excellent supporting cast. Also important for these initial films and for Rogers was Joseph Kane, who directed the first forty-two of the actor's features.[12] These early films permitted Roy Rogers to develop his skill as an actor and set him on the road to becoming one of the most successful Western entertainers in twentieth-century America.

In addition to showing Roy Rogers' evolution as a Western film star, the eighty-three films that established his public persona and entrenched him as a significant cultural figure also reflect American society and values in the 1930s and 1940s. The films themselves can be divided into three or four categories in regard to theme, style, and Roy Rogers' persona.

Twenty-two of the first two dozen Roy Rogers Westerns were period films set in the nineteenth century and related to such topics as the Texas Republic (*Ranger and the Lady*, 1940), the Pony Express (*Frontier Pony Express*, 1939), the Civil War (*Southward Ho*, 1939), Reconstruction (*Robin Hood of the Pecos*, 1941), cattle rustling (*Shine on Harvest Moon*, 1938), and railroads (*Nevada City*, 1941). In these early films Rogers portrayed a variety of characters ranging from Pony Express riders and Confederate military officers to Wild West gunmen. In two films he played dual roles (*Billy the Kid Returns*, 1938, and *Jesse James Returns*, 1941). Although Roy Rogers used his new name in the stories of his first ten films, in 1940 Republic screen writers for some reason began preparing scripts in which he played characters with names such as Steve, Jerry, Bill, Clint, Brett, Vance, and Jeff. He also portrayed Buffalo Bill, Jesse James, Bill Hickok, and Billy the Kid. In none of the first twenty-four film stories was "Roy Rogers" an instantly recogniz-able personality who was known and respected in the fictional frontier com-munities in which he lived. Although he always gained that respect by the end of the film, Roy Rogers usually did not start out with it; he had to prove himself to the other characters and perhaps even to the film-going public. Why Republic decided to give Roy Rogers alternatives names in his film roles is not clear, but as mysteriously as the studio started the practice it stopped it in 1941 with the release of *Red River Valley*.[13]

While the story lines, production values, and acting made these films quality productions, the inclusion of George "Gabby" Hayes in the cast added a dimension that set them apart from most low-budget Westerns. Hayes' con-siderable acting skills and the "Gabby" character that he created marked him as the most effective and popular sidekick in B Westerns. The outline of the "Gabby" persona first revealed itself in the early 1930s when Hayes appeared in Westerns with Ken Maynard, John Wayne, and Bob Steele. It became more apparent in his role as "Windy Holiday" in the *Hopalong Cassidy* series, but it was Roy Rogers Westerns of the early 1940s that Hayes brought it to per-fection and established "Gabby Whittaker" as an institution. Indeed, begin-ning in 1943 and continuing for a decade, Hayes ranked as one of the Top Ten Western money makers in the *Motion Picture Herald* fame poll, the only Western sidekick to receive such continuous recognition. While Hayes' pop-ularity was based on "Gabby," it was also tied to Roy Rogers. The two actors made more than forty films together, and in the stories "Gabby" Hayes enlarged upon Roy Rogers' role as a Western hero, often attributing super-human qualities to him. Hayes' enhancement of Rogers' heroic attributes in the films in turn amplified Rogers' off-screen image as an American cowboy hero.[14]

Beginning with *Red River Valley*, Rogers' Westerns had contemporary settings and themes with the star once again using his own name. While he remained the basic cowboy hero, Rogers became a recognizable celebrity in these films and often portrayed a radio, rodeo, or recording star; occasion-ally he was a ranch foreman, deputy sheriff, or undercover agent. Rogers' con-temporary image also revealed itself in a more stylish Western wardrobe of tight pants, colorful shirt, flashy boots, and tall white hat. Music also received a new emphasis when Rogers' old friends, the Sons of the Pioneers, joined him at Republic. Despite the presence of the Pioneers and the increased use of music, action remained the primary ingredient in the fourteen Rogers West-erns released between December 1941 and October 1943. The plots of these films focused on the traditional themes of cattle rustling (*Ridin' Down the Canyon*, 1942), bank robberies (*Idaho*, 1943), land grabbing (*Sunset on the Desert* and *Sons of the Pioneers*, 1942), and range wars (*Man from Music*

Mountain, 1943), but the script writers incorporated radios, automobiles, trucks, airplanes, and telephones into the stories. Only one film possessed a World War II theme (*King of the Cowboys*, 1943) which had Roy Rogers working as an undercover agent tracking down saboteurs.

Perhaps most important for Rogers' career in the early 1940s was Gene Autry's decision to enlist in the armed services for World War II. With Autry absent, Republic Studios immediately boosted the budgets of Rogers' films and promoted him as "King of the Cowboys." The public relations effort paid off. Within a year Roy Rogers became the number one box-office moneymaker among Western film stars. In this role Rogers also did his part for the war effort by making dozens of personal appearances throughout the country to sell war bonds and entertain GIs. Meshing these patriotic actions with his cowboy image solidly established Rogers as one of America's top Western entertainment heroes.[15]

To capitalize on Roy Rogers' new status as the top box office star, Republic Studios made his films even more elaborate, especially with the inclusion of a separate musical production number at the end of each film. These spectacular productions added several minutes to the films and featured not only Rogers, his singing co-star, and the Sons of the Pioneers, but also costumed singers and dancers performing on lavish sets. The concluding numbers of *Man from Oklahoma* (1945) and *Bells of Rosarita* (1945) are good examples of these elaborate musical features. Herbert J. Yates, the president of Republic Studios, supposedly originated the idea for these musical productions after attending a Broadway performance of *Oklahoma*.[16]

While Yates spent thousands of dollars on the production of Roy Rogers' Westerns and gained thousands more in return, he paid his top Western star a minuscule salary. To survive economically and even to pay the postage to answer his fan mail, Roy Rogers sought other sources of income. He made public appearances, organized his own rodeo, and in 1944 starred in *The Roy Rogers Show*, a Western musical variety program, on the Mutual radio network.[17] Income also came from record sales. In the late 1930s and early 1940s Rogers recorded for Decca and the American Record Company, and then in 1945 he signed a contract with RCA Victor Records. It was also in the mid–1940s that Roy Rogers comic books first appeared and other items began to be merchandised under his name.

Instrumental in helping Rogers manage his career and develop financial security was W. Arthur Rush, a Hollywood talent agent who began to represent the Western star in 1942. It was a remarkable professional and personal relationship, based only on a handshake, that lasted until Rush's death in 1989. Art Rush's marketing of Roy Rogers occurred because of the actor's film stardom, but at the same time the rodeo, public appearances, comic books, and other items added to his image of a cowboy hero.[18]

Rogers worked hard at developing this Western image, making it fit the stereotypical American cowboy. He refused movie parts that might tarnish the image and avoided such things as smoking and drinking in public. He was sensitive to his youthful audiences and the impact that he had upon their lives.[19] He enjoyed his work and liked the Western persona he molded for himself to the extent that a fusion seemed to occur between his public and private life. Roy Rogers, perhaps more than any other screen cowboy, absorbed his Western persona.

As Rogers developed his career and shaped his image in the 1940s a woman entered his life who would affect his future profoundly. Dale Evans starred first with Rogers in *The Cowboy and the Senorita* (1943). A big band vocalist and radio performer, Dale Evans arrived in Hollywood in 1941 and gained a movie contract with 20th Century–Fox. After leaving Fox she became a vocalist on the *Chase and Sanborn Hour* (the Charlie McCarthy radio show), and ultimately signed a contract with Republic Studios where she played minor roles and was featured in rustic country musicals. Then, Republic executives decided to blend Evans' acting and singing talents with those of their top Western star.[20]

Roy Rogers and Dale Evans made twenty-eight Westerns together between 1944 and 1951 and created a romantic screen combination that was unique in Western films. Dale Evans portrayed heroines who were smart, independent, and resourceful but at the same time feminine and appropriately submissive to Roy Rogers' masculine and heroic roles. The musical skills of the two stars, added to their originality and stunning good looks, produced a special kind of chemistry that enthralled audiences. Dale Evans made personal appearances with Rogers and was a regular on his NBC radio program, *Saturday Night Round-up Starring Roy Rogers* in 1946–47. Through their professional relationship Rogers and Evans became friends, and with the death of Rogers' wife Arlene in 1946, that friendship deepened into love. On an icy and snowy New Years Eve in 1947 Rogers and Evans were married at the Oklahoma ranch of a friend. The marriage began a strong personal and professional partnership that continues in the 1990s.

With their marriage, Republic executives removed Dale Evans from Roy Rogers' films, thinking that fans would not tolerate a married couple doing Westerns. Evans made considerable adjustments as she became a homemaker and the mother of Rogers' three small children. In an uncertain and fearful state of mind Dale Evans sought meaning and direction in her life through a renewed faith in Christianity. Indeed, Christianity became the primary force in Dale Evans' life and one which she and Rogers ultimately blended with their public performances. Although Evans left Rogers' films she appeared with him on his Mutual radio program, *The Roy Rogers Show*. Indeed, fans complained so bitterly about her absence from the Westerns that in 1949 Republic relented and again starred her with Rogers on the screen. She made six Westerns in 1949 and 1950 before leaving again to give birth to their daughter, Robin, a victim of Downs syndrome. Evans returned to Republic in 1951 to co-star in Rogers' last two Republic Westerns.[21]

Roy Rogers' post–World War II Westerns differed markedly from those with lavish musical numbers made in the middle 1940s. William Witney, veteran supervisor of many of Republic's action serials, assumed directorial duties from Frank McDonald in 1946 and gave the Rogers Westerns a hard edge with more action. While music was not ignored, it became less important and themes dealing with contemporary issues emerged as the focus of the stories. Rogers dealt with traditional smugglers, thieves, and murderers as he solved modern-day problems related to organized crime (*Heldorado*, 1946), conservation of natural resources (*Springtime in the Rockies*, 1947; *Down Dakota Way*, 1949), the oil business (*Apache Rose*, 1946), and even the Cold War (*Spoilers of the Plains*, 1951). Witney's originality revealed itself in action sequences, especially in the fight scenes when Rogers and the villains mixed it up in water and mud puddles, under the hooves of cattle and horses, in burning barns, and on horseback while swinging empty rifles. These physical encounters occasionally resulted in the villains battering Rogers to a bleeding and unconscious state. In thrashing the hero and using blood Witney added a touch of realism to Rogers' Westerns and gave him a more human dimension.[22]

The determined elements of Roy Rogers' character came into focus in 1951 when his contract with Republic Studios expired, and he began discussions for renewal. In these talks Rogers insisted on a clause that would permit him to do television. He recognized that the new entertainment medium offered significant financial opportunities. Republic Studios likewise understood the moneymaking possibilities of marketing old movies for television and quietly began to edit Roy Rogers' features to fit the television format. Rogers had a unique provision in his contract with Republic which permitted him to control his name, voice, and image. When he and his agent, Art Rush, learned of Republic's actions, they used this provision and sought a court injunction to prevent the studio from releasing Rogers' Westerns to television. Roy Rogers' legal challenge to Republic Studios in regard to control of his image and his films is unique among Hollywood stars. Rogers won the first stage of the legal battle in the fall of 1951, only to have the decision reversed a few years later. In the meantime Rogers and his managers organized a production company and began filming the thirty-minute *Roy Rogers Show* for television. With the contract dispute and lawsuit Roy Rogers' fourteen-year career at Republic Studios came to an end, but the new and more powerful medium of television introduced him to a fresh generation of fans and added to his stature as the nation's number one cowboy hero.[23]

The Roy Rogers television show, set in fictional Paradise Valley, was an adventure program which dealt with traditional Western themes, but like his most recent movies all included plots that related to contemporary issues.

Roy Rogers on Trigger (courtesy of Ray White, Department of History, Ball State University, Muncie, Indiana).

Many of the shows featured children, most expressed a moral value, and some preached a Christian message. All the programs focused on Roy Rogers the Western hero taking action against the villains of Paradise Valley, usually in conjunction with his two sidekicks, Dale Evans and Pat Brady. Rogers' horse Trigger and his dog Bullet also figured prominently in the plots. More than

100 episodes of the show were filmed and aired on network television between 1951 and 1957, and the show continued as a part of network programming until 1962 when it went into syndication. The series provided Roy Rogers and Dale Evans with a bridge from movies to television, and since they controlled their production company, they determined the content of the shows, especially the strong emphasis on morality and Christian values. *The Roy Rogers Show* was their personal version of what Western entertainment should be.

Roy Rogers' and Dale Evans' decision to incorporate moral and Christian themes into their television show evolved over a period of years and coincided with a religious transformation in their personal lives, as well as one within the nation as a whole. Although Roy Rogers grew up in the Protestant Christian environment of southern Ohio, as an adult he expressed some skepticism regarding religion because of his experiences when visiting thousands of sick and disabled children in hospitals; he could not fully accept a God who permitted such illnesses and disabilities to occur among innocent children. However, Dale Evans' spiritual rebirth in 1948 influenced him, and his skepticism faded. In 1949 the couple became charter members of the Hollywood Christian Group, an organization of show business people that met weekly in each other's homes for prayer and testimony. Billy Graham, who appeared in Los Angeles that same year with the star-studded crusade that made him a national figure, emphasized the relationship between religion and show business. He attended one of the Hollywood Christian Group's meetings, became friends with Rogers and Evans, and eventually asked them to testify at his crusades. These events were part of a larger national spiritual revival in the late 1940s and early 1950s during which millions of Americans showed an increased interest in religion. This spiritual upsurge possessed a civic quality that combined patriotism with religious belief, especially as the Cold War intensified and the United States became locked in international competition with the Soviet Union—a nation that officially denounced religion. Part of being American was being religious, and a citizen's personal religious faith comprised a basic component of his or her patriotism.[24]

Within this atmosphere Roy Rogers and Dale Evans incorporated Christianity into their entertainment activities. In 1949 they recorded one of Rogers' compositions, "May the Lord Take a Likin' to You" (RCA 20/21-0373), and in 1950 they produced their first spiritual album, *Hymns of Faith*, for RCA (LPM-3168). The following year they concluded one of their radio programs with a patriotic religious song, "What This Country Needs Is a Talk with the Lord," which expressed the civil piety that seemed to be sweeping the country. In 1952 Roy Rogers altered his traditional Western rodeo and public appearances by including in each performance a patriotic-religious segment, and at a Sunday matinee performance of the Houston Fat Stock Show he even chose to answer publicly a letter from a young fan whose friends claimed it was "sissy" to go to Sunday School.[25] Roy Rogers' and Dale Evans' deliberate use of religious themes in their public performances fit both the national mood of the 1950s and their own personal religious convictions. Indeed, they felt a moral responsibility to their young audiences to set an example and to instill values. In this respect they felt it was natural and right to join their spiritual and professional life, which they did with simple straightforward words, stories, and songs.

Although Western entertainment heroes traditionally represented strong moral values in their dramatic presentations, Roy Rogers was almost alone in overtly meshing religious values and Western adventure. It is difficult to measure the impact of this decision, but apparently it had no adverse effect upon his image or status as a Western performing star. Indeed, he reached the peak of his professional career in the 1950s, just at the time he chose to express religious themes in his public performances. In addition to his weekly appearances on radio and television and his numerous public appearances, he endorsed more than 400 products, mainly toys and clothes for children. Both his and Dale Evans' faces and names appeared on thousands of lunch boxes, pajamas, bedspreads, cap pistols, and puzzles, as well as in millions of comic and juvenile adventure books. All of these media and commercial products entrenched Roy Rogers' image in the minds of Americans and enhanced his stature as a Western entertainment celebrity. But more than that, they established Roy Rogers as an American icon, especially as his life and career extended into the late twentieth century and his youthful admirers of the 1950s became adults.[26]

Roy Rogers and Dale Evans' concern about the moral and religious values of their young fans may have arisen from the fact that they themselves were parents. When the couple married, Rogers had two daughters and one son (Cheryl, Linda Lou, and Dusty), and Evans a grown son (Tom Fox) from previous marriages. In 1950 Robin Elizabeth, their only natural child, was born. Tragedy struck in 1952 when Robin died from complications arising from Downs syndrome. The death devastated the family, but recovery came through the adoption of three children (Sandy, Dodie, and Debbie) and Dale Evans' publication of *Angel Unaware*[27] (1953), a book about Robin's impact upon the Rogers' life. The couple also assumed the guardianship of a teenage Scottish girl (Marion) whom they met while on tour of the British Isles in 1954. Although Rogers and Evans had an extremely busy professional career, they nevertheless focused on their family and attempted to make its life as normal as possible. Occasionally they included the children in their public performances. Cheryl, Dusty, and Dodie appeared in episodes of the television series, and during the summer the children sometimes performed with their parents at state fairs or other public performances. In 1959 the family recorded an album of spiritual music, *Jesus Loves Me* (RCA CAL-1022), and about the same time Dusty appeared with his father on the cover of several issues of the Roy Rogers comic book.[28] Rogers and Evans, like millions of other American parents in the 1950s and 1960s, coped with the problems and issues of growing children and teenagers. Although the Rogers family in reality may not have been completely typical, it represented the values of the period, and American parents applauded Roy Rogers and Dale Evans for providing wholesome entertainment and positive role models for their children.[29]

In the 1960s Roy Rogers continued to entertain but not with Western television and radio adventures; he focused more on personal appearances, musical variety television shows, and recordings with Capitol records. He was ready to slow the pace of his professional life and felt that Westerns needed a rest too, especially since there were so many of them on television. The political and social activism of the 1960s, which centered on the civil rights movement and the Vietnam War, may have dated Rogers' Westerns. The social ferment of the 1960s certainly destroyed the general political and social consensus of the 1950s into which Rogers Westerns fit, and the nation polarized along ideological lines. Within this polarization Roy Rogers remained true to the patriotic/religious views that he had developed during the early days of the Cold War. While he did not become overtly involved in the ideological battles of the 1960s, he nevertheless expressed himself when he felt the case merited it. The millions of youngsters who grew up with Rogers in the 1950s fantasizing about adventures in Paradise Valley were likewise caught up in the tumult and confusion of the 1960s. Political and social issues seemed more complicated than those of the previous decade, and the solutions of the past did not seem to fit. In fact, Westerns themselves became more complex with multidimensional heroes and plots. The hero that Roy Rogers portrayed in his movies and television and radio series lost its appeal as the nation agonized over problems that no hero seemed able to solve.

In the midst of this social and political turbulence tragedy struck the Rogers family a double blow. In 1964 Debbie, their adopted twelve-year-old Korean child, was killed in a car-bus accident while on an outing with a church group. Within two years their son Sandy died a tragic alcohol-related death while in the Army in Germany. At a party after some tough military maneuvers Sandy's buddies challenged him to prove his manhood by drinking. The amount he consumed rendered him unconscious, and left unattended overnight in his bunk, he died. Rogers' and Evans' recovery from their children's deaths came from their strong religious convictions and their positive outlook on life. A USO tour of Vietnam to entertain American troops eased the pain. They also continued to perform publicly by hosting television shows and making personal appearances.[30]

Rogers' image assumed a more rustic flavor in the early 1970s when he recorded three country music albums for Capitol Records. Although he had always performed and was identified with country music, he was noted mainly for his Western songs, especially ballads. In these new recordings he substituted his popular Western style for that of contemporary country music and vocalized such tunes as "Okie from Muskogee," "Money Can't Buy Love," and "Lovenworth"; the latter two songs rose to the top of the country charts.[31] In the 1970s he also recorded some spiritual songs with Dale Evans for Word records[32] and one album for 20th Century Records, *Happy Trails to You* (1975, T-467), out of which came a best selling and nostalgic single, "Hoppy, Gene, and Me." That nostalgia heightened in 1976 when Rogers starred in his first movie since the early 1950s, *Mackintosh and TJ*, a modern-day Western in which Rogers portrayed a wandering elderly cowboy who befriends and helps a delinquent teenage boy in West Texas.

It was also during the late 1960s and early 1970s that Roy Rogers entered the fast-food business with a chain of restaurants that bore his name. Although he was not involved in the direct management of the chain, Rogers made appearances at openings and did public relations work for the franchise. Located mainly in the eastern part of the United States, the Roy Rogers franchise expanded rapidly during the 1970s and numbered more than 600 by the late 1980s. Just as with his merchandising in the 1950s, the restaurants maintained and added to Rogers' image of a celebrity cowboy hero.

While the restaurant chain helped to perpetuate Roy Rogers' image, his work with the Sons of the Pioneers to provide a sound track tune for the feature film *Smokey and the Bandit 2* (1980), and his appearance on such television programs as the *Muppet Show* (8/79) and *The Fall Guy* (1984), indicated that he was still an active and working professional entertainer fifty years after the start of his career.[33] The production of a two-record album (*Many Happy Trails*, Teletex C-7702) with Dale Evans and son Dusty in 1983 indicated the same thing. A revival of interest in Roy Rogers' films also occurred in the mid–1980s when the Nashville Network introduced *Happy Trails Theater*, a weekly program featuring one of his movies with Rogers and Dale Evans reminiscing about their entertainment careers.

The variety and longevity of Roy Rogers' professional career has made him an institution, an icon with which millions of Americans identify. His name, which evokes immediate recognition, is often used by script writers or humorists to create a visual image or make a point that everyone understands. Bruce Willis, in the movie thriller *Die Hard* (1988), used "Roy Rogers" as his code name. Humorous references to Roy Rogers and Dale Evans turned up in episodes of the television sitcoms *Golden Girls* and *Designing Women*. This identification comes in part from the Western cowboy image that he created and has portrayed in all aspects of his professional life. The image of an honest, open, warm-hearted cowboy who stands for traditional American values, especially the democratic spirit. He is a softer John Wayne, who both on and off the screen makes people feel that he is one of them and not a remote distant celebrity. His natural acting style, his music, and his use of self-deprecating humor lets people know who he is, sets them at ease, and establishes a personal connection that uniquely binds him to the American people.[34]

Notes

1. I overheard a fan make this remark to a friend at the conclusion of one of Roy Rogers' appearances at the Cincinnati Bicentennial in July 1988. Rogers had just finished a forty-five minute question and answer session with his fans in the broiling noon-day sun at Fountain Square.

2. The biographical material on Roy Rogers is voluminous and ranges from book-length works to studio- and press-agent biographies. Most important is the autobiographical work *Happy Trails: The Story of Roy Rogers and Dale Evans* with Carlton Stowers (Waco, Texas: Word Books, 1979); also important is Elise Miller Davis, *The Answer Is God: The Inspiring Personal Story of Dale Evans and Roy Rogers* (New York: McGraw-Hill Book Company, 1955); Miller spent several months interviewing and traveling with Rogers and Evans; Roy Rogers, Jr.'s, *Growing Up with Roy and Dale* (Ventura, California: Regal Books, 1986) done with Karen Ann Wojahn provides an honest, personal, and positive view of the Rogers' family life; Dale Evans Rogers' numerous books provide an abundance of biographical material mixed with her spiritual beliefs. One of the best is *The Woman at the Well* (Old Tappan, N.J.: Fleming H. Revell, 1970); hundreds of articles about Roy Rogers have appeared in such fan magazines as *Modern Screen, Photoplay*, and *Motion Picture*, and fat files of clippings on Roy Rogers can be found in the Margaret Herrick Library of the Academy of Motion Picture Arts and Sciences (Beverly Hills, California), the Country Music Foundation Library (Nashville, Tennessee), and the Roy Rogers–Dale Evans Collectors Association (Portsmouth, Ohio). Gary Kramer, Philip Loy, Mark Mock, Michael R. Pitts, Kathryn White, and Dawn Wortinger provided valuable suggestions for the interpretation of the biographical material.

3. Lucky Evelyn Koleman, "Vacationing with the Roy Rogers," *Double R-Bar Ranch News* [fan club newsletter in Country Music Foundation library, Nashville, Tennessee] (May 1951), pp. 6–7.

4. Rogers and Evans, *Happy Trails*, pp. 29–32; Davis, *The Answer Is God*, pp. 15, 18–20.

5. Davis, *The Answer Is God*, pp. 24–25; Rogers and Evans, *Happy Trails*, pp. 36–39.

6. Roy Rogers, "The Truth About My First Wife," *Modern Screen*, Vol. 49, No. 12 (November 1955), pp. 29, 83–85.

7. Ken Griffis, *Hear My Song: The Story of the Celebrated Sons of the Pioneers*, JEMF Special Series No. 5 (Los Angeles: The John Edwards Memorial Foundation, 1974, 1977), pp. 11–19; Tim Spencer, "We Sang for Our Supper," *Western Stars*, Vol. 1, No. 3 (October–December 1949), pp. 8–11. Rogers, *Happy Trails*, pp. 45–46.

8. Rogers and Evans, *Happy Trails*, pp. 43–47.

9. A number of publications have appeared dealing with the development of the B Western singing cowboy. Douglas B. Green has produced several significant pieces on the subject including "The Singing Cowboy: An American Dream," *The Journal of Country Music*, Vol. 7 No. 2 (May 1978), pp. 4–61. Green's penetrating evaluation of Autry's significance in popularizing country music through his movie career can be found in *Stars of Country Music*, edited by Bill C. Malone and Judith McCulloh (Urbana: University of Illinois Press, 1975), pp. 155–171; also see Green's chapter "Gene Autry, Bob Wills, and the Dream of the West," in *Country: The Music and the Musicians* (New York: The Country Music Foundation and Abbeville Press, 1988), pp. 108–150; Bill C. Malone deals with the subject in *Country Music, U.S.A.*, revised edition (Austin: University of Texas Press, 1985), pp. 141–152; Richard Maurice Hurst, *Republic Studios: Between Poverty Row and the Majors* (Metuchen, N.J.: The Scarecrow Press, Inc., 1979), pp. 136–57. David Rothel has much important information on all of the B Western singers in *The Singing Cowboys* (New York: A.S. Barnes & Company, Inc., 1978). For firsthand accounts of their own experiences in getting into the movies as singing cowboys see Rogers and Evans, *Happy Trails*, pp. 49–58, and Gene Autry, *Back in the Saddle Again* (Garden City, N.Y.: Doubleday & Company, 1978), pp. 35–64.

10. For information on Leonard Slye's name change see Rogers, *Happy Trails*, pp. 55–56; *Motion Picture and Television Almanac 1956* (New York: Quigley Publishing, 1955), pp. 790–91, provides information on Rogers' ranking as a moneymaking star.

11. The *Double R-Bar Ranch News*, Roy Rogers' fan club newsletters, reveals that women presided over many of his regional fan clubs and were more active than male fans in collecting clippings and photos of the star. See file in Country Music Foundation Library, Nashville, TN.

12. For information on Joseph Kane's career see Harry Sanford, "Joseph Kane," *Close Up: The Contract Director*, edited by Jon Tuska (Metuchen, N.J.: The Scarecrow Press, 1976), pp. 143–87.

13. The best reference for Roy Rogers' films is Bob Carman and Dan Scapperotti, *Roy Rogers, King of the Cowboys: A Film Guide* (n.p.: Robert Carman, 1979). It provides a review and credits for each of Rogers' Republic features plus information on his other films.

14. No full-scale biography of Gabby Hayes exists, but the best short review of his career as it relates to that of Roy Rogers is David Rothel, *The Great Cowboy Sidekicks* (Waynesville, NC: WOY Publications, 1984), pp. 41–63; also see John A. Rutherford biographical sketch of Hayes and a three-part filmography in "Gabby," *Under Western Skies*, No. 7 (July 1979), pp. 25–45; No. 12 (January 1981), pp. 25–61; No. 21 (November 1982), pp. 5–56. The filmography covers only the early Rogers Westerns; For Rogers' view of Hayes see Rogers and Evans, *Happy Trails*, pp. 61–63.

15. Rogers and Evans, *Happy Trails*, pp. 71, 74–76; William Weaver, "The Biggest Money-Making Stars of 1943," *Motion Picture Herald*, Vol. 153, No. 13 (December 25, 1943), pp. 14–16; Rothel, *The Singing Cowboys*, pp. 120–22; H. Allen Smith, "King of the Cowboys," *Life*, Vol. 15 (July 12, 1943), pp. 47–48+.

16. Hurst, *Republic Studios*, pp. 147, 151–53.

17. Beginning in 1944 as a musical variety program, *The Roy Rogers Show* aired alternately on two networks until 1955. It originated with the Mutual Broadcasting Company in 1944 running for one season before being picked up by the National Broadcasting Company in the fall of 1946. The show returned to Mutual in 1948 where it remained until 1951 when NBC resumed broadcast for its final four years. See Ray White, "The Roy Rogers Show: A Decade of Radio Adventure, 1944–1955," Part I, 1944–1951 in *Roy Rogers–Dale Evans Collectors Association* [Newsletter], Vol. V, No. 33 (September/October 1988), Vol. 5, No. 34 (Winter 1988-89), unpaged.

18. Interview with Art Rush, North Hollywood, California, February 12, 1987; for Rogers' views about Rush see Rogers and Evans, *Happy Trails*, pp. 66–69.

19. Herbert Yates attempted to get Rogers to play the role of a cocky and alcoholic newspaper reporter in *Behind the News* (1942), but the star vehemently refused, not wanting to change the Western image that he had established for himself. In his autobiography Rogers says the film was *Front Page* and that Lloyd Nolan was given the lead; Republic did not make *Front Page* but did produce *Behind the News* starring Nolan. See Rogers and Evans, *Happy Trails*, pp. 64–65; Rogers relates the same story in one of the discussions that he and Evans had on a 1987 episode of *Happy Trails Theater*. For information on Rogers' awareness of the image that he presented to his young fans see Lucy Greenbaum, "A Sinatra in a Sombrero," *New York Times Magazine* (November 4, 1945), p. 42.

20. Rogers and Evans, *Happy Trails*, pp. 114–116.

21. Rogers, *Woman at the Well*, pp. 67–76; Carman and Scapperotti, *Westerns of Roy Rogers*, pp. 146–57, 170–73.

22. For information on William Witney's career see Francis M. Nevins, Jr., "Ballet of Violence: The Films of William Witney," *Films in Review*, Vol. XXV, No. 9 (November 1974), pp. 523–44; Francis M. Nevins, Jr., "William Witney," in *Close Up: The Contract Director*, pp. 188–227; William Witney, *Trigger Remembered* (Toney, AL: Earl Blair Enterprises, 1989).

23. Rogers and Evans, *Happy Trails*, pp. 145–50; William R. Weaver, "Rogers Ver-

dict Sends TV into Vertical Spin," *Motion Picture Herald* (October 27, 1951), pp. 13–14; "Rogers Ruling Favors Pay-TV," *The Hollywood Reporter*, Vol. CXVLI, No. 21 (October 22, 1951), pp. 1, 6; *New York Times*, October 30, 1954, 15:5.

24. Rogers, *Woman at the Well*, pp. 68–75, 86–87; Rogers and Evans, *Happy Trails*, pp. 125–28; the organization of the Hollywood Christian Group is detailed in *Jane Russell: An Autobiography* (New York: Franklin Watts, Inc., 1985), p. 143; the story of Billy Graham's Los Angeles crusade in 1949 is told in Marshall Frady, *Billy Graham: A Parable of American Righteousness* (Boston: Little, Brown and Company, 1979); the post–World War II religious revival in the United States is covered in Sydney E. Ahlstrom, *A Religious History of the American People* (New Haven: Yale University Press, 1972), pp. 949–63, and *Eerdmans' Handbook to Christianity in America* (Grand Rapids, MI: William B. Eerdmans Publishing Company, 1983), pp. 423–37.

25. Rogers and Evans, *Happy Trails*, pp. 152–53.

26. Interview with Art Rush, North Hollywood, California, February 12, 1987; the number and variety of products that Roy Rogers Enterprises produced and marketed can be seen in advertisements in such magazines as *Life*; see "Roy Rogers Shoots for Santa," *Life*, Vol. 35 (November 16, 1953), pp. 77–80; in 1953 Roy Rogers Enterprises produced an 80-page catalog of its merchandise: Elliott V. D. Bogert, *Catalogue and Merchandising Manual* (1953); see also Elliott V. Bogert, *1953 Program for Profit: Roy Rogers, King of the Cowboys, Monarch of Merchandising* (Roy Rogers Enterprises, 1952), 19pp., and Elliott V. Bogert, *1954 Roy Rogers Program for Profit*, designed with you the retailer in mind (Roy Rogers Enterprises, 1953), 16pp.

27. (Westwood, N.J.: Fleming H. Revell Company, 1953).

28. The last eleven issues of the Dell Roy Rogers comic book, #134–#145, November-December, 1959–September-October, 1961, featured Roy Rogers and Dusty on the front covers.

29. One fan from Pennsylvania in 1951 named her son after Roy Rogers and hoped that he would grow up to be as fine a man as the Western star. She wrote the fan club, "If more men loved and brought up their children as Roy does, we would have a much better world," *Double R-Bar Ranch News* (January 1951), p. 6.

30. Dale Evans tells the story of Debbie and Sandy in *Dearest Debbie* (Westwood, N.J.: Fleming H. Revell Company, 1965), and *Salute to Sandy* (Westwood, N.J.: Fleming H. Revell Company, 1967).

31. Roy Rogers country/western albums on Capitol records included *The Country Side of Roy Rogers* (1970, ST-594); *Roy Rogers: A Man from Duck Run* (1971, ST-785); *Take a Little Love and Pass It On* (1972, ST-11020).

32. *In the Sweet By and By* (1973, WST-8589); *The Good Life* (1977, WSA-8761).

33. The soundtrack tune that Rogers and the Sons of the Pioneers performed, "Ride Concrete Cowboy, Ride," was recorded on MCA Records (1980, MCA-41294). In the spring of 1989 Rogers and country/western singer Randy Travis recorded "Happy Trails" for an album of duets that features Travis with several prominent recording artists.

34. Subsequent to the writing of this chapter, on July 6, 1998, Roy Rogers died in his sleep of congestive heart failure at his home in Apple Valley, near Victorville, California, at the age of 86. He was survived by his wife of 50 years, Dale Evans, his children, Roy Rogers, Jr. ("Dusty"), Cheryl Barnett, Linda Lou Johnson, Dodie Sailors, Marion Swift and Tom Fox, 15 grandchildren and 33 great-grandchildren.

JAMES M. STEWART: AN AMERICAN ORIGINAL

by Michael K. Schoenecke

In *The Western Films of John Ford*, J. A. Place aptly notes that Jimmy Stewart's versatility as an actor allowed him to be "used in more different ways by directors than any other actor of his stature."[1] Jimmy Stewart's films, including *Mr. Smith Goes to Washington* (1939), *The Philadelphia Story* (1940), *It's a Wonderful Life* (1946), *Harvey* (1951), *Rear Window* (1954), *Vertigo* (1958), seventeen Westerns, and fifty-four other films remain successful today because of their intrinsic entertainment value and because Stewart's films reflect and embody the most fundamental and universal concerns of people. In fact, if any cinematic actor could challenge John Wayne as the greatest Western hero, that actor would be Jimmy Stewart. As Archie P. McDonald succinctly notes, Wayne personified "Super-America," and he became "an embodiment of our nationalism, our jingoistic, self-image of success...."[2] Jimmy Stewart's Western roles, on the other hand, personified ordinary Americans and their frustrations, expectations, and glory. As Americans flocked to theaters to watch a Stewart Western, they saw in Stewart a man they regarded as a close relative, a man whose cinematic character became an American Everyman.

James (Jimmy) Maitland Stewart, the first child and only son of Alexander Maitland and Elizabeth Ruth Jackson Stewart, was born on May 20, 1908, in Indiana, Pennsylvania, a small town nestled in the foothills of the Alleghany Mountains. When Stewart's grandparents moved to Indiana in 1853, they opened the J. M. Stewart hardware store which, like the other local stores, serviced the farmers in this predominantly rural community. These Presbyterian Stewarts were of Scots-Irish stock and conservative by nature; they believed in and supported small town, middle-class American values such as honesty, pride, dignity, and industry. Stewart openly and willingly embraced these values, and his life on and off the screen has conveyed these characteristics to film audiences.

James Stewart's childhood was similar to that of most boys of his time. Although this tall, unusually thin young man initially wanted to be a magician, he developed a dedicated interest in the Boy Scouts of America, chemistry, radio, the accordion, and model airplanes. Most of all, the young Stewart admired his father, a sometimes gruff but self-reliant man who supported his son's wildest aspirations. When his father enlisted for service in World War I, young Stewart not only assumed the masculine roles of the household, such as locking up the hardware store and the house for the evening, he also spent much of his time writing and producing plays about World War I. These patriotic plays, entitled *The Slacker* and *To Hell with the Kaiser*, were performed in the basement of the Stewart house. Patience, sincerity, dedication, and intensity were fortifying characteristics that Stewart learned not only from his parents but from life itself. These values would later become marking points for his cinematic characters.

In 1928 Stewart attended Mercersburg Academy where he ran track, sang with the glee club, and because he was an exceptional artist, he worked on the school's yearbook. Although Stewart wanted to attend the Naval Academy after he had completed his studies at Mercersburg, his head-strong father insisted that his son attend Princeton University. While he was at Princeton, Stewart's above average academic standing was balanced by a number of extracurricular activities. For example, he studied architecture, in which he earned a degree, and he played the accordion with the Triangle Club, which contributed to his great fame and fortune in later years. After Stewart was graduated from Princeton in 1932, his thoughts turned to graduate school; however, his friend Josh Logan, who was more interested in Stewart's accordion playing than his acting ability, persuaded him to perform with the University Players, a reputable amateur performing society.

Since it was the time of the Great Depression and he had no job offers from an architectural firm, Stewart accepted Logan's invitation to join the University Players. He moved to West Falmouth, where he was assigned to the Old Silver Beach Tearoom, which was located next to the theater. One night, while Stewart entertained dinner guests with his lively accordion wizardry, he was approached by the company director who promised him a small role in a company production if Stewart would not ruin anyone else's appetite. Stewart accepted a walk-on role in *Magnolia*, a bit part in *It's a Wise Child*, and a small part as a chauffeur in *Goodbye Again* before he played Officer Gano in *Carrie Nation*, a role which became responsible for his professional life as an actor. At the completion of *Carrie Nation*'s theatrical run, Stewart vacillated between returning to Indiana to work in the family hardware store and pursuing an advanced degree in architecture at Princeton. When New York producer Arthur Beckhard asked him to repeat his role as Officer Gano at the Biltmore Theatre in New York, Stewart accepted the offer and moved to New York where he shared a small apartment with his close friends Henry Fonda, Josh Logan, and Myron McCormick.

When *Carrie Nation* closed in New York, Stewart once again entertained thoughts of returning to Indiana, but Beckhard decided to stage *Goodbye*

Again, and he asked Stewart to repeat his role as the chauffeur. The play had better than 200 performances, and audiences and critics praised young Stewart's performances. With such good luck behind him, he decided to pursue, at least temporarily, an acting career in theater. Although his next few theater jobs were as stage manager in *Camille* and *Spring in Autumn*, which did provide him with a bit part, Stewart accepted a role in *All Good Americans*, which led to his part as the warm, idealistic Sergeant O'Hara in *Yellow Jacket*. By October 1934, Stewart had secured a major role in *Divided by Three,* starring Judith Anderson. While many outstanding young actors such as Henry Fonda struggled to acquire even minor theatrical roles, Stewart, who never realized how talented he truly was, seemed to stumble upon part after part.

In 1935 Stewart signed his first Hollywood contract, which was extendable over seven years, with Metro-Goldwyn-Mayer. He received a guaranteed income of $350 per week. Although Stewart's New York theatrical career had never been spectacular, he became an outstanding and successful Hollywood actor within one year. When Stewart arrived in Hollywood, Henry Fonda met him at the airport, offered to share his apartment with him, and helped the conservative Stewart become comfortable with the Hollywood lifestyle, which for this six-foot, three-inch, 138-pound young man was a tremendous adjustment. Although Stewart's physical stature seemed too slender for filming, Margaret Sullivan, Fonda's ex-wife, asked Universal to borrow him from MGM so he could co-star with her in *Next Time We Love* (1936). Stewart's cinematic career mushroomed in 1936 when he appeared in eight films with such top Hollywood headliners as Clark Gable, Jean Harlow, Joan Crawford, and William Powell. This exposure brought him to the attention of Frank Capra and Columbia Studio; Capra cast Stewart in *You Can't Take It with You* (1938) and *Mr. Smith Goes to Washington* (1939).

Stewart's pre-war Hollywood days were extremely fruitful. During this time he established himself as an actor capable of playing a variety of parts and as an appealing actor who demonstrated emotional substance balanced by a sense of humor. The Academy of Motion Picture Arts and Sciences also recognized Stewart's talent by nominating him for Best Actor in 1939 for his role in *Mr. Smith Goes to Washington*. Although Robert Donat won for his performance in *Goodbye Mr. Chips*, Stewart won the following year for his portrayal of Mike Connor, a cynical yet vulnerable journalist, in *The Philadelphia Story* (1940). Even though Stewart's Hollywood career was now established, he believed that America would become involved in the war. He began to concentrate on flying so that he could qualify as a military pilot when America entered World War II.

On March 21, 1941, Stewart was accepted into the United States Air Force after being deferred earlier by the draft board because his 140 pounds was underweight. Because he enlisted one year before Pearl Harbor, he was the first Hollywood star to join the military for World War II. Since he owned his own plane, a two-seat Stinson 105, and clocked as many hours as he could, he was assigned to the Air Corps. This assignment cost Stewart $11,979 a month in salary; his salary in Hollywood was estimated to be $12,000 a month. Although his age qualified him for an immediate release from any military action, Stewart refused to accept it. In fact, whenever he was treated as a star rather than as one of the troops, he resented it. Perhaps the one way he did use his star status occurred when he pulled a few strings so that he could be treated like anyone else.

The Air Corps assigned Stewart to Moffet Field, California, where he served as an instructor for bombardier cadets. He received his promotion to lieutenant in August 1942, and in November 1943 was reassigned to England where as a captain he flew twenty-five missions over enemy territory with the Second Air Division, Eighth Air Command. He and his crew named their plane "Nine Yanks and a Jerk." When he returned to the United States in September 1945 as Colonel Stewart, he was awarded the Air Medal and the Distinguished Flying Cross, the Oak Leaf Cluster, and seven battle stars; later, the French government honored Stewart for his distinguished service with the Croix de Guerre with Palm. In 1957 he was nominated to the rank of brigadier general; however, Senator Margaret Chase Smith of Maine opposed the promotion by arguing that Stewart was being promoted because of his public stature as an actor. Stewart's fellow officers and servicemen succeeded in overcoming the objection, and Stewart received the rank of brigadier general in July 1959; later that year he was elected to the Princeton University board of trustees. Stewart remained actively involved with the Air Force Reserve for twenty-seven years until his age (60) required him to retire. Upon retirement he toured Air Force bases and addressed the men on duty; the Air Force later awarded him the Distinguished Service Medal, accompanied by a commendation for his total service to the military.

When Stewart returned to the United States following his military service, he returned home to Indiana, Pennsylvania, looking for peace and quiet; however, *Life* magazine, hoping that they could be the first to do a feature story on the Hollywood veteran's wartime experiences, invaded Indiana. *Life*'s attempt to capture a few words about Stewart's role in the military was cut short because he refused to talk.

Stewart's wartime experiences had changed him. When he returned to Hollywood, his contract with MGM had lapsed, but Louis B. Mayer generously offered to extend the contract as a small token of his appreciation for Stewart's military service; however, Stewart, who doubted his cinematic talent, surprised everyone when he rejected Mayer's offer. When Stewart failed to make a living as a flyer, he listened to Frank Capra's idea about starring in a film entitled *It's a Wonderful Life* (1946). Although Capra was concerned that the plot was too corny, Stewart agreed to star as George Bailey, a man who returns to his family after contemplating suicide. With the help of an angel and a visit to the future, Bailey learns that whatever one's problems, family and friends can make life wonderful. Stewart's performance earned him his third Oscar nomination for Best Actor, and the film is a classic piece of Americana as well as a cinematic masterpiece. Aware that unscrupulous Hollywood promoters might also attempt to use his wartime experiences as a promotional gimmick, Stewart's future contracts denied Hollywood promoters the opportunity to refer to his military service and later to his service in the United States Air Force Reserve in their publicity campaigns.

When Stewart first moved to Hollywood, his father encouraged him to find a girl and settle down; however, the star-struck Stewart, who had a tendency to fall in love with all the leading ladies, took a long time to divest himself of dating legendary actresses. On August 9, 1949, Stewart married Gloria Hatrick McLean, who had two young sons from a previous marriage: Ronald, who died in Vietnam, and Michael. Since Stewart preferred a normal home life amid the emotional chaos of Hollywood, Gloria, who was bright, humorous, and strong-minded, proved to be a logical choice. They became the parents of twin girls, Kelly and Judy, on May 7, 1951. The Stewarts continued to live a low-profile life in Beverly Hills where Stewart enjoyed working with his photographic equipment, picnicking, and walking his dogs.

Jimmy Stewart's cinematic Western career began with *Destry Rides Again* (1939), which proved to be profitable at the box office as well as for the careers of Stewart and Marlene Dietrich, with whom Stewart shared equal billing. Director George Michael loosely based his version of *Destry Rides Again* upon Max Brand's story which Universal Studios had filmed in 1932 with Tom Mix in the title role. The Stewart vehicle, like Mack Sennett's *His Bitter Pill* (1916) and Laurel and Hardy's *Way Out West* (1937), parodies B Westerns popularized by such stars as Buck Jones, Ken Maynard, Tim McCoy, and Hoot Gibson, who built their films around action-packed chases and fistic encounters in the 1930s.

Stewart's film takes place some time around the 1870s in the town of Bottle Neck's Last Chance Saloon, which is owned by a villain, Kent (Brian Donlevy). The saloon's chief attraction is the singer-hostess Frenchy (Dietrich). Kent runs the town and tells the mayor to appoint a new sheriff; the mayor then selects Wash Dimsdale (Charles Winninger), the town drunk, who, to everyone's surprise, sobers up and takes his new job seriously. In an attempt to restore order in this raucous cowtown, Wash sends for Tom Destry (Stewart), the son of a famous marshal for whom Wash once worked. Although some of the townspeople, who have listened to Wash's hyperbolic tales, fear the arrival of a young, gun-happy deputy, these fears soon dissipate when an unarmed Tom Destry gets off the stage carrying a parasol rather than six-guns. While Destry accumulates the needed evidence to reveal Kent's crimes, he gradually earns the respect of Frenchy and the townspeople. Once Kent's men kill Wash, Destry, who is an expert shot, straps on his father's guns and leads

Tom Destry (James Stewart) (center, with birdcage) tells the sheriff (Charles Winninger) and the Bottle Neck townspeople that he doesn't carry guns because he doesn't believe in them. *Destry Rides Again*, 1939, Universal Pictures.

the good people on a raid. During the final shoot-out between Kent and Destry, Frenchy steps in front of a bullet destined for Tom, who then shoots and kills Kent.

Stewart's amusing portrayal of the pacifist deputy who prefers not to carry guns was a "boots-and-saddle variation" of Jefferson Smith in *Mr. Smith Goes to Washington*. When Kent challenges Destry to a gunfight, Destry humorously replies, "You see, if I had carried a gun, one of us might have got hurt, and it might have been me." Such lines obviously parodied the B Western's shoot-'em-up gunfights and the hero's eagerness to fight, and Stewart's role as the naive, docile, idealistic deputy provided great entertainment to audiences who did not take the B Western tradition too seriously.

In *Winchester '73* (1950), the partnership of James Stewart/Anthony Mann, who called the film his "favorite Western," provided the premise for all future mature Westerns that attempted to develop psychologically intense films. Aware that the hero's relationship with the gun was of such extreme importance for this film, Stewart "studied a long time learning how to use it. His fingers became completely at home with it.... Knowing how to use something is the only way to achieve Western realism."[3] Like Glyn McLyntock, Lin McAdam (Stewart) is a man with a secret: he plans to hunt down and kill Dutch Henry Brown (Stephen McNally), his brother, who killed their father by shooting him in the back. McAdam is a fairly easy-going, self-effacing individual until he sees his brother. During a Fourth of July celebration, a shooting match supervised by Wyatt Earp (Will Geer) is held to determine who will receive a new Winchester '73, the gun that won the West. Lin and Dutch Henry easily out-perform their competitors. By temporarily sublimating his hatred in order to outshoot Dutch Henry, Lin claims the repeating rifle, which symbolizes Lin's superior morality and their father's principles. When the cowardly Dutch Henry and Steve Miller ambush Lin in his hotel room and steal the rifle, *Winchester '73* follows Lin's journey as he demonstrates his ability to defend his honor, to accomplish his mission, and to conquer his personal problems. During the final shootout in the streets of Abilene, an exhausted Lin endures the punishing test of not only surviving the hail of bullets fired from his brother's gun but by killing his brother and thereby restoring his psychological balance and order in society. This desire to join a community was demonstrated earlier in the film when Lin and High Spade (Millard Mitchell), his traveling companion, help the cavalry fight off an Indian attack. Stewart's Western screen persona in *Winchester '73* increased his public appeal. Many viewers, however, were stunned by the new Stewart hero. In one instance, Lin encounters the crazed Waco Johnny Dean (Dan Duryea) in a saloon. Wanting information about his brother's whereabouts, Lin grabs Dean's arm, viciously twists it behind his back, and slams his face into the counter while Dean begs for mercy. The role of Lin McAdam allowed Stewart to explore the emotionally torturous realm of an individual consumed by hatred.

Bend of the River (1952) furthered the collaboration between Jimmy Stewart and Anthony Mann that eventually produced five of the best Westerns ever made; Stewart's "single-mindedness," his willingness to do anything to achieve realism on screen, "interlocking with Mann's conception of character,"[4] provided Mann with the opportunity to draw on Stewart's talent to convey humor laced with cynicism. Glyn McLyntock (Stewart) was the antithesis of the traditionally soft-spoken, amiable Stewart image to which film audiences had grown accustomed. The "new" Stewart Western hero, at least in those films directed by Mann, was a quiet man who sought to purge himself of his post–Civil War outlaw past as a Missouri raider and reestablish a clearly defined relationship with society. As Emerson Cole (Arthur Kennedy), a former Missouri raider and McLyntock's alter ego, ride in an equally framed two-shot, Cole asks, "What are you running away from?" McLyntock replies, "A man named Glyn McLyntock," to which Cole then asks, "What happens when he catches up with you?" A pensive McLyntock says, "He died on the Missouri border." After some thought, Cole answers,

Millard Mitchell and James Stewart in a scene from *Winchester '73*, a Universal International Picture.

"No, he'll catch up with you one day." Cole, being McLyntock's evil side, has caught up with him. While McLyntock, Cole, and some of the new settlers take their supplies to their camp, they encounter some miners who offer to buy the supplies. The greedy Cole, willing to sacrifice the food that would save the lives of innocent children and women for a fast buck, and the miners steal the loaded wagons as well as two hostages. In a bitter battle, McLyntock drowns Cole, and the rushing water carries him away—symbolically purifying McLyntock of his past and galvanizing McLyntock's relationship with the settlers and his new life.

The obsessed Stewart hero does not always travel alone. Although he is often accompanied by a male companion, as in *Bend of the River*, *The Naked Spur* (1953), and *The Far Country* (1955), the companionship does not last because the hero unites with a woman; on the other hand, in *Winchester '73*, *The Man from Laramie* (1955), and *The Cheyenne Social Club* (1970), the male relationship does endure as a partnership and as a tolerance as well as a search for friendship.

During the 1950s, America's initial post-war attention focused on the status of minorities, particularly blacks, in modern society. *Broken Arrow* (1950) examined America's confusion regarding racial relations. Tom Jeffords'

Robert Ryan, Ralph Meeker, Janet Leigh, James Stewart, Millard Mitchell in a scene from *The Naked Spur* (Metro-Goldwyn-Mayer).

(Stewart)—the hero, a Civil War veteran, a cavalry scout, and a friend to the Indians—adjustment to society depends more upon society's acceptance and willingness to accommodate the Indian, who is regarded as an alien. Delmer Daves' film, like Mann's *Devil's Doorway* (1950), presents Indian customs and mores with sympathy and authenticity. Realizing that the Indians possess such desirable human characteristics as kindness, honesty, and fair play, traits which all races admire and attempt to perpetuate, Jeffords tries to reconcile the conflict between Indians and whites. He falls in love with and marries, in an Apache ceremony, Sonseeahray (Debra Paget), an Indian princess. Their marriage suggests that racial harmony can be achieved if people accept one another as human beings. As Jeffords tells the peace-loving, noble Cochise (Jeff Chandler), Indians and whites must alter their thinking and behavior so that true racial harmony can be achieved. Although peace finally comes, Sonseeahray is killed by renegade whites, an event which satisfied the demands of conventional morality concerning miscegenation.

In *The Evolution of the Western*, Andre Bazin boldly writes that "anyone who wants to know what a real Western is" and wants "to know the finest of them all," should see *The Naked Spur* (1953).[5] Howard Kemp's (Stewart) psychological torture and self-destructive desires, coupled with violent reprisal, becomes most explicit. Ever since his girlfriend sold his ranch and ran off with another man while he was fighting the Civil War, Kemp has worked as a ruthless bounty hunter, killing for money so he can buy back his ranch. His coarse amorality and materialism mirror his disillusionment with a deceitful world. And again it is the war that serves as the turning point in Kemp's heretofore peaceful life. Anxiety arises, however, because Kemp can never totally submerge his basic humanity and yearning for the old way of life. In a moment of romantic weakness, he reminisces about the joys of his former life and what his life will be like when he reclaims his farm: "I had neighbors, you know ... the Websters had four sons, each skinnier than the other; always comin' over to lend a hand; didn't give you much chance to get lonesome. The house—the house ain't much, but it's just prime cattle country. The fella that owns the ranch now, he's willin' to sell." Only after considerable physical violence and mental anguish bordering on insanity does Kemp transcend his desire for an insatiable revenge and accept Lina Patch's (Janet Leigh) offer to start a new life.

Stewart and Mann's fourth cinematic collaboration, *The Far Country* (1955), tells how a quick-draw, egotistical wrangler, Jeff Webster (Stewart) whose motto is "Nobody does a favor for nothin'," remains on the periphery of a villainous society until that society forces him to abandon his selfishness by acting against it. The film's opening image of a far mountainous region mirrors Webster's cold, uncompromising psychological state; he prefers to observe the world's actions, "live and let live," rather than develop relationships with others. As he tells the equally self-centered Ronda Castle (Ruth Roman), a saloon owner who is attracted to him: "I don't need help.... I can take care of me ... that's the only way." When Castle saves his life and suggests that Webster could at least say thank you, he sarcastically responds by saying, "That's a term I seldom use." When Skagway's corrupt Judge Gannon (John McIntyre) and his men steal Webster's cattle, Webster resteals them and drives the herd across the border to Dawson. Although he is unaware that Gannon will try to get even, Webster remains unconcerned until the judge and his men ambush Webster and his friend, Ben (Walter Brennan), at their gold claim. Ben is killed, but before he dies he gives Webster his small bell. After Kemp alerts Gannon that he is coming back to Skagway to revenge Ben's death, Webster's horse strolls into town with Ben's bell ringing. During the final shootout, Castle is killed when she tries to warn Webster, who then kills Gannon. Ben's death and his bell signal Webster's acceptance of and need for other people while Castle's death symbolizes the end of his non-social self.

By 1955 standards, *The Man from Laramie*, a Western version of *King Lear*, was a brutal film as well as the last film Anthony Mann and Jimmy Stewart made together. The lean, heroic Will Lockhart (Stewart), who expresses more humanity and warmth than any of the previous Stewart/Mann heroes, has isolated himself from society by abandoning his Army post in Laramie, Wyoming, so he can hunt down those responsible for selling guns to the Apaches and indirectly causing his young brother's death. When he arrives in Coronado, New Mexico, he meets Barbara Waggoman (Cathy O'Donnell), the niece of the almost literally and figuratively blind Alec Waggoman (Donald Crisp), who controls the town. Later, when Lockhart visits the salt lagoons, he is ambushed by Dave (Alex Nichols), Alec's brutal biological son, and he and his men lasso and then drag Lockhart through a fire, destroy his wagons, and kill his mules. Stewart performed such stunts as these himself to maintain authenticity.Determined to gain revenge. Lockhart follows the Waggoman gang back to town where he beats up Dave before fighting Vic Hansboro (Arthur Kennedy), Alec's foreman and adopted son, who sold the guns to the Indians to vent his range on Alec for mistreating him. Lockhart's dogged investigative persistence exposes Hansboro as the one responsible for giving the Indians the repeating rifles and for killing Dave. After traveling over rough, rocky terrain, Lockhart finally catches Hansboro. He exclaims, "I came one thousand miles to kill you," but he cannot kill him, so he leaves Hansboro to the Indians to destroy. Lockhart, unlike the previous Stewart/Mann creations, is less insane and truer to his social nature even though "danger is," as the title song says, his "specialty."

Anthony Mann agreed to direct *Night Passage* (1957), but he resigned before the film went into production so he could direct screenwriter Dudley Nichols' *The Tin Star*. Stewart was angered by Mann's departure, and the two cinematic giants never worked together again. Grant McLaine (Stewart) has exchanged his railroad detective's guns for an accordion because of his past involvement in theft, although some people believe that he took the blame for others. When railroad owner Ben Kimball (Jay C. Flippen) decides to give McLaine an opportunity to prove his honesty, McLaine tries to deliver a payroll to some angry railroad field workers who are on the verge of quitting. All previous attempts have failed because Whitey Harbin's (Dan Duryea) gang, which includes the Utica Kid (Audie Murphy), McLaine's younger brother, kills and robs all the runners. McLaine fails to persuade the Utica Kid to leave the gang until the final showdown when Whitey and his gang trap McLaine. Whitey and the Utica Kid are killed, but McLaine delivers the payroll.

Arthur Schlesinger once lectured American society that "it is fatal not to maintain an unrelenting attack on all forms of racial discrimination."[6] During the 1950s and 1960s, many social-problem films addressed racial tolerance and racial pride. Included in this group are *The Well* (1951), *A Medal for Benny* (1945), *My Man and I* (1952), *Bad Day at Black Rock* (1954), *The Searchers* (1956), and *Two Rode Together* (1961). The latter two films were directed by John Ford, and thematically parallel one another. In both films a white man sets out to rescue a white woman and children who have been captured by the Indians. Whereas *The Searchers'* Ethan Edwards (John Wayne) is motivated solely by his hatred of Indians, *Two Rode Together*'s mercenary Guthrie McCabe (Stewart) executes his mission solely for his ten percent take. In that sense, McCabe, who is more concerned with money than with principles, is seen as a corrupt version of Ethan Edwards. At the end of the film, McCabe rejects society when he rides off, but then McCabe and the audience realize that McCabe's "What's in it for me?" morality is no worse than the hypocritic white society that breaks deals and refuses to pay for services rendered. Stewart's portrayal of the morally ambiguous and furtive McCabe required great acting talent, and even John Ford said that Stewart, unlike such natural actors as Wayne, Cooper, and Gable, "did a whale of a job manufacturing a character the public went for. He studied acting."[7] In turn, Ford utilized Stewart's talent by creating a character who possessed a sense of humor as well as hatred.

The Man Who Shot Liberty Valance (1962), one of John Ford's masterpieces, is noted for its critical, melancholy statement about the settling of the West. Like *Donovan's Reef* (1962), *Liberty Valance* concentrates on three characters and their world—Ransom Stoddard (Stewart), a famous senator; his wife Hallie (Vera Miles), who was once in love with Tom Doniphon (John Wayne), the archetypal frontier individualist. When Ranse and Hallie are asked why they have returned to Shinbone to attend Tom's funeral, Ranse, with Hallie's approval, gives them his painful explanation. Stoddard's tale mirrors the dark, dangerous, chaotic landscape peopled by individuals such as the violent and abusive Liberty Valance (Lee Marvin), who horse-whipped the idealistic, civilized Ranse. Stoddard symbolizes the advancement of civilization and enlightenment on the frontier, but he is unable to duel physically with the men of the West. When Stoddard and Valance confront one another in a shootout, they fire simultaneously. Valance drops dead under the livery stable lamp. Stoddard, holding his wounded arm and thinking that he has killed Valance, stumbles into the restaurant where Hallie binds his wound. Doniphon, who has responded to Hallie's plea to help Stoddard, has killed Valance, but he tells Stoddard to marry Hallie, become the man that people believe him to be, and, of course, be known as the man who shot Liberty Valance. Stoddard's story, however, will not be printed because, as the young reporter tells him, "This is the West. When the legend becomes fact, print the legend."

When the fifty-five-year-old Jimmy Stewart agreed to appear in *How the West Was Won* (1963), he joined a cast of major stars and thousands of actors and extras who participated in the most lavish Western spectacle of its time. The story covers fifty years of adventure for the Prescott family—Zebulon (Karl Malden), Rebecca (Agnes Moorehead) and their daughters Eve (Carroll Baker) and Lilith (Debbie Reynolds)—as they travel to free land in the West through the Ohio Valley. When they camp alongside the Ohio River, they meet the buckskin-clad Linus Rawlings (Stewart) who saves them from Colonel Hawkins' (Walter Brennan) river pirates. Linus pursues the family to ask for Eve's hand in marriage, but he is too late to save Zebulon and Rebecca, who drown when their raft capsizes. Linus and Eve marry and build their farm on the spot where Eve's parents are buried. When the Civil War breaks out, Linus joins the Union Army, and is killed in action. The rest of the film follows the lives of Zeb, Linus and Eve's son, who moves to Arizona, and Lilith, who marries a wealthy gambler. Stewart's portrayal of the fiesty Linus Rawlings is typical of his energy and conviction to play a man twenty years younger than Stewart was at the time of the filming. The makeup artist also helped Stewart look much like the frontiersmen who helped tame the West.

Cheyenne Autumn (1964) is close in spirit to *Broken Arrow* because it portrays the Cheyennes as the victims of governmental genocide. Stuck in the middle of this cinematic dirge, which traces the 1,200-mile, agonizing trek of the Cheyenne to their northern homeland, is a comic episode set in Dodge City. Dressed in a perfectly spotless, well-tailored suit and Panama hat is a self-absorbed, laconic Wyatt Earp (Stewart) who is trying to enjoy a quiet poker game with Doc Holliday (Arthur Kennedy) and Major Jeff Blair (John Carradine). When a few young rebel warriors kill some soldiers, the Dodge City newspaper claims that "marauding savages" are loose and that the community is in danger. Earp and Holliday are then pressured into forming and leading a posse against the Indians; however, they deliberately lead the posse in the wrong direction. As Tag Gallagher notes, the Dodge City episode, with its "Ionesco-like dialogue and pantomime," is clearly a hilarious parody of Wyatt Earp as well as Western film audiences' "inability to think or to see beyond the cliches of our specific cultural determination."[8]

The Rare Breed (1966) provided Stewart with the opportunity to portray a slightly decent, yet offbeat drifter cowpoke named Sam Burden. Sam is exposed to the determined, spunky British cattle breeder Martha Price (Maureen O'Hara) and her daughter Hilary (Juliet Mills), who have come to the St. Louis Stockman's Exposition in 1884 to sell Vindicator, their prize Hereford bull. Believing that cross-breeding Vindicator with longhorns will produce a better beef stock capable of surviving the rough, cold Texas winters, Martha and Hilary convince Sam of the goodness of their cause; as a result, Sam readjusts his thinking and dedicates his life to raising this new breed. Although Sam discovers Vindicator's corpse when the spring finally comes, he also discovers a Hereford calf tailing its longhorn mother. At film's end, Sam reaps the reward of a "rare breed" of cattle and, having fallen under the gentle influence of Martha, he marries her.

Firecreek (1968), like Westerns such as *Welcome to Hard Times* (1967) and *McCabe and Mrs. Miller* (1971), shows the deterioration and the failure of the Firecreek community because they cannot form a unified forceful defense of their lives and property in emergency situations. Johnny Cobb (Stewart), a two-dollar-a-month sheriff and a full-time farmer, is a quiet, gentle person whose withdrawal from the community in favor of his backward settlement symbolizes his failure. When Larkin (Henry Fonda) and his gang threaten the townspeople and falsely accuse and then kill Arthur, a simpleminded stable boy, for murder, Cobb recognizes his role and knows that he must reestablish tranquility and justice through the purging of vengeance. "The day a man decides not to face the world, he'd better step out of it." After a fierce battle, Larkin dies when Evelyn (Inger Stevens), who is attracted to Larkin romantically yet knows that he will not reform, shoots him. Despite the thematic resemblance between *Firecreek* and *High Noon* (1950), this grim town of losers lacks promise, and the character of the wasted Johnny Cobb suggests that America's heroes, unlike Marshal Kane, are pushed into violence rather than acting on principles.

As early as *Winchester '73*, Stewart had ridden only a sorrel stallion named Pie in his Westerns films. Although owner Stevie Myers turned down Stewart's offer to purchase Pie, she did allow him to use the horse whenever he wanted to ride. *Bandolero!* (1968) was not only the last Western film in which Stewart rode Pie or any other horse but the last film in which he played a "good baddie." Stewart was cast as the lusty Mace Bishop who waylays a hangman in order to help his brother Dee (Dean Martin) and his gang, who have killed a rancher and robbed a bank, escape from the Val Verde jail. After the men escape their execution, they and Maria (Raquel Welch), the murdered rancher's widow, head into Mexico while Sheriff Johnson (George Kennedy) and his posse hotly pursue and capture the Bishop brothers in an abandoned pueblo. Mexican bandits then attack and kill the posse, forcing Johnson to release Mace and Dee so they can present a common defense against the bandits. Both brothers, however, are killed; Sheriff Johnson and Maria, who has fallen in love with Dee, return to Val Verde. *Bandolero!* succeeds as a noisy, brisk tale replete with lively, affectionate dialogue as Mace tries to persuade Dee to give up his life of crime.

Noted for its vicious, patriarchal stereotypes of the happy, comely prostitute who is proud of her profession, *The Cheyenne Social Club* (1970), directed by Gene Kelly, gave Stewart and Henry Fonda the opportunity to work together once again. As Will Wright notes, *The Cheyenne Social Club* is a story where "the drama and the action remain serious, not put on, and the comedy derives from the unlikeliness and yet success of the heroes."[9] The better portions of the film occur at the beginning and at the end when John O'Hanlan (Stewart) and Harley Sullivan (Fonda) travel across the vast Western landscape while Harley talks on and on about his family, his dogs, and his doings. O'Hanlan is a Texas cowpoke who inherits a profitable bordello, although the townspeople call it a social club, when his brother dies. The straitlaced O'Hanlan's decision to change the house into a saloon meets immediate opposition from the women as well as the town, but he only alters his decision when he realizes that the women will be left destitute. Later he discovers that Jenny (Shirley Jones), the madam, has been abused by the outlaw Corey Bannister (Robert J. Wilkie). O'Hanlan earns the townspeople's respect when he kills Bannister. Realizing, however, that Bannister's kin will continue the feud, O'Hanlan makes Jenny the owner and he and Harley return to Texas to work as cowpokes.

The Shootist (1976) was the last Western for Stewart, who was gradually making his exit from cinema in the mid–1970s. Although he had been turning down parts, he agreed to play Doc Hostetler as a tribute to John Wayne, a long-admired friend. When John Bernard Books (Wayne) arrives in Carson City, Nevada, he visits the doctor who tells him that he has "two months—six weeks—less—no way to tell" to live. When Doc gives Books an awful-tasting painkiller to ease the pain in Books' lower back and groin, he goes on to tell Books that the relief is only temporary: "If you're lucky, you'll lose consciousness." Then, as Books prepares to leave, Doc adds, "One more thing; I would not die the death I've just described—not if I had your courage." Books dies when a cowardly bartender shoots him in the back with a shotgun; as the townspeople, including Doc Hostetler, come into the saloon to see what has happened, Doc understands that Books has staged his own death to avoid further physical agony.

Stewart continued to read scripts into his eighties; however, his primary focus became his campaign for the salvation of the African elephant. Illegal poaching had reduced the elephant population from 1.3 million to 40,000 animals in about ten years. Although the Stewarts were originally hunters, they became crusaders for the conservation of game.

Referring to Stewart, John Ford once said that "people just seem to like him." Onscreen or offscreen, Stewart came across as a humble person who not only survived but overcame brushes with an uncertain world. When the American Film Institute honored Stewart with their Life Achievement Award in 1980, fellow actor Dustin Hoffman spoke for all filmgoers when he said, "Mr. Stewart, you made my parents happy. You've made me happy. I'm making sure you make my children happy. And if this world has any kind of luck, you're going to make my grandchildren happy." Stewart's cinematic career spanned six decades as generations of Americans responded to his likableness, his drawl, and his awkward manner that personified him as a slow but courageous winner against extreme odds.

Notes

1. Place, J. A., *The Western Films of John Ford* (New York: Citadel Press, 1975), p. 25.

2. Archie P. McDonald, "John Wayne: Hero of the Western," *Shooting Stars: Heroes and Heroines of Western Film*, Archie P. McDonald, ed. (Bloomington: Indiana University Press, 1987), p. 109.

3. "Entretien avec Anthony Mann" ["Interview with Anthony Mann"], *POSITIF* (September 1968), p. 26.

4. Jean-Claude Missiaen, "A Lesson in Cinema," *Cahiers du Cinema in English*, No. 12 (December 1967), p. 46.

5. Bazin, Andre, "The Evolution of the Western," *What Is Cinema?* vol. 2; ed. and trans. Hugh Gray (Berkeley: University of California Press, 1971), p. 156.

6. Arthur Schlesinger, Jr., *The Vital Center*, new ed. (London: Andre Deutsch, 1970), p. 191.

7. John Ford as quoted by George Capozzi, Jr., *The John Wayne Story* (New Rochelle: Arlington, 1972), p. 91.

8. Tag Gallagher, *John Ford: The Man and His Films* (Berkeley: University of California Press, 1986), p. 431.

9. Will Wright, *Sixguns and Society: A Structural Study of the Western* (Berkeley: University of California Press, 1975), p. 30.

Barbara Stanwyck: Uncommon Heroine

by Sandra Schackel

"Barbara Stanwyck, an intrepid citizen who has shown no fear of man, terrain, or scripts over a long and illustrious career, is tackling all three in *Cattle Queen of Montana*," reported the *New York Times* when the film opened in that city in 1954.[1] Thirty years into her movie career, Stanwyck indeed had demonstrated her ability as a versatile and accomplished actress, appearing in more than eighty roles by the late 1950s. Nominated for four Academy Awards in her career, none of them for Westerns, Stanwyck professed to love that genre best; she starred in ten Western movies during the 1940s and 1950s.[2] In these films, Stanwyck brought to the Western heroine a spunky determination and spirit of independence unusual for women in Westerns in this era. So successful was she, and so enamored of Westerns was the American public, that success followed her to the small screen as head of the Barkley clan in *The Big Valley* television series in the 1960s.

Stanwyck's film and television roles contrast with her private life. These roles mirror, in part, her longstanding need for security and independence, hence the many portrayals of strong, assertive women. Yet behind this image she remained vulnerable and sensitive to the pressures of the profession as well as cultural expectations that limited the lives of most women. In many ways, Stanwyck lived out roles on the big screen that eluded ordinary women because society was not yet ready to allow women those kinds of freedoms. Through such acting, Stanwyck was ahead of her time in the 1940s and 1950s in Western films that allowed her to portray women who take charge of the ranch, the county, and the people around her.[3]

Roles for women in Westerns, and indeed much of cinema, traditionally have been limited to two stereotypes: the bad woman/prostitute and the good woman/civilizer. Variations on these themes include the saloon singer, the whore with a heart of gold, the spunky ranchwoman, the frontier schoolteacher, and the pioneer mother. Nearly always, the Western heroine depends on a man in some capacity, and if she rejects or otherwise denies male counsel, she is penalized for her "unnatural" behavior through death, banishment, or, at the least, loss of the hero's love. These prescriptive roles for women were well fixed in Western cinema until the 1970s, when a third stereotype appeared, the strong, independent heroine who can take care of herself and expects to do so. Several actresses, including Candace Bergen in *Soldier Blue* (1970), Kathleen Lloyd in *The Missouri Breaks* (1970), and Jane Fonda in *Comes a Horseman* (1978), illustrate this image.[4]

Prior to the 1970s, Barbara Stanwyck frequently played a Western heroine who challenged the stereotypical female image. For example, in *Maverick Queen* (1956) and in *Forty Guns* (1957), Stanwyck moved beyond the civilizer role to play tough, take-charge women. As a result, part of her popularity in both movies and on television stemmed from her ability to carry out adventurous, demanding tasks not usually assigned to women in films prior to the 1970s. Although she starred in a wide variety of roles, including comedies, for the most part Stanwyck is remembered for her portrayals of strong, determined women who met men on even terms or dominated them from the onset.

Stanwyck's treatment of strong-willed, independent women was not limited to Westerns but dominated most of her other films as well. In Academy Award–nominated *Double Indemnity* (1944) Stanwyck is the mastermind behind both the seduction of insurance salesman Fred MacMurray and their bizarre plot to kill her husband. Similarly, in *The Lady Eve* (1940) and *Ball of Fire* (1941), Stanwyck remains the boss despite falling in love with the men she intends to trap. In time, Stanwyck's choice of roles came to reflect a tension between the narrow confines of female destiny and her drive to expand beyond those constrictions. Very much a product of the times when a woman was expected to put marriage before career, she nonetheless rose to stardom on the strength of roles that diverged from the traditional formula. In doing so, Stanwyck proved to be a role model for later actresses.[5]

Born Ruby Stevens on July 16, 1907, in Brooklyn, Stanwyck was orphaned at the age of four and spent the next ten years of her life in foster homes. Although Hollywood lore frequently capitalized on her waif-like early years, Stanwyck insisted it was not that grim: "Foster homes in those days weren't cruel—they were just impersonal."[6] By her early teens, Stanwyck had discovered her love for entertaining by dancing to hurdy-gurdy music in city streets. At age fifteen she landed a job as a chorus girl and eventually appeared with the Ziegfeld Follies and in other stage revues. She gradually worked her way up the show business ladder, securing the lead in a Broadway play in 1926. The following year she made her screen debut in a silent film, *Broadway Nights*, and in 1928 followed her vaudeville performer husband, Frank Fay, to Hollywood, where she signed contracts with both Columbia and Warner Bros.[7] By then, Ruby Stevens had become Barbara Stanwyck, but she would never lose the traits she had developed in her early years—a gritty determination, a strong sense of independence, and the desire to excel in her profession.[8]

Stanwyck starred in her first Western in 1935, playing the title role in *Annie Oakley*, but her interest in Westerns had been with her since childhood. As a youngster growing up in the tenements of Brooklyn, her idol was Pearl White, the silent heroine of the *Perils of Pauline* serials of the early movie industry. Stanwyck explained in an interview in 1981, "I came from very poor surroundings and I had to work my tail off just to get a penny, a *penny*, so that I could see her. She's influenced me all my life."[9] Stories of the West made an impression also. Stanwyck spoke warmly of the pioneers who opened the West to settlement. In her words, "all the immigrants coming over on the covered wagons and atop the trains, the little Jewish peddler with his calicos and ginghams on his back, the good men, the bad men, they all made this country."[10] To Stanwyck, westerners were America's aristocracy and the heros and heroines America's royalty. Little wonder that Ruby Stevens, starting out with little but her natural talent, would aspire to become part of that royal western family.

Annie Oakley marked Stanwyck's first film in the genre of which she would someday be queen. Directed by George Stevens and cast opposite Preston Foster and Melvyn Douglas, Stanwyck played a winsome if accommodating tomboy sharpshooter signed on by the manager (Douglas) of Buffalo Bill's Wild West show. A crack shot, Annie shows up world champion Toby Walker (Foster), who is "scornful of shooting against a half-baked kid, and a girl at that," until it is suggested that she should be the star of the show and Foster should seek another job.[11] By now romance has blossomed between the two, but Foster's ego is on the line, and Annie backs down, deliberately missing her target during one of their performances.

Throughout this mildly amusing film, Stanwyck wavers between believing in her superior abilities and wanting to maintain a relationship with Foster, a relationship shaped by deference, not dominance. As Annie, Stanwyck is sweet, vulnerable, charming, and agreeable, hardly the strong, assertive woman she would become in future Western roles. At the same time she was shooting the film, she was undergoing a difficult period in her personal life because of her divorce from Frank Fay. Always a private person, the actress endeavored to keep her private life separate from her public life. To cope with her personal disappointment, she diverted her energy to her career.

Four years and her first Academy Award nomination later, Stanwyck starred as Molly Monahan, the Irish "spitfire" daughter of a railroad engineer in Cecil B. De Mille's epic, *Union Pacific* (1939). In this saga of the struggle to build the transcontinental railroad, Stanwyck is the postmistress of "End of Track," the town that moves westward with the railroad's progress. Serving as the spunky, good woman stereotype, she is pursued by two competing suitors: Joel McCrea, the troubleshooter sent out from Washington, and Robert Preston, the gambler determined to stop him. Stanwyck is the mediator, the facilitator who unites East and West, and in the process, herself with McCrea.

Barbara Stanwyck in a still from one of her Western films.

Despite her sauciness, Molly is still "tamed enough" to be a suitable match for the hero, and as mediator further fulfills the civilizer role.

One of the most popular hits of a blockbuster year in films that saw the release of *Stagecoach*, *Gone with the Wind*, and *The Wizard of Oz*, *Union Pacific* marked the beginning of Stanwyck's career as a stuntwoman. Though filmed in black and white, the movie had plenty of color—and action. The list of De Mille–style events included two spectacular train wrecks, a mail-car robbery, an Indian massacre, and numerous saloon brawls and horseback chases through wild Wyoming. "That makes *Union Pacific* the largest con-glomeration of thrills and cold-blooded murder since Pauline was in Peril," reported the *Brooklyn Daily Eagle*.[12] "Pauline," however, held her own, leap-ing off and on boxcars, chasing (and catching) a wagon, and battling attack-ing Indians, prompting her co-star McCrea to note that Stanwyck was involved "in everything. She is fearless and has more guts than most men."[13] Unlike many other female stars, Stanwyck prided herself on doing her own stunt-work and continued to do so during the filming of *The Big Valley* in the 1960s. For her courage and bravery, the actress gained the admiration and respect of film crews and co-stars alike throughout her career.

Stanwyck's next Western, *The Great Man's Lady* (1942), allowed her much latitude in her stunts. This Western was one of Stanwyck's favorites because of the challenge the role presented. Physically demanding, the script called for her to slide down bannisters, elope on horseback, get married on the prairie in a rainstorm, shoot and dress rabbits, throw crockery, and sur-vive a flood in which her twin babies drowned. Stanwyck thrived on action and always welcomed it in her work.

Sometimes this determination on her part caused unexpected conse-quences for other cast members. For example, while working with veteran actor Walter Huston on the set of *The Furies* in Tucson in 1950, Stanwyck decided to do a dangerous riding scene herself although a double was avail-able. Although not eager to do so, Huston agreed to do his own riding as well, because he was not going to be outdone by a woman.[14] Actor and actress became close while making this movie, and Huston's death shortly after filming was completed deeply saddened all the cast and crew.

Stanwyck's doing her own stunt work frequently made directors ner-vous. In *The Moonlighter* (1953), a poorly received, low-budget, 3-D West-ern, director Roy Rowland recounted a scene in which the heroine tumbled down a waterfall into a fast-moving river in the High Sierra: "She was capa-ble of doing her own stunt work and completely unafraid. She always wanted to do her stunts, but we could not risk the possibility of an accident. Barbara understood this, but she still pleaded."[15] She got her opportunity when her stunt woman was not available to shoot the waterfall scene. Although bruised from the many rocks she encountered on her plunge into the river—on her back, on her side, on her stomach—Stanwyck never complained or held up the film. This air of professionalism and dedication characterized her entire career.

One other dramatic scene, one in which she traded bullets with Ward Bond, helped "save" this film for Stanwyck. The reaction of a reviewer to this scene revealed gender expectations in the 1950s: "Stanwyck, stylishly thin and looking mighty small beside a horse, fights it out with rifles with Ward Bond and wins." The reviewer also noted that, "This, as anyone who has ever seen a Western knows, is practically impossible. Bond may lose a screen battle here and there but never to a wisp of a woman with rifles at fifty yards."[16] Such action was unexpected to moviegoers because it exceeded cultural prescriptions for women in Western film. Although Stanwyck carried it off well, this scene apparently caused audiences to "fidget a bit."[17]

The actress' physical endurance on the set brought high praise from both Ronald Reagan, Stanwyck's co-star in *Cattle Queen of Montana* (1954), and the Blackfeet Indians who appeared in the movie filmed in their homeland near Glacier National Park. Reagan recounted a bathing scene in a mountain lake where the water temperature was in the mid-forties. Although there was a double available, Stanwyck knew that her face should be seen, rather than that of her double, shot from a distance. "She came out blue, but did not hesitate to do another take," reported the cameraman.[18] The Indians were so impressed with Stanwyck's stamina and bravery that they gave her their tribe's most revered name, "Princess Many Victories," and made her a member of their Brave Dog Society, citing her "very hard work—rare for a white woman."[19] Stanwyck followed this experience with other demanding riding scenes and stunt work in *The Maverick Queen* (1956) and *Forty Guns* (1957).

Although Stanwyck was one of the few major female stars to risk injury in action scenes, some B Western actresses were doing similar stunts. Betty Miles, for example, wrestled a gun away from her co-star in *The Return of Daniel Boone* (1941) and climbed onto a runaway stage in *Sonora Stagecoach* (1944).[20] But Stanwyck's developing reputation included more than stunt work; her choice of roles clearly shaped her style. She went beyond the heroines in B movies who, in the 1940s, gradually were moving away from dependent daughters and submissive ranchwives. Stanwyck became the prototype of the spunky ranchwoman who could ride the range and run the ranch as well as the wranglers, predating Jane Fonda's various Western roles in the 1960s and 1970s.[21] As a result, a great part of Stanwyck's appeal came from her ability to engage in adventures usually assigned to men. Equally appealing were her grit and determination, the result of having grown up independently. This strong sense of independence is apparent in many of her Western roles, including Molly Monahan in *Union Pacific*, Sierra Nevada Jones in *Cattle Queen of Montana*, and Kit Banion in *The Maverick Queen*.

Yet this public image is frequently in conflict with the private Barbara Stanwyck, who placed great value on the traditional roles of wife and mother. Perhaps because her formative years lacked a fully functioning family situation, Stanwyck developed an urgent need to create a stable family in her adult years. She was deeply disappointed when her marriage to Frank Fay failed in 1935, leaving her with recurring custody battles over their adopted son Dion, then three years old. Her second marriage, to actor Robert Taylor in 1939, also ended in divorce after thirteen years of struggling to maintain a marriage as well as two thriving movie careers. Like many women in later decades, Stanwyck found herself caught between the worlds of domesticity and career. Not surprisingly, perhaps, Stanwyck credited her work, not her private world, with providing meaning to her life. "My work is responsible for all the good things that have come into my life...," she remarked late in the 1950s. "I feel most completely alive when I'm starting a new picture."[22]

Quite in contrast to her personal life is the "stand-by-your-man" role she played in *The Great Man's Lady* (1942), made during her marriage to Taylor. As Hannah Semplar, the thirty-three-year-old actress ages from sixteen to 109. Told in a series of flashbacks over a one hundred year period, the movie is a classic paean to the theme of woman's self-sacrifice. Devoted to her husband Ethan Hoyt (Joel McCrea) and to his dream of building a city in the wilderness, Hannah places his needs before hers, sublimating her desires to his. As a pioneer bride, she fiercely protects her husband and shields him from those who would interfere with his goals. But when he attempts to manipulate the townspeople over the coming of the railroad, Hannah sadly recognizes his moneygrubbing ways and leaves him. Thinking her dead, Hoyt remarries, and rather than blemish his career by reappearing in his life, Hannah sacrifices herself to obscurity.[23]

Stanwyck's personal life did not mirror Hannah Semplar's self-sacrifices. Instead, the Stanwyck-Taylor marriage underwent difficult times during the 1940s, when Stanwyck's popularity seemed to decline. Still, she and Taylor, to all appearances, remained the happy Hollywood couple despite frequent separations because of professional requirements. Fan magazines touted the stars' seeming devotion to one another and their "perfect" Hollywood-style marriage, much as they would the Janet Leigh–Tony Curtis marriage in the 1950s. In reality, great differences separated the two stars that apparently could not be reconciled. For example, although Taylor loved to fly airplanes and ride motorcycles, Stanwyck disliked both and preferred to spend what little time they had together at home. More serious problems included rumors of Taylor's dalliances away from home and Stanwyck's need for control in the marriage. Finally unable to deny their unhappiness, the couple announced their divorce late in 1950.

Coincidentally, *The Furies*, released the same year, mirrored some of the emotions Stanwyck had experienced in her marriage. Ambition, revenge, jealousy, and passion color this dark, moody Western set on a New Mexico ranch. Walter Huston plays a self-made cattle baron; Stanwyck is his iron-willed daughter. The two actors are well matched in principles, capabilities, and drive. Having no intention of sharing her father's affections with her new rival, Judith Anderson, Stanwyck throws a pair of scissors at her during her first visit to the ranch. Initially, Huston admires his daughter's pluck and accedes to her wishes, reinforcing the stereotype of the manipulative, dominant female. In time, however, the love between father and daughter turns to hatred after the cattle baron hangs her friend, a leader of a group of squatters on their ranch, appropriately named "The Furies." Stanwyck then teams up with a gambler (Wendell Corey), though she "admits that she doesn't like being in love but capitulates when that man does come around," and together they attempt to force her father into bankruptcy.[24] Despite the viciousness of Stanwyck's character in this film, she is brimming with energy, her riding is strong, and she is comfortable in her western surroundings.[25]

Stanwyck completed six Westerns in the 1950s, and in each she portrayed a clear-headed, hard-driven woman intent on keeping either her land, her child, her saloon, or her man. Sometimes she must become the villain to do so, as in *The Violent Man* (1954). In this film, she plays a scheming ranch wife in love with her disabled husband's brother. She is unable to save her land or be with the man she wants in this violent melodrama, but that does not stop her from trying.[26]

As Sierra Nevada Jones in *Cattle Queen of Montana*, Stanwyck is a rancher's daughter who is determined to file on her deceased father's land. After trailing a herd of cattle from Texas to Montana, she runs into competition from a land-grabbing local villain. Overcoming a weak script, Stanwyck holds her own against both the villain and local Blackfeet Indians who side with the villain. Here she goes beyond the traditional woman-as-civilizer role; she can take care of herself more than adequately, and when she uses a gun, she is doing what the first men on the frontier did—establishing order. But in this film she is not acting entirely on her own, for she received her mission from a man, her father, who filed the claim in her name and then brought her to Montana the following year. Frequently in Westerns, the female provides the motivation for the action rather than initiates it. In this film, her father's death sanctions her actions in retaining the family land. Still, she does not accomplish her goal alone. Ronald Reagan is the mysterious gunman and government undercover agent who helps her recover her land and vanquish the Indians. After the last battle he remarks, "You have all you want now," to which she replies, "Including you?" This simple ending reflects the mores of the 1950s, when the heroine, even one as competent as Sierra Nevada Jones, is not fulfilled without a man/husband to complete her life.

In 1956, Stanwyck starred opposite Barry Sullivan in *The Maverick Queen*, a title she earned by rounding up stray cattle—mavericks—and branding them as her own. As Kit Banion, Stanwyck also owns the Maverick Saloon, most of the town, and works closely with the Wild Bunch—very closely, since she is in love with Sundance (Scott Brady). A love triangle soon develops, however, when she falls in love with a new faro dealer (Sullivan) she has hired. But he proves to be a Pinkerton detective on the trail of the Wild Bunch. The climax to this weak Western comes when Kit dies in Sullivan's arms after an earlier speech in which she tells him that, despite her

Virginia upbringing, she is not "fit" for him. By the standards of the day, the bad woman cannot have the hero, and she had become the bad woman by virtue of her maverick business dealings, although she "did what she had to do to get where she is."[27]

Stanwyck and Sullivan co-starred in another Western in the 1950s, *Forty Guns* (1957). Samuel Fuller wrote, produced, and directed this violent film, initially called *Woman with a Whip*—a title that symbolized Stanwyck's determination to be her own master. Again, Stanwyck plays an outlaw woman, a "stallion-riding leader of a band of hired gunmen" who go everywhere with her. And, as the movie's title song reveals, "There was something about her since she was sixteen that attracted the men to the Maverick Queen, most dangerous woman the West's ever seen!"[28] When the U.S. Marshal (Sullivan) and his brother (Gene Barry) arrive to establish law and order in Cochise County, Arizona, Stanwyck is less than friendly. Soon, however, an attraction develops, based on opposition to one another, and this attraction dooms their lives and leads to the film's final dramatic confrontation.[29]

When the marshal jails Stanwyck's brother (John Ericson), she and her forty gunmen ride into town to free him. Ericson then kills Barry on his wedding day, provoking Sullivan to kill him. In the closing battle, Ericson uses his sister as a shield, but Sullivan, ignoring his personal feelings toward Stanwyck, shoots them both, killing Ericson. The original script called for Sullivan to kill both Stanwyck and Ericson, but the studio objected, and she was only wounded instead. The final scene finds Sullivan leaving town and Stanwyck, humbled, running after him. Again, because of stringent cultural prescriptions for acceptable female behavior, the bad woman cannot win the good man, so despite her prowess, this heroine is left loveless. American film critics denounced this picture but Europeans applauded it, and it possibly served as an inspiration for the violence of the Sergio Leone–style "spaghetti Westerns" of the 1960s.[30]

Stanwyck's next Western took the form of a captivity narrative that explored the sensitive issue of racial mixing. "Go ahead and hate me, Hook" ran the storyline on posters for *Trooper Hook*, released in 1957. "Hate me because I saved myself from Apache torture … because I gave their chief a son!"[31] In this film, her last Western on the big screen, Stanwyck moved away from the dominating, villainous female role and played a woman whom whites scorned because she was captured by Apache Indians and subsequently gave birth to a son. As Cora Sutliff, Stanwyck is a brave, determined woman whose love for her son gives her the strength to face, and live down, the disapproval of a prejudice-driven community. Joel McCrea, her leading man for the sixth time in her movie career, plays Hook, a cavalry sergeant who "rescues" her and returns her to her husband. Upon her return, both her husband and the townspeople shun her for becoming the sexual partner of the Apache chief rather than killing herself. Her only hope for compassion and understanding comes from the tolerant Hook, with whom, after her husband's death, she eventually finds love. Although she clearly deserved the community's respect for enduring her captivity, the climate of the 1950s was not conducive to sympathy or understanding of the issue of miscegenation.[32]

Although *Trooper Hook* was Stanwyck's last feature-length Western film, she did not forsake her favorite genre. Then over fifty years old, she was well aware of the liability, in American culture, of aging, but was adamant that she still had something to contribute to her profession. Mindful by the mid-1950s of the possibilities of acting for television, she conceived the idea of a Western series starring a woman, but she could not convince the networks to offer one. "They want action shows and have a theory that women don't do action," Stanwyck angrily retorted. "The fact is, I'm the best action actress in the world. I can do horse drags and jump off buildings, and I have the scars to prove it."[33] By the fall of 1965, Stanwyck's lobbying for a Western series finally bore fruit, and she debuted as Victoria Barkley in ABC's *The Big Valley*.

After forty years in film, often portraying the self-willed heroine, Stanwyck had a clear idea of how she wanted to play Victoria, the heroic matriarch of the Barkley clan. And it was not in velvet and lace but as "a real frontier woman, not one of those crinoline-covered things you see in most Westerns."[34] Before she accepted the role, she made sure that the producers understood her interpretation of the lead character. "I'm a tough old broad from Brooklyn," she told them. "Don't try to make me into something I'm not. If you want someone to tiptoe down the Barkley staircase in crinoline and politely ask where the cattle went, get another girl. That's not me." Nor was Barkley a "mother knows best" character; she was a woman who was willing to argue and disagree with her children. Despite her sexist language, Stanwyck's feminist leanings were clear in her interpretation of the script. As a result, in *The Big Valley* Stanwyck transferred to television the strong, independent Western heroine she had developed on the silver screen.

Set in the 1870s in California's San Joaquin Valley, the series centered on the powerful and wealthy Barkley family and their interactions with settlers in the surrounding area. Although initial reviews were lukewarm, the show improved and soon gained an enthusiastic following. As the widowed matriarch with three sons and one daughter, Stanwyck appeared in all but seven of 112 episodes. She either completely carried the segment, shared it with a variety of talented guest stars or some member of the family, or appeared briefly when someone else starred. Linda Evans appeared as Audra, the only Barkley daughter; Richard Long played Jarrod, the oldest son and a lawyer; Peter Breck played Nick; and Lee Majors was Heath, the illegitimate son of Victoria's late husband. Again ahead of the times, Stanwyck wanted Majors to play the widow's illegitimate son, but the network was horrified at the idea and retained the original casting of Majors as his father's bastard child.[35]

The cast of television's *The Big Valley* with Barbara Stanwyck as matriarch Victoria Barkley surrounded by her children: Linda Evans (Audra), Lee Majors (Heath), Peter Breck (Nick), Richard Long (Jarrod), and Charles Briles (Eugene, called Gene by the family; he was dropped from the cast during the first season episodes and said to be away at college).

Lew Ayres guest stars as Jason Fleet, cattle rustler, who becomes involved in the life of Victoria Barkley (Stanwyck) in "Presumed Dead," on ABC-TV's *The Big Valley*.

A close family relationship developed among the cast. As Stanwyck had done with others throughout her career, she made a special effort to help a less-experienced Evans and Majors. Under the actress' nurturing guidance, both novices improved their acting skills and came to love and respect their mentor. Evans, who would become a television superstar for her role in *Dynasty* in the 1980s, grew especially fond of Stanwyck. She said of Stanwyck's effect on her career: "She taught me the most important thing in my career, which is to be a professional ... and when I work with people, they always say 'you can tell who taught you about the business because you're very professional.' I'm very grateful to her for that."[36] The special affection that developed among *The Big Valley* cast members was important to Stanwyck. Here, late in life, was the sense of family that had eluded her. Understandably, her disappointment was keen when the series was canceled in 1969, and *The Big Valley* set no longer served as her surrogate home.

The Barkley heroine was a significant role for Stanwyck. It was the first and only adult Western featuring a woman who went beyond the limited roles of saloon singer, prostitute, spunky ranchwoman, pioneer wife, or some other variation of the good woman/bad woman dichotomy.[37] Victoria Barkley was Stanwyck at her strongest—clear-headed, capable, loving, and strong. She loved the role and gave it her utmost, winning an Emmy for her performances in 1966 and additional nominations in 1967 and 1968. But she insisted that she was no "female Ben Cartwright" and took exception to reviewers who frequently compared the Barkley clan to the Cartwrights of NBC's equally popular *Bonanza* series. "Our family is much stronger," she insisted. "Our family behaves like any normal family. We fight, argue, discuss things.... The woman I'm playing has plenty of battles with her boys. She's a very vital person. So are her sons. They have minds of their own."[38] Despite Stanwyck's protestations, the two series were indeed similar, since both starred lone parents who were ready with advice and guidance for their grown children and occasionally enjoyed an adventure or romance on their own.[39]

Stanwyck's role in *The Big Valley* was her last as a Western heroine. The series was dropped in 1969 as a result of weak Nielsen ratings and the decline in popularity of the Western genre, although the program continued to air in syndication during the 1970s and can still be seen. The actress continued to perform in television specials into the 1980s and was nominated in 1983 for an Emmy for her outstanding performance as the wealthy, domineering matron, Mary Carson, in the mini-series *The Thorn Birds*. Because she looked younger than her years, Stanwyck needed special makeup to "age" her appropriately for the role. Once again on horseback, Stanwyck kept up with the rest of the cast, despite her seventy-five years.[40] Her final TV appearance came in 1985, as Constance Colby Patterson in *Dynasty II: The Colbys*, a weekly series that made its debut that November and reunited Stanwyck with her *Big Valley* daughter, Linda Evans.

Stanwyck lived out the few remaining years of her life quietly in her long-time Beverly Hills home. Just as she had refused to conceal either her age or her graying hair, the actress had come to terms with the inevitability of aging in youth-obsessed southern California. "You have to know when you've had your hour, your place in the sun," she advised. "To be old is death here. I think it's kind of silly. Be glad you're healthy. Be glad you can get out of bed on your own." Finally, at age eighty-two, Stanwyck followed longtime friends and sometimes rivals, Bette Davis and Joan Crawford, in death, succumbing to congestive heart failure on January 20, 1990. At her request, no funeral service was held, and the actress was buried quietly and without fanfare.[41]

Throughout her long and illustrious career, Barbara Stanwyck maintained a public persona that masked a complex, private person. She became one of Hollywood's greatest stars although she failed to win the profession's highest accolade, an Oscar. In her own inimitable fashion, Stanwyck explained away her disappointment. "I've had my time and it was lovely. I'm grateful for it. Now I have to move aside and make room for somebody else. I'm not jealous of anybody. Well, I take it back. Maybe Miss Hepburn because she won three academy awards. But sing no sad songs for Barbara Stanwyck. What the hell! Whatever I had, it worked, didn't it?"[42] From a street-tough city kid, she grew into a versatile and accomplished actress on the strength of her roles as aggressive, determined women. In many ways, Stanwyck lived out roles on the big screen that ordinary women might have emulated but for cultural constraints that prevented them from doing so.

Throughout her career, a tension existed between the strong Western women she so often portrayed in film and her private life. Her film roles mirror, in great part, her longstanding need for security and independence. Two divorces and a continually unhappy relationship with her son Dion Fay seemed to reinforce her determination to succeed.[43] How much of this personal unhappiness accounts for the strong roles she chose is unclear, but the parallels are suggestive.

In her Western roles, then, Stanwyck was far more than a faint-hearted heroine waiting for the hero to rescue her. Although she was not quite the totally independent woman who appeared in the 1970s, personified in the films of Jane Fonda such as *Comes a Horseman* and *The Electric Horseman*, she represented the necessary bridge between the submissive good woman stereotype and Fonda's assertive women. Clearly, she was a forerunner to Fonda and as such, served as an important role model for other actresses. One of the many interpreters of Western heroines—Maureen O'Hara, Joanne Dru, and Jean Arthur are others—Stanwyck took the civilizer role and expanded it beyond the standard approach. Also contributing to her success was her ability as a stuntwoman, for in this activity she directed her energies and determination into physically demanding and sometimes dangerous scenes that commanded the respect of the public as well as of her co-stars and film crews.

Doing her own stuntwork further enhanced her roles as strong, assertive women. Equally important was her contribution to television as the "founding mother" of this image on the small screen, a role that contrasted sharply with the traditional wife and mother portrayed by such actresses as Harriet Nelson and Donna Reed. In *The Big Valley*, Stanwyck pioneered the role she had developed in films, thus fulfilling one of her long-held dreams and illustrating the essence of her career as an uncommon heroine.

Notes

1. *New York Times*, January 26, 1955.
2. Although Stanwyck never won a coveted Oscar, she was nominated for *Stella Dallas* (1936), *Ball of Fire* (1941), *Double Indemnity* (1944), and *Sorry, Wrong Number* (1948).
3. Although many films made in the 1940s are noted for their strong women's roles, those with admirable heroines often appeared alongside others portraying evil or helpless women. War-theme films, which earlier had stressed women's competence, were replaced by the end of the decade with films that glorified domestic and romantic life. This trend continued into the 1950s. See Molly Haskell, *From Reverence to Rape: The Treatment of Women in the Movies* (New York: Holt, Rinehart and Winston, 1974), and Marjorie Rosen, *Popcorn Venus: Women, Movies and the American Dream* (New York: Avon Books, 1974).
4. Sandra Schackel, "The Civilizer, the Saloon Singer, and Their Modern Sister," in Archie P. McDonald, ed., *Shooting Stars: Heros and Heroines in Western Film* (Bloomington: Indiana University Press, 1987), 196–217. Also see Cheryl J. Foote, "Changing Images of Women in the Western Film," *Journal of the West* 22 (October 1983): 64–71.
5. Stephen Harvey, "The Strange Fate of Barbara Stanwyck," *Film Comment* 17 (March-April 1981): 34, 36. In addition to some of her Western films, ten of Stanwyck's non–Western classics are now available on video. See Gerald Peary, *American Film* 14 (July-August 1989): 60–63.
6. Ella Smith, *Starring Miss Barbara Stanwyck* (New York: Crown Publishers, Inc., 1974), 1. Several good biographies of Stanwyck exist, although they tend to focus either on her film career or on her private life. Smith's work is an excellent discussion of the actress' films, while those that focus for the most part on her personal life include: Jane Ellen Wayne, *Stanwyck* (New York: Arbor House, 1985); Al DiOrio, *Barbara Stanwyck: A Biography* (New York: Coward-McCann, 1983); and Jerry Vermilye, *Barbara Stanwyck* (New York: Pyramid Publications, 1975).
7. Smith, *Starring Miss Barbara Stanwyck*, 1–11.
8. Joseph Lewis, "Barbara Stanwyck: A Fiery Devotion," in Danny Peary, ed., *Close-Ups: The Movie Star Book* (New York: Workman Publishing Company, 1987), 441–43; DiOrio, *Barbara Stanwyck*, 206; Smith, *Starring Miss Barbara Stanwyck*, 125, 263.
9. Bernard Drew, "Stanwyck Speaks," *Film Comment* 17 (March-April 1981): 43.
10. Drew, "Stanwyck Speaks," 45.
11. Smith, *Starring Miss Barbara Stanwyck*, 75.
12. Quoted in Smith, *Starring Miss Barbara Stanwyck*, 125.
13. Smith, *Starring Miss Barbara Stanwyck*, 125.
14. Drew, "Stanwyck Speaks," 45.
15. *Ibid.*
16. Quoted in Smith, *Starring Miss Barbara Stanwyck*, 247.
17. Smith, *Starring Miss Barbara Stanwyck*, 247.
18. *Ibid.*, 255; DiOrio, *Barbara Stanwyck*, 180.

19. Wayne, *Stanwyck*, 150; DiOrio, *Barbara Stanwyck*, 180.

20. Jon Tuska, *The American West in Film: Critical Approaches to the Western* (Westport, Connecticut: Greenwood Press, 1985), 227–28.

21. For example, *Cat Ballou* (1965); *Electric Horseman* (1969); and *Comes a Horseman* (1978).

22. DiOrio, *Barbara Stanwyck*, 182.

23. Jay Hyams, *The Life and Times of the Western Movie* (New York: Gallery Books, 1983), 61–62; Smith, *Starring Miss Barbara Stanwyck*, 151–52.

24. *New York Times Film Reviews*, August 17, 1950.

25. Smith, *Starring Miss Barbara Stanwyck*, 229.

26. Brian Garfield, *Western Films: A Complete Guide* (New York: Rawson Associates, 1982), 338; Smith, *Starring Miss Barbara Stanwyck*, 255.

27. Phil Hardy, *The Film Encyclopedia* (New York: William Morrow and Company, 1983), 249–50; Smith, *Starring Miss Barbara Stanwyck*, 259.

28. Western Pressbook Collection, Inventory, DeGolyer Library, Southern Methodist University, Dallas.

29. Phil Hardy, *Samuel Fuller* (New York: Praeger Publication, 1970), 124–28; Nicholas Garnham, *Samuel Fuller* (New York: Viking Press, 1972), 141–43.

30. Hardy, *Film Encyclopedia*, 254; Smith, *Starring Miss Barbara Stanwyck*, 263; Hyams, *Life and Times*, 93.

31. Western Pressbook Collection. Several films, beginning with *Broken Arrow* in 1950, explored the issue of miscegenation, including *The Searchers* (1956), *The Tin Star* (1957), and *Two Rode Together* (1961).

32. Smith, *Starring Miss Barbara Stanwyck*, 263; John Linihan, *Showdown: Confronting Modern America in the Western Film* (Urbana: University of Illinois Press, 1980), 73–78. Although the pro–Indian film, *Broken Arrow*, has been lauded for its liberal attitudes toward Native Americans, the viewing public remained suspicious of racial mixing. Reflecting popular biases, the Indian princess died shortly after her marriage to the white hero.

33. Vermilye, *Barbara Stanwyck*, 131.

34. Wayne, *Stanwyck*, 157.

35. Smith, *Starring Miss Barbara Stanwyck*, 293.

36. DiOrio, *Stanwyck*, 202–203.

37. Gary A. Yoggy, "When Television Wore Six-Guns: Cowboy Heroes on TV," in McDonald, *Shooting Stars*, 218–57.

38. Wayne, *Stanwyck*, 168; DiOrio, *Stanwyck*, 203–204; Smith, *Starring Miss Barbara Stanwyck*, 293–94.

39. Rita Parks, *The Western Hero in Film and Television: Mass Media Mythology* (Ann Arbor: UMI Research Press, 1982), 140.

40. Wayne, *Stanwyck*, 194.

41. *New York Times*, January 22, 1990.

42. Wayne, *Stanwyck*, 136.

43. Wayne, *Stanwyck*, 181, 197. As of 1984, Stanwyck had not seen her son, from whom she had been estranged, for more than thirty years. She rarely discussed their relationship, leaving Fay and others to speculate that he had disappointed her because, as a child, he was fat, freckled, and awkward.

WILL THE REAL INDIANS
PLEASE STAND UP?

by Jacqueline K. Greb

A few years ago, a short Western documentary about the Cherokee Indians in eastern Oklahoma during the nineteenth century was filmed in the town originally set aside as a capital of the Cherokee Nation of Oklahoma. *Tahlequah: Indian Territory* (1988) told the story of the Cherokee with a compilation of pictures, reenactments, oral histories, and art work. The director set up the reenactments with a professional finesse that clearly illustrated his expertise in film technique. After spending a frustrating hour trying to work with inexperienced actors, he began to doubt the quality of the final product. When told that the actors, full-blooded Cherokee Indians, were literate, but in Cherokee, not in English, the director's eyes brightened with understanding. Recruiting Sam Nofire (a Cherokee-speaking extra) to translate, the director again set to work. He gave directions slowly, clearly, and visually with satisfactory results. Sam Nofire and the other actors understood what was expected of them and they successfully rose to the challenge.

This director had agreed to do the project for less than half his normal fee because he was interested in "learning more about the Trail of Tears and Indian Territory." Like most Americans, he was infatuated with Indians, especially as presented first in the pulp novels and the Wild West shows of the nineteenth century and then in the motion pictures of the twentieth century. His knowledge of Indians came from Western films which treated Indians as the props necessary to bring out the cavalry, as the savage contrast to the heroic lead character, or as victims of a social evil for which the white society seeks a solution. In "A Fistful of Westerns," the introduction to a collection of essays titled *Western Movies* (1979), the editors discuss the most frequently used critical approaches to Western film. The list includes the "auteur" which argues that a picture is shaped by the director, the "Western as history," the "Western as allegory," "decades" approach, the "structuralist" view, and finally, the "genre" approach.[1]

No matter which analytical approach a critic chooses, Indians seldom rise above the conception created by miles of celluloid and decades of written and visual reinforcement. The early pulp novels about Buffalo Bill Cody, written by Ned Buntline and later by Cody himself, presented all Indians as those who lived on the plains, wore feathers, rode horses, had tepees, used bows and arrows, and hunted buffalo. These props were combined with humans who had no culture, no family life, little depth, were savage and cruel, and were in one way or another expendable. When translated into film, these props and characteristics combined to create the American filmgoer's image of Indians which has survived to the present. Rarely did an American Indian play the role of an American Indian in American Western films. Will Sampson, a Creek praised for his portrayal of Chief Bromden (*One Flew Over the Cuckoo's Nest*, 1975) said, "A lot of Italians have played Indians. Some day I'd like to play an Italian... Actually, the part I've always secretly wanted to play is Rommel, the desert fox."[2]

This stereotypical portrayal of Indians drew critical attention almost with the first motion picture. In 1911 a short review titled simply "The Make-Believe Indian" appeared in *Moving Picture World*, the first journal that dealt exclusively with the movie industry. The reviewer states that after viewing a recent release a group of Indians "justly resented the untrue, unreal, and unfair representations of themselves and their habits." The anonymous author closed the piece with a sentence that is appropriate as the theme of this article: "It is to be hoped that some of our Western manufacturers will yet produce a series of films of *real* Indian life."[3]

In 1989 a television miniseries based on Larry McMurtry's novel *Lonesome Dove* had forty Indians in the cast but Frederic Forest, who won the coveted role of the villainous Blue Duck, a major speaking part, only reinforced the film image of American Indians.[4] A year earlier Lou Diamond Phillips, playing the part of Chavez y Chavez in *Young Guns* (1988), managed to maintain the traditional film image of Indians and simultaneously attract young viewers with such 1980s concerns as drug use and peer loyalty. Phillips, like those who portrayed Indians before him, is not of Native American descent. Chris Cain, the film's producer/director, defended his selection of Phillips with "You start looking around for somebody who can play an Indian believably, he's the first guy who comes to your mind."[5] An interesting observation since Phillips' interpretation of Chavez y Chavez in *Young Guns* is remarkably like his portrayal of an "East L.A. Cholo" in *Stand and Deliver* (1988).

More recently a controversy arose when director/producer Robert Redford selected Lou Diamond Phillips to play the Navajo lead in the Tony Hillerman novel, *Dark Wind*. "Redford's casting representative Tricia Tumey said the director of that movie also conducted a search for a few Native American actors but failed to find the perfect person."[6] Although Redford's work in past celluloid portrayals of ethnic subjects such as the Hispanic in *Milagro Beanfield War* have been honest efforts, the selection of Phillips may have resulted from a concern for the economic future of the film rather than for authenticity. Redford is again trying to cast the Hillerman characters Joe Leaphorn and Jim Chee, this time for *A Thief of Time*. Casting calls have been held in areas where concentrations of Native Americans live such as the Four Corners (where the novel takes place) and South Dakota.

In the past these casting calls have resulted in such popular stars as Robert Blake, Jeff Chandler, Charles Bronson, Elvis Presley, Debra Paget, Robert Wagner, Loretta Young, Burt Lancaster and Charlton Heston playing roles as American Indians. Not until 1970, when Chief Dan George appeared in *Little Big Man*, was an Indian cast "in a major role in a big-budget movie."[7] This was not the first appearance of Indians in speaking roles; they had grunted through hundreds of films beginning with the early silent productions.

The role of the American Indian in Western films is seldom more meaningful to the plot than any other prop no matter who is cast in the part. Beginning with early silent era productions, Indians were treated as "a part of the setting to a greater extent than he is ever a character in his own right."[8] Indians were relegated to the background so far that James Robert Parish was comfortable ignoring them in his introduction to *Great Western Stars* (1976). He wrote, "Of course, the Western movies would not have been nearly so enjoyable or presentable had there not been the bevy of gingham-clad heroines ... the salty, comic sidekicks ... or dastardly screen villains. Then also where would the Westerns and their stars have been without their faithful steeds..."[9] Parish excludes Indians from this list of necessities for good Western films just as he does houses, mountains, saddles, and trees.

A producer's concern for authenticity was the same whether hunting for great scenery or in the portrayal of Indians—what looked good on film was what counted. The film *Rooster Cogburn* (1975), filmed in Oregon, contained beautiful scenery with snow-topped mountains, river rapids through deep canyons, and lush high mountain valleys. Rooster (John Wayne) was a marshal going from Ft. Smith, Arkansas, to Webber's Falls, Indian Territory (Oklahoma), a land of rolling hills. He stops at a mission where Katharine Hepburn, a schoolteacher and the daughter of a murdered missionary, is burying her father and the mission Indians killed by the outlaws Rooster is chasing. The mission was a wooden structure nestled in the pine trees and surrounded by the tepees of Indians who had accepted the faith of the missionary. Pine trees grew in the gentle rolling hills of Indian Territory but the Indians who lived at the mission came from the southeastern United States where log cabins were in use by Indians as early as 1800. Even before the adoption of the log cabin, the southeastern Indians used clay and thatch as building materials for their rectangular houses.

The lack of concern with presenting authentic Indians and Indian culture began in the silent film era and remained in Western films thereafter. In the early silent film *The Mended Lute* (1919) a Dakota Indian couple escaped from danger in a canoe, "a conveyance unknown to the tribe" as a means of transportation.[10] Even more serious was a "version of *The Last of the Mohicans* (1920) when Wallace Beery, playing the role of Magua, stalked through the forest sporting rolled-down socks."[11] In *She Wore a Yellow Ribbon* (1949) director John Ford, using his favorite location in Monument Valley, Arizona, had John Wayne and the cavalry fighting Indians who would not have been found in that part of the country. Like directors before him, John Ford was more concerned about the visual image than the need to present Indians accurately.

Even though directors such as Ford knew the importance of the visual image to the success of a film, they also realized that Indians were necessary to the "reality" of the Western. In 1948 the "political rehabilitation of the Indian" began with the release of *Fort Apache* (1948). Fully half of Ford's over one hundred films were Westerns, and many were major milestones in the history of the genre. His *Stagecoach* (1939) not only became a classic but also raised the Western to an artistic high. *The Searchers* (1956) opened new ground as one of the earliest explorations of the "Indian Question"—although from the white perspective rather than from that of the American Indian. With *Cheyenne Autumn* (1964) Ford made an honest attempt to present the Indian perspective, but with non–Indian actors. Ford began with a simplistic view of Indians which changed to a "subtle and in many ways alarming examination of the impact of Indians (and their culture) on frontier whites in *The Searchers*."[12] The link between early Ford Westerns, that point where he began to present Indians on their own terms, such as *By Indian Post* (1919), *Stagecoach* and *Drums Along the Mohawk* (1939), where Indians were props, to *The Searchers* is found in *Fort Apache*, the first film in a loose-fitting trilogy.

Fort Apache glorified the winning of the West by the United States Cavalry. The central focus is a patriotic view of American society in microcosm where individuals of divergent backgrounds (Confederate, Irish) and different goals work together and play together to the benefit of all. In spite of the often erratic nature of the film, for the first time John Ford "confronts Indian culture on its own terms." For the first time in a Ford film Indians have culture, lives, and, most importantly, "legitimate complaints against white society."[13] Captain York, played by John Wayne, not only shows respect for Cochise, played by Miguel Inclan, but he also treats him as an equal. In *She Wore a Yellow Ribbon* and *Rio Grande* (1950), the rest of the loose trilogy, Indians gain more culture, normal life experiences, and human traits.

After John Ford opened the door, there came other attempts at a more realistic presentation of Indians. *Broken Arrow* (1950) has Cochise (Jeff Chandler) and Tom Jeffords (James Stewart) treating each other like friends and brothers as they try to bring peace to a small portion of the West. The story line allows the viewer to venture into the tribal marriage rituals as Tom Jeffords and an Apache woman develop a deep compassionate relationship.

True to American images of mixed marriages at the time, the Indian woman died, but her death was followed by the uncharacteristically peaceful Cochise telling Jeffords he could not break the peace by seeking revenge. Jeffords responds positively to the words of his friend and the peace is maintained.

The portrayal of Indians that began in 1949 and 1950 with the John Ford Westerns changed little during the following decade. Directors did begin to explore subjects previously considered taboo to Western films and the Indians in them. In *Daughter of the West* (1949), Harold Daniels explored the saga of a woman regaining her Navajo heritage during the 1880s after spending most of her life in a convent. In *Comanche Territory* (1950) the Seventh Cavalry and Maureen O'Hara bring rifles to the Indians so they can fight silver-hunting intruders on their land, an experiment in the presentation of white land grabbers as the bad guys. MGM was so fearful of the recriminations for the film *Devil's Doorway* (1950), about an educated Indian who won a Congressional Medal of Honor during the Civil War, that it was not released until after the positive reaction *Broken Arrow* received made it "safe."[14]

The military prowess of the Seminole allowed Indians led by Anthony Quinn to surround the cavalry in the swamps as they hunted for an enemy they could not find in *Seminole* (1953). By 1955 another element was added in the *Indian Fighter* when the bathing scenes of actress Elsa Martinelli brought nudity and blatant sexuality to the mainstream Western. Further, the film is noted for director Andre de Toth's attempts to show Indian culture accurately as it relates to nature. Ford's *The Searchers* presents an anti–Indian John Wayne neurotically determined to seek revenge for an event that happened in the past. He, unlike Jeffrey Hunter's half-breed Indian character, is not the usual Ford hero who had come to civilize the West but instead is one of those savages who must be destroyed before society and civilization can move forward.

The use of cinema to affect emotion and reality in both setting and story is evident in Samuel Fuller's *Run of the Arrow* (1957). The Sioux, no longer primitive, do have a distinctive culture in this sympathetic treatment that sidesteps reality. A subtle, if comic, attempt to treat Indian problems accurately is evident in the Oscar-winning *Cat Ballou* (1965) with such incidents as the Indian ranch hand (Tom Nardini) telling Jane Fonda's character, on her homecoming, that her father was the only one who would hire an "Indian," and later at a dance, telling her trouble would follow her dancing with him. She understands this only when the local racists try to run him off.

The end of the 1960s saw the production of two films impacting the development of the portrayal of Indians in different ways. *Smith* (1969), a minor Disney film, featured Glen Ford and Chief Dan George defending an Indian boy who was charged with murder. Even though George gives an impassioned speech for the defense in the courtroom and the Indian actors were directed by Jay Silverheels, the portrayal of Indians was no different from that of other films of the decade. But for the first time an Indian character, played by a real Indian, gave an intelligent speech in a white setting where it made a difference. *Tell Them Willie Boy Is Here* (1969) featured major stars in a project which briefly revitalized the Western genre. Abraham Polonsky, in his first film since being blacklisted in 1951, directed; Robert Redford, fresh from his success in *Butch Cassidy and the Sundance Kid* (1969), starred; and Robert Blake appeared in an Indian role. He had begun his career as Little Beaver in the *Red Ryder* Western series (1940). The star-studded list of credits gave credence to a liberal American self-hate film with meaning in every word of the dialogue which mirrored the activist feelings of the Vietnam era.[15] The film, although not a great Western, proved that Westerns could make a statement. Other statement Westerns from the period included *Billy Jack* (1971), *When the Legends Die* (1972), *Ulanza's Raid* (1972), and *The Outlaw Josey Wales* (1976).

The majority of "Indians" in these films are members of other ethnic groups playing a role. Real Indians often were asked to play an Indian role quite new to them. This newness goes beyond the persona most actors assume for a role. During the filming of *Valley of the Sun* (1941) Juan Concha, "leader of some Taos Indians performing in the film, asked his tribesmen to work overtime to finish up a scene. Replied one: 'Nope, we tired playing Indian. Go home.'"[16] They had to learn to be Indians of a different tribe for the roles and like other actors, they were ready to go home at the end of a normal day of shooting. Little attention was paid to tribal differences by casting directors, producers, and directors. This remains true even among real Indians with credited roles.

The number of Indians listed in the credits of films from the last days of silent pictures until the present can be counted on two hands. In *The Western: The Complete Film Sourcebook* (1983), compiled by Phil Hardy, each film is listed with the six major players, director, producer, writer, and the cinematographer. Films not discussed in detail are listed in the final pages with at least two major stars. In the 400 pages of the volume less than ten Indians are listed among the six major characters for any film. Jim Thorpe, Chief Thunder Cloud, Jay Silverheels, Iron Eyes Cody, Will Rogers, Jr., Chief Dan George, Eddie Little Sky, and Will Sampson make up the list. By taking a closer look at each, one can see a gradual change, slow though it may be, in the way Indians have been portrayed in Western movies.

As Rayna Green points out, the Wild West shows which preceded the silent films, and the silent films themselves, often had real Indians playing Indians. Then, she writes, "Quickly, whites invaded the screen the way they had invaded Indian Country ... and did little to diminish the disappearance of real Indians from that stage."[17] There were Indians who survived the invasion but with reason. Jim Thorpe, a Sac and Fox Indian born in Indian Territory, was one of the greatest athletes of all time. He had a minor role in

Wild Horse Mesa (1932), a film based on a novel by Zane Grey about the coming of barbed wire to the West. He played an Indian chief in the musical *Treachery Rides the Range* (1937). After his phenomenal success on the playing fields of the Olympics in 1912, in baseball with the New York Giants and Cincinnati Reds (1913–1919), and professional football teams of the 1920s, his name was a draw for any movie.

Unlike Thorpe, who was a draw at the box office, Chief Thunder Cloud survived by doing what he was told without question. Through the changes from stage to silent film to talkies, Chief Thunder Cloud was one Indian who survived. A Cherokee who quickly became "Hollywood's mainstay on Indian lore for many years,"[18] he first appeared in the list of major credits for *Rustler's Paradise* (1935), a typical low-budget film of the period. He made an appearance the next year in another Harry Carey film, *Wagon Train* (1936). The picture was one of Carey's best, in part because of the work of cinematographer Robert Cline. During this period Thunder Cloud was hired more for his technical advice than for his acting. His next appearance was perhaps his most famous. He played Tonto in the landmark Western series, *The Lone Ranger* (fifteen chapters, 1938). Chief Thunder Cloud's reaction to the part may explain why he lasted so long in Hollywood. Thunder Cloud failed to voice concern about the name Tonto, which means fool in Spanish. During the same series he even sat under a sun lamp to make his skin the dark tan moviegoers expected in Indians.[19]

Chief Thunder Cloud acted in situations designed for South Asian Indians. Ironically, in 1944 he was hired to teach Navajos how to scalp, wear war bonnets and other Cheyenne paraphernalia for the film *Buffalo Bill*, and to replace Ken Maynard as a trail blazer in *Outlaw Trail*.[20] After a series of low-budget films and some major credits as technical advisor, Thunder Cloud made his final screen appearance in 1952. True to his entire film career, his final film, *Buffalo Bill in Tomahawk Territory* (1952), was full of stock footage and dialogue. Chief Thunder Cloud survived in the world of make-believe as few other Indians have managed to do.

Others who survived were Iron Eyes Cody, a Cherokee, and Jay Silverheels, a Mohawk. Both came on the movie scene during the final years of Chief Thunder Cloud's career and they learned from his experiences. Iron Eyes Cody recently caught the public eye with a public service television announcement about land and water pollution. The sight of an older Indian in traditional dress riding through the beauties of nature which abruptly gave way to a trashed meadow and polluted lake moved the nation. The piece ended with a close-up of a giant tear rolling down the face of this proud representative of the nature other Americans had destroyed.[21]

Although greater public recognition came with the piece, Cody already was well known in the film world as an actor and technical advisor for his knowledge of Indian culture and history. Cody's first screen credit was the film *Crashin' Thru* (1939), the last singing Mountie effort. His next credited role was as Crazy Horse in *Sitting Bull* (1954), for which he was also the technical advisor. Although reviewers did not directly comment on Cody's role—they did comment on Dale Robertson and J. Carrol Naish—he won high praise for the accuracy of the film as it presented Indian culture and events. For the most part, reviewers agreed that the film contained "the most accurate description of the events that led up to the Battle of the Little Big Horn."[22]

Iron Eyes Cody could not work the success of one small-budget film into stardom. He continued to work as a technical advisor but was relegated to playing minor roles in low-budget Westerns. *El Condor* (1970), a forgettable film shot in Spain, gave him work as did *Greyeagle* (1977). At least in *Greyeagle* an attempt was made to present the true life of American Indians with Cody as technical advisor and a star, unlike *El Condor*, which had a gold-stealing plot set in Mexico. Although he did not become a major star, Iron Eyes Cody managed to remain on the fringes of the world of make-believe for more than forty years.

Jay Silverheels, on the other hand, spent the last forty years as one of the most recognized Indians in the world, not for himself, but because as Tonto he followed the Lone Ranger into the hearts of children all over the world. Born in Canada to a father who was the most decorated Canadian Indian soldier in World War I, Silverheels was named Harry Smith. Silverheels, like Thorpe, won recognition in sports before venturing into films. He won honors in such diverse activities as hockey, boxing, track, and football before being discovered by Joe E. Brown, the noted comedian. His pre–Tonto roles were lackluster with the exception of the educated, articulate Indian he played in *The Cowboy and the Indians* (1949).[23]

The Tonto role which Silverheels first played in 1949 provided him with steady employment in television and then in two films—*The Lone Ranger* (1956) and *The Lone Ranger and the Lost City of Gold* (1958). However, the role was a stereotypical sidekick who was inarticulate, faithful, and trustworthy. This was basically the same Indian portrayed in films from the early "talkies" to the present time. Rayna Green sums up the effect of such a character thusly, "The rare Indian who actually played an Indian role ... suffered the fate of becoming a stereotype or negative role model for young Indian people, the same fate often suffered by black actresses like Hattie McDaniel (Mammy in *Gone with the Wind*)."[24]

Silverheels played memorable roles in other films as an actor and technical advisor, a trade he refined under the leadership of Chief Thunder Cloud. He was considered a stable, veteran actor when he won nondescript roles in *Broken Arrow* (1950), *War Arrow* (1953), and *Drums Along the Mohawk* (1954). During his career he played characters opposite such luminaries as Elizabeth Taylor, Tyrone Power, Gene Autry, Errol Flynn, and Audie Murphy, but many argue that his major contribution to films was off the screen.

Jay Silverheels broke new ground for Native American actors as the Lone Ranger's faithful Indian companion Tonto.

As a technical advisor on numerous Westerns, Silverheels found that there were few trained Indian actors. He set up the Indian Acting Workshop in Los Angeles to help aspiring Indian actors break into television and movies. Not everyone agrees that the results of the workshop have been positive. For example, many reviewers of Walt Disney Productions' *Smith* (1969) agreed that the stereotype Indian reared its head the way characters were portrayed in the film. Jay Silverheels served as technical advisor on the film and most of the Indian actors were from his Indian Acting Workshop.[25] At any rate, he continued the effort to get more Indians involved in the entertainment industry, and with only 105 actors and technicians listed in the American Indian Registry for the Performing Arts in 1988,[26] there was much work to be done.

Of the four recognized film actors to come on the scene since the production of *Broken Arrow*, the least productive in films was Will Rogers, Jr. Rogers, who is of Cherokee Indian heritage, played a credited role in only three minor films. None of the films was exceptional but Rogers did have the unique opportunity of playing his father in the *Will Rogers Story* (1951). Like his father, Rogers was primarily a journalist although he did do a television morning talk show called the *Good Morning Show* on CBS.[27] Periodically he can still be seen doing public service announcements or promoting Time-Life *History of the West* books. Most of his energy is devoted to his real estate business rather than to any aspect of the media.

Chief Dan George, a Squamish Indian, was another Indian actor who arrived on the scene during the past thirty years. With his flowing white hair, shiny eyes, and quick smile, George was, along with Silverheels and Iron Eyes Cody, easily recognized by an adoring public. After working as a logger and longshoreman for more than twenty-five years, George began playing small roles in the 1960s. Although some of his best work was in his native Canada—*Cariboo County* (CBS), *Cold Journey* (Canadian National Film Board)[28]—two of his efforts in this country deserve closer inspection.

Before his death in 1977, Chief Dan George gave two of the four most important performances by an Indian actor in the past twenty-five years (the third was Will Sampson's Chief Bromden role in *One Flew Over the Cuckoo's Nest* [1975]; the fourth was Graham Green in *Dances with Wolves* [1990]). In 1969 Chief Dan George worked with Silverheels on Disney's *Smith*. In the film, in defense of an Indian boy charged with murder, George gave a lengthy courtroom speech about the true relationship between the Whites and Indians. This speech was closer to the truth than the educated, articulate, groundbreaking role Silverheels played in 1949 in *The Cowboy and the Indians*.

The second major Chief Dan George performance was as Old Lodge Skins in *Little Big Man* (1970). Never before had an Indian actor played a major role in a big-budget movie or received an Academy Award nomination for a role in a Western.[29] Chief Dan George was nominated in the Best Supporting Actor category and even though he did not win, the recognition he received gave a tremendous boost to Indian actors. Without compromising his heritage, George played the role of Old Lodge Skins with conviction and with the comic timing necessary to make such a role work. The debate about the film centers not around its portrayal of Indians, but on its faithfulness to the Thomas Berger novel of the same name. In fact, reviewers contend that the re-creation of the Washita River Massacre of 1868 in the film is the most truthful portrayal of any film version of a confrontation between Indians and the United States government. In *Little Big Man*, the major star—Dustin Hoffman as Little Big Man—is criticized while the lead Indian actor—Chief Dan George—is praised.[30]

Another actor who won the praises of contemporary moviemakers and critics was Will Sampson. Sampson was a Creek who won an Academy Award nomination for his portrayal of Chief Bromden in *One Flew Over the Cuckoo's Nest*, his first film role. Born in 1933, he thought of himself as a painter and artist rather than as an actor. His paintings have been exhibited in such prestigious galleries and museums as the Amon Carter Museum, the Smithsonian Institute of Art, and the Library of Congress. "As a young man, he frequently supported himself by selling his sketches and paintings. His works—mostly Indian themes, cowboy scenes and western landscapes—are found today in many prestigious private collections."[31]

The six-foot, five-inch Sampson looked like he stepped out of a Catlin painting or a Curtis photograph with high cheek bones, impassive stare, and an air of dignity tinged with menace. Known in filmdom as an independent because he insisted on playing an Indian realistically, Sampson took a firm stand in his first role, that of Chief Bromden. Director Milos Foreman wanted the stereotypical "Ugh" Indian, to which Sampson replied, "It was 1963—Chief Bromden had gone through high school as a football athlete, had served in the Korean War,

Chief Dan George turned in outstanding performances in *Little Big Man* (1970) and *The Outlaw Josie Wales* (1976).

had perfect diction."[32] Sampson played the role his way and the film academy proved him right when they nominated him for an Oscar.

Sampson followed *Cuckoo's Nest* with equally memorable performances in Robert Altman's *Buffalo Bill and the Indians* (1976), *The Outlaw Josie Wales* (1976), and *The White Buffalo* (1978). In the first film Sampson plays William Halsey, Sitting Bull's interpreter, "a highly educated man who tried to get every bit he could from the Indians." In the second, he is Ten Bears, chief of the Comanches opposite the other outstanding Indian actor of the decade, Chief Dan George (who steals the show with his belief in life and the future). In the third film, Sampson is the Sioux War Chief Crazy Horse "trying to save his dignity, trying to keep as much of his land as possible, yet knowing his people were being overwhelmed." These are the roles and philosophies Will Sampson wants the audience to see when they watch an Indian on the screen.[33]

White Buffalo portrayed Indians, according to Sampson, as "caring individuals rather than stoic savages of so many other films." "Some screenwriters had even consulted him on the accuracy of Indian detail," Sampson, with a note of surprise in his voice, said in an interview with Grace Lichtenstein. Sampson continued, "They're [filmmakers] still using 'em [Indians] as livestock. They somehow just can't seem to bring it around to give the truth about

Graham Greene as "Kicking Bird" in the Academy Award–winning Western *Dances with Wolves* **(1990).**

Crazy Horse (Will Sampson) raises his rifle in greeting in *The White Buffalo*, a United Artists release.

Indians." When he died in 1988 at the age of fifty-three, Sampson left behind a legacy of accuracy and a determination to correct the way Indians are portrayed in art and films. As he stated at the end of an interview, "Mountains, thunderstorms, lightning, rain—they awe me. Man doesn't."[34] Will Sampson was true to his heritage to the end.

Eddie Little Sky, a Lakota Sioux, worked at Disneyland as a dancer and entertainer until Walt Disney put him to work in Disney Production films. One of his first roles was in *Tonka* (1958) with Sal Mineo in the lead role, followed by a leading role in the small production company effort titled *Journey Through Rosebud* (1972). Not an outstanding actor, Little Sky is better known in the Indian entertainment society for his participation in pow-wows and as the author of *I the Actor* and *The Other Side of Me*.

Little Sky learned the traditions of the pow-wow from his elders who taught him the importance of the "costumes, dance and songs as well as their traditional values"[35] in the Sioux society of which he was a part. He often speaks to youth groups about the importance of their heritage and the role of the elders in the perpetuation of traditional society. Eddie Little Sky has taken it upon himself to explain to Indian youth why their heritage is different from that shown and represented in the films they watch. Young Indians in Oklahoma wonder why the character Sam Starr in *The Long Riders* (1980) "was the typical Hollywood Indian, with only a vest covering his bare chest, and his hair down to his shoulders. The real Sam Starr wore proper suits, had close-cropped hair, a broad-brimmed hat and tried to look like a white man." In an interview even Little Sky noted that even such highly praised works as *A Man Called Horse*, in which eighty percent of the dialogue was in the Sioux language, used a Kiowa song as background music for the titles and credits.[36] The film was about the Sioux, not the Kiowa.

In 1981 Iron Eyes Cody's interview with Stan Steiner was published in *American West*. Speaking for all Indian actors, he declared that there may not have been as many as ten movies in which Indians were not insulted.[37] Eddie Little Sky, Will Sampson, and the others discussed in this essay have expressed the same concern in a variety of ways. When will an Indian be shown returning from a hunt with food for the family or successful against the white man, and, with his wife, happily enjoying his children? Certainly the 1990 film *Dances with Wolves* presents, for the first time in a major work, Indian life and customs and presents a more accurate interpretation; but the headlines still belonged to Kevin Costner, actor and director. Although Costner, who upon accepting his Academy Award for the film of the year had his speech translated in Lakota Sioux by Doris Leadercharge, made an honest effort to give credit to the American Indians.

Certainly steps are being taken to present American Indians more realistically in films, but it's time for the pace to pick up from a crawl to a run. Bonnie Paradise, executive director of the American Indian Registry for the Performing Arts in Hollywood, recently stated that "the time has come for this [stereotyping Native Americans and their culture] and the only way ... is for every Indian... to do something about it."[38] An accurate portrayal of the role of American Indians in the American West is "closer today than in the early days of motion pictures, but what price has been paid for the stereotype Indian American children have grown up with during the past fifty years as they sat in the Saturday matinee watching the cavalry race to the rescue? Perhaps the great Western film director John Ford was correct when he "found the ideal framework for the expression of his poetic vision of America, a new nation carved out of a savage land at great cost, a price he suggests in his last work (*Cheyenne Autumn*)—too high for what America actually becomes."[39]

Notes

1. William T. Pilkington and Don Graham, eds. *Western Movies* (Albuquerque, 1979), pp. 1–13.

2. Grace Lichtenstein, "He Refuses to Be an 'Ugh-Tonto' Indian," in *New York Times Sunday* (June 6, 1976), p. 15.

3. "The 'Make-Believe' Indian," in *Moving Picture World* 8 (March 4, 1911), p. 473.

4. Pat Hilton, "Indians Breaking Film, TV Barriers," *USA Weekend* (July 22–24, 1988), p. 6.

5. Fred Schrers, "Young Guns or the Western Rides Again," *Premiers* (August 1988), pp. 44–45.

6. Nancy Lofholm, "Indians Seek 'Thief of Time' Roles," *Daily Sentinel* (February 14, 1992), p. 1B.

7. Phil Hardy, *The Western* (New York, 1983), p. 325.

8. John G. Cawelti, *The Six-Gun Mystique* (Bowling Green, Ohio, 1971), p. 37.

9. James Robert Parish, *Great Western Stars* (New York, 1976), p. iv.

10. Paul O'Neal, *The End of the Myth*, Time-Life Edition, *The Old West Series* (Virginia, 1979), p. 218.

11. *The End*, p. 218.

12. *Western Movies*, p. 48.

13. *Western Movies*, p. 47.

14. *The Western*, p. 192.

15. Pauline Kael, *5001 Nights at the Movies: A Guide from A to Z* (New York, 1982), p. 582.

16. *The End*, p. 219.

17. Rayna Green, "The Tribe Called Wannabee," *Folklore* 99 (Number 11, 1988), p. 41.

18. Roger W. Axford, Dr., *Native Americans: 23 Indian Biographies* (Pennsylvania, 1978), pp. 96–98, and Frank H. Gille, *Dictionary of Indians of North America*, Vol. II (Minnesota, 1980), pp. 157–58.

19. James F. Denton, "The Red Man Plays Indian," *Collier's* 113 (March 18, 1944), p. 18.

20. *Red Man*, p. 19.

21. Iron Eyes Cody, File #63 Box 24, Cherokee National Archives, Tahlequah, Oklahoma.

22. *The Western*, p. 235.

23. Marion E. Grindley, *Indians of Today* (Los Angeles, 1971), p. 126.

24. "Wannabee," p. 41.

25. *The Western*, p. 316.

26. "Indians," p. 6.

27. Barry T. Klein, *Who's Who Reference Encyclopedia of the American Indian* (New York, 1986), p. 229.

28. Gille, Vol. I, p. 271.

29. *The Western*, p. 316.

30. *Western Movies*, p. 119.

31. Gary Robinson, "Mourners Gather in Okmulgee to Observe the Passing of Will Sampson—1933–1987," *Muskogee News* (June 9, 1987), p. 4.

32. 'Ugh-Tonto,' p. 15.

33. 'Ugh-Tonto,' p. 15.

34. 'Ugh-Tonto,' p. 15.

35. "Eddie Little Sky," *Red Earth '87 Program* (Oklahoma City, 1987), p. 46.

36. David Jones, "Oklahomans Fight to Change an Image," *Tulsa Tribune Weekend* (June 1, 1979), proof copy.

37. Stan Steiner, "Real Horses and Mythic Riders," *American West* 18 (September-October, 1981), p. 57.

38. "Indians in Film Form Coalition," Associated Press Wireservice release, June 28, 1992.

39. Jim Kitses, "The Western," in Donal E. Staples, ed., *The American Cinema* (Washington, D.C., 1976), p. 341.

FACES WITHOUT NAMES

by Jim Collins

"Hey, I know him! That's what's-his-face!" you say as you spot one of those actors you just *know* but cannot name. Then you turn to whomever it is you are seeing the movie with and say, "By the way, who is that guy?" We have all done it hundreds of times. Who is that guy? After all, you have seen him more times than you care to count, but for the life of you, his name is impossible to remember.

Do not despair; there are thousands of such actors in the world of television and the silver screen. They make the "good guys" look better and the "bad guys" look worse than they could be. In fact, some of them are "good" or "bad" guys in different films. They simply are not as noticeable as the star of the show, who plays the hero, or the arch villain, who more often than not is a guest star on television or the co-star on the silver screen. Still, they are a necessary part of the motion picture and of the television series. They are faces without names, the indefatigable character actor.

Think about it. How could Jimmy Stewart's Ransom Stoddard have been so good if it were not for the evil gunfighter portrayed by Lee Marvin in *The Man Who Shot Liberty Valance*? How could those thirty-seven Western television shows have gotten by week after week back in the late 1950s if it had not been for character actors such as Claude Akins, Lee Van Cleef, Jack Elam, and Leo Gordon? If you are old enough to remember those shows, you will realize that Larry Hagman's J. R. Ewing was not the first "man you love to hate!" It was the above-named character actors, and many more like them, who kept coming back week after week to bite the dust again, that we really loved to hate.

Just about every genre of fiction that you can think of has been transported in story form to the big or small screen, including mystery, thriller, historical, horror, science fiction, fantasy, and romance, to name but a few. Each genre has been put on the screen, and each has had its fair share of character actors in supporting roles. Without the character actors in supporting roles there would be little worth watching, but the character actor is seldom given his due.

Of all the genres of fiction, why has the Western been the best and most often transformed type of story to come to the screen? The answer is simple.

The life of the frontiersman and American cowboy was pretty cut and dried during the nineteenth century in which they lived. Contrary to today's way of living, which becomes more complicated daily, the cowboy had to deal with right and wrong in a simple manner. The penalty for stealing and killing was death, if you lived long enough to make it to the trial. There was no such thing as plea bargaining, and if you lived by the gun, you more than likely would die that way. The cowboy also had a great deal of respect for womanhood, often to the point of being fearful of the weaker sex, and you can see why this type of man was so easily made into a hero on the silver screen. He was a man who could hold up every moral conviction that our country stood for and keep on coming, even when he had been shot down once or twice. It was good material, and you would not be ashamed to let your kids go see a movie with a hero with those kinds of standards, at least not eighty years ago, when moviemaking was still in its childhood and the cowboy was still a recent part of our national scene, and not just a myth, as some would have you believe today.

There are dozens of good character actors who are quite memorable for their parts in Western movie pictures, and many also made their name in the television arena. In some cases, these actors were able to work profitably in both areas. What follows is a look at a dozen or so of the better known character actors.

The beginning is always a good place to start, so follow me back to the Los Angeles of 1910, when the town was no more than a sleepy village with a valley of orange groves outside of it. Filmmaker D. W. Griffith recently had moved to California to take advantage of the seasonable weather available nearly all year around, not to mention the better background scenery. He also had put together a stock company of players, comprised in part of the likes of Mary Pickford and the Gish sisters, Dorothy and Lillian. And one of the stock players who would go on to make a name for himself was **Harry Carey**.

Born January 16, 1878, in the Bronx, New York, Harry Carey was what today we would call a handyman. He spent a good deal of his youth trying a hand at various professions, even attempting to write melodramas, before joining Biograph, Griffith's company, in 1909. By 1917, after appearing in a number of Griffith's productions, Carey had become a star of both Westerns and other action pictures, many directed by John Ford. Carey made twenty-six productions with John Ford, often playing a character by the name of Cheyenne Harry. Far from shy, he occasionally collaborated with Ford on the scripting, producing, and directing side of the camera.

Harry Carey may be one of the few actors who began his movie career as a star and went on to become even better known as a reliable character actor, and that is exactly what happened when "talkies" replaced the silent films in the late 1920s. He spent nearly twenty years in his second career, giving a standout performance in *Mr. Smith Goes to Washington* (1939), and appearing in *The Spoilers* (1942), *Duel in the Sun* (1946), and *The Angel and the Badman* (1947), before he died in Brentwood, California, of coronary thrombosis September 21, 1947.[1]

Carey's son, Harry Carey, Jr., carried on the family tradition and became an excellent character actor as well. One of his first films was *The Three Godfathers* (1949), a John Ford film which the director dedicated "to the memory of Harry Carey—bright star of the early Western sky."[2]

While Harry Carey was becoming a movie star in 1917, a strapping young Britisher by the name of **Victor McLaglen** served as a captain with the Irish Fusiliers in World War I. Born on December 10, 1886, McLaglen served as a boy soldier in the Boer War (1899–1902), worked as a prizefighter in Canada, and performed in vaudeville and the circus. In 1920 he played in a film in England, the first of many silent films he would make in the 1920s. But England was not the only market for his work; he made his first film in the United States in 1924. It turned out to be a memorable film since McLaglen thereafter was billed with a nickname taken from the title of that first film, *The Beloved Brute*.[3]

In Hollywood he was often cast in lead and supporting roles that typified McLaglen—big, savage, soft-hearted men of action who were usually of the military mold. Like a number of the well-known character actors, McLaglen soon became friends with John Ford, who put him to good use in his films. Although he won his only Academy Award for his role in *The Informer* (1935), McLaglen is best remembered as the tough and playful Irish Sergeant Major Quincannon of Ford's well-known cavalry trilogy, consisting of *Fort Apache* (1948), *She Wore a Yellow Ribbon* (1949), and *Rio Grande* (1950). Working with John Wayne in the Ford trilogy allowed him to become familiar with the Duke, and enabled McLaglen to turn in one of his best performances opposite Wayne in *The Quiet Man* (1952). He was active in films in the United States during much of the 1950s, making one picture a year until his death in Newport Beach, California, on November 7, 1959.[4]

Walter Brennan, another early entry into the motion picture business, was also a veteran of service in the war to end all wars. Born July 25, 1894, he chose the acting field over his training as an engineer, and appeared in vaudeville and in stock companies. He supported himself as a bank clerk and lumberjack before enlisting for service in World War I. It was not until 1923, after he had made and lost a fortune in real estate, that he showed up in Hollywood and began to work in films as an extra and a stuntman. By the 1930s Brennan began to get roles that made him a recognizable face. But the one thing that had the greatest impact on his career was an accident that knocked out his teeth in 1932. From then on he had a ready form of comic relief in being able to remove and replace those false teeth he carried with him for the rest of his life.[5]

Walter Brennan made over 100 films in his fifty-year career, in most of

Walter Brennan in his Academy Award–winning portrayal of Judge Roy Bean in
***The Westerner* (1940).**

them portraying what had come to be known as the epitome in the "old-timer"
on the frontier, or at least his modern-day counterpart. He hardly every strayed
from this role, playing mostly honest, understanding old-timers who have
been up the creek, over the mountain, down into the cave and back. As a character actor, he is best remembered for being the first supporting actor to
receive three Academy Awards; his first for *Come and Get It* (1936); his second for *Kentucky* (1938); and an outstanding performance as a crooked, hard-
bitten, and very real Judge Roy Bean in *The Westerner* (1940).

After nearly thirty years as a successful character actor, Brennan alter-
nated between the movies and two television series during the late 1950s and
the 1960s. *The Real McCoys* (1957–1963) was the first original show to bring
the modern-day country boy to the big city and was the inspiration for such
successful shows as *The Andy Griffith Show*, *The Beverly Hillbillies*, *Petticoat Junction*, and *Green Acres*. Grumpy old Amos McCoy was the spitting
image of everyone's grandfather, and if he was not ... well, he should have
been! The show was so successful that if you did not see it the first time
around, you can likely find it in reruns on one of the television channels. *The
Guns of Will Sonnett* (1967–1969) featured Brennan as an old ex-cavalry scout

of the 1870s, in search of his son. Walter Brennan was in his seventies by then and no longer had to *act* like an old-timer. Yet he still fit the saddle and the character as though he were born to them.

By the late 1960s Walter Brennan had become an institution. He parodied himself in one of his last films, which was also one of his best. In *Support Your Local Sheriff* (1969), he parodied the role of Old Man Clanton he had played in *My Darling Clementine* (1946). Brennan died in Oxnard, California, on September 22, 1974.

The year 1929 is usually remembered as the year of the Wall Street Crash and the beginning of the Great Depression. In the movie industry it was a year of transition that brought the "talkie" into popularity. Along with the new "talkie" came two new faces to the screen. They were a couple of University of Southern California football players who were spending their summer as prop men to make extra money. Director John Ford picked them out of the crowd to play screen roles, and they formed a three-way friendship that lasted the rest of their lives. Nearly everyone has heard this story of how John Wayne got started in the movies, but few realize that his friend **Ward Bond**[6] shared his move into acting.

Born on April 9, 1903, in Denver, Colorado, Ward Bond was a big, muscular man who, like Wayne, had his college years interrupted by a movie career. Bond started his career with Wayne, being placed with him in many of their early films as a sidekick to Duke. Like Wayne, Bond acted in approximately 200 films over an active career on the screen. Wayne became a leading man, and Bond became a character actor of note. He was quite versatile in his roles, sometimes playing a brutal heavy in movies such as *The Mortal Storm* (1940). More frequently, he was seen as the rugged but kindhearted lawman or friend of the hero, and most of those roles were in Western movies.[7]

Ward Bond is best remembered as the wagonmaster, Major Seth Adams, in the long-running *Wagon Train* (1957–1965) television series. His fatherly but tough image was one of the things that made this Western series one of the most popular series in history. Unfortunately, Bond died in Dallas, Texas, on November 5, 1960, following a heart attack, halfway through the eight-year run of *Wagon Train*.

Lee J. Cobb has been one of the most successful character actors. Born on December 8, 1911, in New York City, he originally showed promise as a child violinist, but a broken wrist put an end to his musical career. He ran away from home at the age of seventeen and spent seven years crisscrossing the country to Hollywood and back to New York in several attempts to start a movie career. In 1937 he began to appear in films, usually in character roles as a menacing heavy or sometimes as an imposing patriarch, a brooding community leader, or a business executive, although he did have some leads.[8] His stage career peaked when he created the Broadway version of Arthur Miller's Willy Loman in *Death of a Salesman*.

Ward Bond (left) starred as Major Seth Adams, wagonmaster, on *Wagon Train*, while Robert Horton played the scout Flint McCullough.

Cobb began his acting career with some forgettable Westerns, but later acted in such well-made Westerns as *Mackenna's Gold* (1968), *Coogan's Bluff* (1968), and *Lawman* (1970). Perhaps his best role was that of Judge Henry Garth on the Western series *The Virginian* (1962–1971), although Cobb was only with the series from 1962 until 1966. He left the series after he and James

During *The Virginian*'s first four seasons, Academy Award–winning actor Lee J. Cobb was featured as Judge Henry Garth, owner of the Shiloh ranch, with Roberta Shore as his daughter Betsy.

Drury, who co-starred as the Virginian, could not stand each other's ego on the set. Cobb left the set and the program, but tried his hand at a second, albeit short-lived series, *The Young Lawyers*, in 1970. He then did several movies in Italy in the early 1970s before his death in Los Angeles, California, on February 11, 1976.

One of the most versatile of Hollywood's character actors was **John McIntire**. Born June 27, 1907, in Spokane, Washington, McIntire began his career in radio and did not appear in movies until after World War II, when he looked older than his age. For the next fifteen years he gave more than credible performances, three of his best being Anthony Mann pictures in which he played what has been described as a "top-hatted conniver": *Winchester '73* (1950), *The Far Country* (1954), and *The Tin Star* (1957).[9] He often played in movies opposite his wife, actress Jeanette Nolan.

On television, John McIntire seems to have been the perfect replacement for a series star. When Ward Bond died during the *Wagon Train* series, McIntire completed the second half of the series' eight-year run from 1961 to 1965 as the new wagonmaster, Christopher Hale. And when Lee J. Cobb walked off the set of *The Virginian*, once again John McIntire filled the void for two seasons (1967–1968) as Clay Grainger, the new owner of the Shiloh spread. Clay Grainger's wife, Holly, was played by Jeanette Nolan.

John Ford was instrumental in the discovery of various actors whom he started on the way to stardom. One of the few actual "cowboys" he discovered to play in his Westerns was **Ben Johnson**, who was born on June 13, 1920, and raised in Pawhuska, Oklahoma. Johnson became a champion rodeo rider. During the early 1940s, when Howard Hughes was filming *The Outlaw*, the eccentric billionaire hired Johnson as a horse wrangler. Afterwards Johnson found work as a stuntman and double. When Ford "discovered" Johnson, he placed him in the last two of his cavalry pictures, *She Wore a Yellow Ribbon* (1949) and *Rio Grande* (1950), playing the part of a young cavalry sergeant.[10] This gave Johnson some exposure, and Ford liked what he saw. In fact, he had enough faith in the young horse wrangler to give him a leading part in a little known Western, *The Wagonmaster* (1950), which turned out to be one of Johnson's best performances. Johnson won an Academy Award for Best Supporting Actor in *The Last Picture Show* (1971), but for the most

Ben Johnson starred in John Ford's *The Wagonmaster* (1950).

part he was cast in Western movies and television Westerns; and his appearances helped lend an air of authenticity to the roles he played. Examples of
this include his appearances in the television mini-series, *The Sacketts* (1979)
and the made-for-TV movie *The Shadow Riders* (1982), both of which co-starred
Tom Selleck and Sam Elliott. Johnson died in Texas on April 8, 1996.

Lee Marvin was one of those actors who made it to stardom by playing
hard-bitten and brutal heavies at the start of his career before proving that he
could play the hero as well. Born on February 19, 1924, in New York City,
Marvin's entry into the entertainment world was accidental. As a Marine in
World War II, Marvin was invalided on the beaches of Tarawa—he got shot
in the end that goes over the fence last. After the war he was working as a
plumber's helper when he was asked to fill in for an ailing actor for a bit role
in summer stock. Afterwards he took up acting and in 1951 landed a part in
his first movie, *You're in the Navy Now*. Tall and rugged, he was typecast during the 1950s as a brutal heavy, mostly in Westerns and crime dramas.[11] Among
his most memorable roles during that time were that of the hoodlum who
throws scalding coffee in Gloria Grahame's face in *The Big Heat* (1953), and
as one of Spencer Tracy's opponents in *Bad Day at Black Rock* (1954).[12]

Marvin's image improved immensely when he gave a weekly performance—more than 100 shows—in the successful *M Squad* (1957–1960), as
tough, capable Chicago detective Lieutenant Frank Ballinger. Somehow, bru-
tality tends to show through as simply being capable when you are on the
side of the law, which says something about how your popularity rises when
you are a "good guy."

Marvin proved he could be a versatile actor when, at the end of his television series, he made one picture a year for the next three years with John
Wayne. *The Comancheros* (1961) and John Ford's *The Man Who Shot Liberty
Valance* (1962) proved that Marvin had not lost his touch in playing mean,
bullying bad guys; *Donovan's Reef* (1963) was a comedy which seemed to be
played for fun by everyone in the cast, including Marvin and Wayne.

Marvin's Academy Award–winning performance in *Cat Ballou* (1965)
transformed him from a character actor into a major star. *The Professionals*
(1966) proved he could hold his own with such competent actors as Burt Lancaster, Robert Ryan, and Ralph Bellamy. *Monte Walsh* (1970) paired him with
Jack Palance in a well-done story of two cowboys in the dying days of the
Old West.

If playing an unsympathetic hero was one of the roles Marvin did best,
it was showcased in an excellent portrayal of a tough Army sergeant in *The
Big Red One* (1980). One of his last films paired him with Chuck Norris as a
tough Green Beret–type commander of *Delta Force* (1986). He died in Tucson, Arizona, on August 29, 1987.

Occasionally two character actors will start out together and be stereo-
typed in roles that are exactly the opposite of those in which they began. Such

was the case with **Bruce Dern** and **Warren Oates**. Both began film careers within a year of each other and had the fortune—or misfortune—to co-star as members of the short-lived *Stoney Burke* (1962–1963) television series. Bruce Dern, as E. J. Stocker, was a responsible member of Stoney Burke's rodeo troop, while Warren Oates, as Ves Painter, was a shiftless con man who was constantly in trouble. Then Bruce Dern emerged in films as a psychotic and or drug-addicted fanatic in his roles. "I've played more psychotics and freaks and dopers then anyone," Dern once stated. Warren Oates, on the other hand, although he went on to play more than his share of "bad guys" and misguided felons, developed into an excellent character actor over the years.

Dern was born on June 4, 1936, in Chicago, and downplays the fact that he is the grandson of a former governor of Utah and the nephew of a Secretary of War in President Franklin D. Roosevelt's cabinet. He dropped out of college to pursue an acting career and, after several supporting roles on and off Broadway, played his first bit part in Elia Kazan's *Wild River* (1960).[13]

In an episode of *Alfred Hitchcock Presents* (1955–1965), Dern played so convincing a role as a hillbilly psycho that he seemed doomed to a career of playing maniacs, perverts, and freaks. If you can recall the convincing madness in the eyes of Kirk Douglas as he played Doc Holliday in *The Gunfight at the OK Corral* (1957), then perhaps that same paranoia and resentment were in Dern's eyes in the Hitchcock episode. Whatever it was, his role was effective and well done.

Dern played the heavy in a number of Westerns, including *Will Penny* (1967), *Water Hole #3* (1967), and opposite Kirk Douglas in *Posse* (1975). Ironically, he was killed by John Wayne in *The War Wagon* (1967), but played the vicious Long Hair who killed Wayne—one of the few times the Duke died onscreen—in *The Cowboys* (1971). The importance of Dern's roles improved and he enjoyed success in comedies during the 1980s.

It is hard to picture Warren Oates as someone who once tested gags for *Beat the Clock*, but that demonstrates the lengths to which people will go to get into show business. Born on July 5, 1928, in Depoy, Kentucky, Oates made his first Western, *Yellowstone Kelly*, in 1959.[14] As a supporting actor he tended to portray a small man, unashamedly a Southerner, in accordance with his Kentucky background, who always had an unshaven reek of low life about him.[15] Still, this persona was effectively done and added to his believability as an actor. He gained prominence as a character actor by appearing in such popular and well-made Westerns as *Ride the High Country* (1962), *The Wild Bunch* (1969), and *There Was a Crooked Man* (1970). This prepared him to play the title role of *Dillinger* (1974), giving a performance which was well received, and led to a role as a style-made thief in *The Brinks Job* (1978). After that he turned up in several mediocre television movies before he died in 1982.

One of the things the character actor has often had to do was provide a

Slim Pickens in a typical pose from the comedy Western *Hawmps* (1976).

bit of comic relief. Some play slapstick well, but when it comes to Westerns, there is nothing better than a droll sense of humor and a straight face. Two of the best characters to accomplish this in Western films have been **Slim Pickens** and **Chill Wills**.

Born on June 29, 1919, in Kingsberg, California, Slim Pickens was a wiry, hoarse character actor who appeared in rodeos from the time he was

Veteran character actor Chill Wills in cavalry garb from one of his countless Westerns.

twelve years of age and was one of the top clowns on the rodeo circuit before he began his film career in 1950.[16] His most memorable non–Western role was in *Dr. Strangelove* (1964). He appeared in many Western movies and television series, but his originality comes through best in such films as *Blazing Saddles* (1974), *The Apple Dumpling Gang* (1975), and *Hawmps* (1976). He died on December 8, 1983.

Chill Wills was born on July 18, 1903, in Seagoville, Texas, and began his performing career during his childhood by appearing in tent shows, vaudeville, and stock companies throughout the Southwest. Although he would not seem a likely candidate, Wills formed his own singing group, Chill Wills and the Avalons, in the 1930s and appeared with them in several Westerns, beginning in 1935.[17] The group disbanded in 1938 when Wills began what would be a fifty-year career as a character actor in the movies, most of them Westerns. A better than average character actor, he was nominated for an Oscar for best supporting actor for his performance in John Wayne's *The Alamo* (1960). His gravelly voice also provided the off-screen voice of Francis, the talking mule, in that series of films.[18] To cap off his career, at the age of seventy-two, in 1975, he released his first singing album. He died in Encino, California, on December 15, 1978.

Not to be neglected, of course, are the character actors who make their living mostly in the realm of television. Because of space requirements, only a handful of the most noticeable of those faces can be discussed here. Although the actors listed here are most often seen in television, nearly all of them have appeared in movies as well. Along with their names is listed a short summary of each man and his work:

Claude Akins (May 25, 1918–January 27, 1994). Although Akins' first film was *From Here to Eternity* (1953), he was best known as a television and motion picture heavy. He starred in two series, *Movin' On* (1974–1976) and *The Misadventures of Sheriff Lobo* (1979-1980).

John Anderson (1923–August 7, 1992). This tall, wiry actor has been seen by many as both a "good guy" and a "bad guy," mostly in Westerns on television and in films. From 1959 until 1961, he played a recurring role as Virgil Earp, brother to Wyatt, in *The Life and Legend of Wyatt Earp* (1955–1961).

R. G. Armstrong (April 7, 1917–). This heavyset, balding actor is usually seen as a heavy-handed villain, and has divided his career between movies—he played the puritanical father, Joshua Knudsen, in *Ride the High Country* (1962)—and television Westerns.

Lyle Bettger (February 13, 1915–). This blond-haired, blue-eyed actor is perhaps best remembered for his villainous roles in which he expressed extreme hatred through the clenching of his teeth. Despite often being typecast as a heavy, he starred in his own series, *The Court of Last Resort*, from 1957 to 1960.

Edgar Buchanan (March 21, 1903–1979). This character actor did for the "old-timer" character on television what Walter Brennan did for the role on the screen, and is best remembered for those types of roles and two series in which he starred, *Judge Roy Bean*, in which he played the title role, and *Petticoat Junction* (1963–1970). In early television he also co-starred with William Boyd in *Hopalong Cassidy* (1949–1951) as his saddle pard, Red Connors.

Jack Elam (left) as Deputy J. D. Smith and Larry Ward as Marshal Frank Ragan appearing in the Warner Bros. television series *The Dakotas.*

Jim Davis (August 26, 1916–April 26, 1981). Often playing corrupt lawmen or downright plug-ugly mean outlaws, Davis is best remembered for his outstanding performances as the patriarch of the Ewing clan, Jock Ewing, on *Dallas* from the program's inception in 1978 to his fatal heart attack in 1981. He was not replaced in that role.

Ted De Corsia (1904–1973). Although he played his share of gangsters, this actor played plenty of villains in Westerns. As tough as he was, he co-starred in the *Steve Canyon* (1958–1960) series as Police Chief Hagedorn.

John Dehner (November 23, 1915–February 4, 1992). If ever there was an actor who could successfully play the villainous banker foreclosing on the widow woman in town, John Dehner was that actor. From hard-bitten lawmen to misguided but basically good fathers, Dehner played the entire range with great success and believability. He also co-starred on a number of television shows, most notably a two-year run (1971–1973) on *The Doris Day Show* (1968–1973). ·

John Doucette (1921–August 16, 1994). Capable of playing storekeepers with an agreeable nature or tough guys who are downright mean, Doucette specialized in Westerns, although he did co-star with Macdonald Carey in *Lock Up* (1959–1961) as Jim Weston.

Jack Elam (November 13, 1916–). Elam is a real scene stealer who has played villainous "bad guys" and comical "good and bad guys" and been effective in both areas. He co-starred in the short-lived Western, *The Dakotas* (1963), followed shortly by a second co-starring role as an over-the-hill gunfighter in *Temple Houston* (1963-1964). His most recent television series was a non–Western titled *Easy Street* (1985).

Paul Fix (March 13, 1901–October 14, 1983). Giving a minor Barry Fitzgerald impression in roles ranging from crooks to benevolent doctors, Fix made over 300 films before his career ended. He is best remembered as fatherly Marshal Micah Torrance in *The Rifleman* (1958–1963).

Leo Gordon (December 2, 1922–). One of the most often seen and nastiest of the Western villains, Gordon has turned his hand of late more to screenplays and is quite good in this field. He was seen occasionally on television and had a co-starring role in a short-lived spinoff from the *Dukes of Hazzard* show called *Enos* (1980-1981).

James Griffith (1919–). This actor could be another scene stealer and did especially well in the 1950s by portraying seemingly easy-going general store clerks on the good side and evil-minded gunfighters and bad men on the outside of the law. From 1959 to 1960 he co-starred in the syndicated series, *The Sheriff of Cochise County* (1956–1960).

Denver Pyle (May 11, 1920–December 7, 1997). One of the most experienced of Western character actors, his career began by playing lean and sneaky characters. During 1955 and 1956 he had a recurring role as real-life gunman Ben Thompson in *The Life and Legend of Wyatt Earp* (1955–1961), but later put on some weight and took to playing the more jovial types, such as his starring role of Uncle Jesse in *The Dukes of Hazzard* (1979–1982).

Ray Teal (January 12, 1902–1976). No one played both sides of the tracks with equal strength better than Ray Teal. A good, solid actor, he was capable of giving off just the right feeling of irritability and sly temperament to be a bad guy, while the next time you saw him he was the friendly local sheriff. In fact, Teal may well have been the best-known sheriff in Westerns, playing the best role of his career as Sheriff Roy Coffee (1961–1971) on *Bonanza* (1959–1973).

Lee Van Cleef (January 9, 1925–1989). Van Cleef's steely look and narrow eyes made him one of the most watched Western villains. When television Westerns began to fade in the late 1960s, he enjoyed enormous success as a brutal hero in the "spaghetti Westerns."

Robert J. Wilke (1911–). Seen quite frequently in the heyday of the televised Westerns, his icy-eyed, taut features could only be described as coming from a man who is "devilish mean." Wilke played convincing villains but had a co-starring role as Marshal Sam Corbett in the short-lived *The Legend of Jesse James* (1965–1966).[19]

It is interesting to note that of the character actors named above, nearly all at one time or another were given the opportunity to star or co-star in a series of their own. Some would likely claim it was pure luck that this happened, but it may prove the truth in the old saying that "every mean dog has his day." After all, these fellows played some real dogs!

Notes

1. Ephraim Katz, *The Film Encyclopedia* (New York: Crowell, 1979), p. 206.
2. Katz, *The Film Encyclopedia*, p. 206.
3. Katz, *The Film Encyclopedia*, p. 758.
4. Katz, *The Film Encyclopedia*, p. 758.
5. David Thomson, *A Biographical Dictionary of Film* 2nd ed., rev. (New York, 1981), p. 67.
6. Katz, *The Film Encyclopedia*, p. 139.
7. Katz, *The Film Encyclopedia*, p. 139.
8. Katz, *The Film Encyclopedia*, p. 250.
9. Thomson, *A Biographical Dictionary of Film*, p. 373.
10. Katz, *The Film Encyclopedia*, p. 621.
11. Katz, *The Film Encyclopedia*, p. 783.
12. Thomson, *A Biographical Dictionary of Film*, p. 390.
13. Katz, *The Film Encyclopedia*, p. 330.
14. Katz, *The Film Encyclopedia*, p. 869.
15. Thomson, *A Biographical Dictionary of Film*, p. 444.
16. Katz, *The Film Encyclopedia*, p. 912.
17. Katz, *The Film Encyclopedia*, p. 1240.
18. Katz, *The Film Encyclopedia*, p. 1240.
19. *The Western* (New York, 1975) (Allen Eyles); David Quinlan, *The Illustrated Encyclopedia of Movie Character Actors* (New York, 1985), and Tim Brooks and Earl Marsh, *The Complete Directory to Prime Time Network TV Shows, 1946–Present* (New York, 1981), were used in compiling the information on television's character actors.

STEVE MCQUEEN
AND THE LAST WESTERN

by Richard Robertson

"But of all the actors I've worked with,
Steve was the most alone."
Norman Jewison, director

Westerns dominated prime-time television in the late 1950s. Beginning with the premiers of *Gunsmoke* and *The Life and Legend of Wyatt Earp* in 1955, the so-called adult Western emerged. The hero of the adult Western did not quite fit into the usual mold. Rather than a cowboy or a marshal, he might be a drifter, a gambler, a paid gunman, or even a bounty hunter. *Cheyenne*, *Maverick*, and Paladin of *Have Gun, Will Travel*, embodied the first three. The last, the bounty hunter, was Josh Randall of *Wanted: Dead or Alive*, played by little-known actor, Steve McQueen.

Born at the start of the Great Depression in 1930 to a young mother, Steve McQueen all his life invented glamorous stories to cover the pain of a father who abandoned his wife and one-year-old child. McQueen's mother drifted in and out of a series of short-lived marriages leaving Steve to be raised by a distant uncle and his kind-hearted former burlesque dancer wife. By the age of fourteen he was on the street and on his own. A series of minor scrapes with the law resulted in a significant period at the Boys' Republic, a reform school which remained close to McQueen's heart throughout his life. In later years, he would impulsively drop in and visit with the boys. The merchant marine, towel boy in a bordello, the Marine Corps, cab driver, odd jobs, and thief: this was the background of the twenty-one-year-old who found himself in New York in 1951 studying with Uta Hagen to be an actor.

The work was sparse. His first parts were tiny ones in the Yiddish Theatre. Lee Strasberg picked him from among hundreds who applied for a place at the Actors Studio. He studied alongside Paul Newman, James Dean, Shelly Winters, and Ben Gazzara, who he briefly replaced opposite Winters in *A Hatful of Rain* in 1956 for his only Broadway appearance. That was the year of Paul Newman's first film triumph in *Somebody Up There Likes Me*.

When *Wanted: Dead or Alive* premiered in 1958, it was the peak year for new Western series on television. Eighteen new series started in 1958 and seven of the top ten shows that year were Westerns. *Buckskin*, *Jefferson Drum*, and *MacKenzie's Raiders* were a few of the more forgettable entries. *The Rifleman* and *Rawhide* were much more successful, launching the careers of Chuck Connors and Clint Eastwood. *Wanted: Dead or Alive* lasted only three years and would not be memorable for its scripts or characters, but it did advance the career of McQueen, who became one of Hollywood's biggest stars of the '60s and '70s.

Josh Randall, the character played by McQueen, made his living by pursuing fugitives and outlaws. He carried their "wanted" posters folded in his shirt pocket. He was a bounty hunter out to turn a profit at the expense of other men's lives. He belonged to no group and lived in no town but prowled the frontier looking for his prey. Because he did not represent the community or the federal government as a sheriff or marshal would, he carried neither the coercive clout of law and authority or the moral legitimacy of the people. Thus, the character was always at a disadvantage for the sympathy of the audience. He represented himself alone and claimed no mission of righting wrongs. Josh Randall was assumed, by all he met, to be motivated by greed. He was unwelcome, even treated as an outcast, wherever he traveled. Since many of the men he sought were innocent or had taken up peaceable and community-serving lives, he often was pitted against both good and bad elements in a town.

Only a special actor could make such a character sympathetic. Vincent Fannelly, executive producer of another television Western, *Trackdown*, looked for an actor with "a hint of menace underneath." McQueen possessed that quality. "I picked him because he was a little guy, you know. A bounty hunter is a sort of underdog. Everyone's against him except the audience. And McQueen was an offbeat guy. He wasn't the best looking guy in the world, but he had a nice kind of animal instinct." In addition to these qualities McQueen had a trim, athletic body and a disarmingly innocent boyish smile which he would flash at unexpected moments.[1]

The *Wanted: Dead or Alive* stories were straightforward and fell easily within the Western genre. They also pointed up a moral. Typical was an episode where a town drunk asks Josh Randall to find the body of his missing son. The townspeople are defensive and insist that the boy is not dead but instead has just run off. Josh is soon ready to give up the search, but the father's deep and obvious love for his son urges him on. Randall is threatened and beaten when he begins to suspect the town's leading employer. No one will oppose this powerful man because he helped rebuild the town when it was down. One citizens states their position: "We owe Jed Miller more than we can pay." Randall counters, "You don't owe him your souls, mister." A gunfight settles the issue in typical Western fashion; Randall kills the villains.

Steve McQueen got the big break he had been waiting for as Josh Randall in
Wanted: Dead or Alive.

He rides out after issuing his verdict, "This town can only do one thing for me, watch me ride out. It'll be the first time in a week I've felt clean."

Josh Randall's highly developed moral sense often worked to his economic disadvantage. In an episode centering around a town election involving an old friend, Randall is forced to choose between saving his friendship or saving his friend's marriage. He chooses the latter and rides out with only the audience knowing what a higher good he has served. In another episode, Randall voluntarily sacrifices his bounty so that a widow can benefit from the money.

Over a three-year period *Wanted: Dead or Alive* cast some of the solid supporting actors of the period including Edgar Buchanan and Ralph Meeker. Occasionally a future star, such as Mary Tyler Moore, showed up as a bit player or in a leading role. In one episode, James Coburn played Jesse Holloway, an old friend of Randall. He is besieged by a crooked gambler and his tough friends. When Jesse is beaten, Josh, looking for help, finds a notebook in his friend's pocket. It lists all the people who owe Jesse favors. Josh proposes to bring in Clay Allison, John Wesley Hardin, Johnny Ringo, and Luke Short, surely the most threatening group of gunslingers imaginable.[2] Before all this can happen, the violent climax occurs. Randall, aided by his friend who rises from a sickbed, polishes off the whole mob. When Jesse's girl objects to all the killing, Josh simply says, "I understand the way you feel about violence. I don't think much of it myself. But if anything's worth having, it's worth fighting for...." To Josh Randall, violence is a tool of his trade.

The violence of the series on screen mirrored a stormy behind-the-scenes production. Steve McQueen was twenty-eight years old when the series premiered in the fall of 1958. He had struggled to make his mark as an actor for years, had seen fellow students of the Actors Studio, including Paul Newman, emerge as film stars while he performed a few plays and occasional television parts. The previous year McQueen had done a creditable job in a low-budget independent film called the *Great St. Louis Bank Robbery* which was shot entirely on location in that city. It did not receive wide distribution and failed to be a breakthrough for him. In February 1958, two months before beginning the filming of his television series, reluctantly, he had taken the teenage lead in a crude, low-budget, sci-fi thriller, *The Blob*. He was embarrassed when compared with Newman's acclaimed starring roles in *Somebody Up There Likes Me* (1956) and *The Long Hot Summer* (1958).

Early reviews of *Wanted: Dead or Alive* were not good because of the violence. It was a violent show and that was part of the point, but McQueen pushed from the first to make Josh Randall less heroic and more realistic. He complained to his wife that a script had him taking on three men at a time. Fights were not unfamiliar to McQueen who had grown up a rough and tumble youth on the streets and in the Marines. Faced with three-to-one odds, he felt that a real person would do just what he had done in similar situations, back away and later fight the men one at a time.[3]

Josh Randall was armed with a unique sawed-off Winchester rifle which he wore in a holster-like hook and clamp on his right leg. McQueen spent long hours mastering the weapon and a quick draw to bring authenticity to his role. Horses were another problem. His mount was a spirited horse named Ringo. They fought for the entire three years of the series. Neither would give in, although McQueen came to admire the horse, admitting, "He beat me."[4]

Ringo was not the only one McQueen fought. He clashed with writers, the producer and director as well. He kept a notebook of his ideas to improve the series and fought for their implementation. He stubbornly refused to give what he called a "phony performance" and even threatened to leave the country rather than compromise his standards. At the end of the first season, when the series had proved to be a success despite the critics, he sat down with Dick Powell and his wife June Allyson whose company, Four Star, produced the series, and after much difficulty negotiated a contract for three more years, 117 episodes. Many of McQueen's ideas were incorporated, and he toured the country on personal appearance tours to publicize the series. With the first money he received ($750/episode to start) he bought a new black Porsche, the start of a collection that would grow to thirty-five cars and four times as many motorcycles. They would sell for more than $1.5 million after his death.[5]

Wanted: Dead or Alive ranked sixteenth overall in its premier season, rose to ninth the following year. It was not a long-running success, and was canceled after the third season when it fell disastrously to twenty-sixth in the ratings probably due to a change in its location on the schedule.[6] Not a high-budget production, it was shot almost entirely in the studio, although some location work was done in Phoenix, Arizona. Indeed, if you watch episode after episode today, you get the uncomfortable feeling that Josh Randall spent all his time in the same town, waking up each day only to find new inhabitants and different names on the buildings.

The fame brought by a successful television series was welcomed by McQueen and his wife, Niele. Up to then, her career as a dancer and singer had appeared more promising than his. She was the one in demand on the stage, in television, and in Las Vegas. They did not know it but Steve was on the verge of spectacular success, a success that would make him an international star while Niele subordinated her role to that of supporting player.

The weekly grind of preparing up to forty shows per season left only a short period for Steve to work elsewhere, but he managed to squeeze in two important film roles in 1959 and 1960. These roles provided his bridge to films when his series was canceled in 1961. In *Never So Few*, McQueen supported Frank Sinatra, Gina Lollobrigida, and Peter Lawford in an action romance set in World War II southeast Asia. "It's your picture, kid," was Sinatra's way

of acknowledging that the film itself was not as good as McQueen's performance.

The following year McQueen made his first Western film. *The Magnifi-cent Seven* was based on the Japanese classic, *The Seven Samurai* (1954) by
Akira Kurosawa. John Sturges directed the American version with a cast
headed by Yul Brynner who plays an aging gunman who is requested to assem-
ble a group of professional gunslingers to protect a poor Mexican town threatened by bandits. Brynner was supported by a strong cast of future film and
television stars including Charles Bronson, Robert Vaughn, James Coburn,
and Horst Bucholz. Eli Wallach played the bandit chief, Calvera.

The story of *The Magnificent Seven* is a simple one. Three peasant vil-
lagers come to an American town looking for fearless gunmen. They observe
Brynner and McQueen as they commandeer a hearse and haul the body of a
dead Indian to Boot Hill for burial against the wishes of the town. Obviously
these are brave men. Their motivation, however, is not justice but boredom.
McQueen as Vin queries Brynner as Chris about the action in Dodge City,
"Seen any action up there?" "No," replies Chris, "people all settled down."
"Same everywhere." This theme, that the West, as they knew it, is passing is
one of the major themes of the film. The peasants plead with Chris to supply
them guns with which to protect their town. Chris suggests they instead hire
men: "Nowadays men are cheaper than guns." The Mexicans say they will
fight but Chris doubts that they comprehend how bloody this fight can become.
"Once it begins, you must be prepared for killing, more killing, and still more
killing until the reason for it is gone."

Chris and Vin take the job and begin to round up other down-and-out
gunmen to accompany them to the village. James Coburn is a specialist with
a knife. Robert Vaughn plays the fast gun who fears that the next fight will
be his last. Bernardo O'Reilly is the name of Charles Bronson's character, a
man who fits in nowhere, a gunfighter who has been reduced to odd jobs. Horst
Bucholz is the young innocent who thinks he wants to become a gunman. He
says to Chris, "Your gun has got you everything you have." To which
McQueen's Vin replies, "Home ... none, wife ... none, kids ... none." What
they have they given up is balanced in the eyes of Lee (Vaughn): "Men you
step aside for ... none, none alive!" The kid says, "This is the kind of arith-
metic I like." "So did I when I was your age," laments Chris.

The strength of the film is less in its action sequences than in its character building. Each character is clearly defined. Lee, played by Robert
Vaughn, is both offensive and sympathetic. On the one hand, he is an oily,
arrogant, dandy who claims to have killed all of his enemies. On the other
hand, he admits privately to terrible fears and nightmares. "I've lost count of
my enemies." He is on the run from his enemies and from himself. He sees
the irony of signing on with a group heading for a bloody fight calling himself "the deserter, hiding out in the middle of a battlefield." The audience

suspects that what he is really after is a quick death in combat that will end his flight and the inevitable decline of his skills. He snatches at five flies on the table with his gun hand and comes away with one. "There was a time when I would have caught all five," he says.

As the story progresses, some of the villagers want the gunmen to leave. They cannot stand the killing. Even the seven gunmen speak of getting out. Chris invokes the code of the West: "You forget one thing, we took a contract." Vin challenges, "It's not the kind any court would enforce." "That's just the kind you have to keep," retorts Chris.

After one clash turns sour, several of the gunmen are captured. Calvera, magnanimous in victory, gives them the chance to save themselves by disarming them and ordering them to ride out, disgraced but alive. Vin reflects on his future, "Maybe I could put my gun away, settle down." But we know that this is against his nature. One of the enduring lessons of the Western is that a man cannot deny his nature. Shane could not; Marshal Kane in *High Noon* (1952) could not, and neither can the seven. They ride back, some of them they know, to certain death. It is a magnificent moment, an heroic moment, in the film.

The climactic battle is desperate, violent, and, of course, victorious for the seven. As Calvera lies dying on the ground, a startled quizzical look on his face, he says, "You came back! For a place like this, men like you. Why?" They make no reply, but the answer had come earlier from Lee when they turned back to town. "Go on Lee, you don't owe anything to anybody," said Chris. "Except myself," was the reply.

The screenplay for *The Magnificent Seven* was written by William Roberts and his best soliloquies are by two unlikely characters. The first, Bernardo O'Reilly, Charles Bronson's taciturn misfit, is adopted by the children of the town during the course of the film. When they compare their own fathers to the heroic gunmen unfavorably, he chastises them. "Your fathers are not cowards. Your fathers are much braver because they bear responsibility. And this responsibility is like a great rock which weights them down, bends and twists them until they are under the ground. This is courage. I have never had that kind of courage." And in the end the lesson of *The Magnificent Seven* is that of the enduring qualities of the land and the people of the land, the peasant farmers. After most of the seven are killed in their victory, the youngest, Chico, decides to stay behind because of love. The old village wise man, played with dignity by Vladimir Sokoloff, speaks the film's moral to the departing Chris and Vin. "Only the farmers remain. They are like the land. You are like the wind, blowing over the land and passing on." In the typical Western ending (not a cliche because it is fitting), the heroes ride off into the distance ... and into the past.

The Magnificent Seven is as much a pleasure to watch today as it was three decades ago. It was not a pleasure to make. Steve McQueen and Yul

Brynner did not work well together. "I think I represented a threat to him," was McQueen's explanation. "He doesn't ride very well, and he doesn't know anything about quick draws and that stuff. I know horses. I know guns. I was in my element and he wasn't."[7] It might also have been the result of the strong cast, including many future stars, and Brynner's inability to dominate the screen. Brynner had started his film career with a series of blockbuster hits: *The King and I* (1956), *The Ten Commandments* (1956), *Anastasia* (1956), and *The Brothers Karamazov* (1958). After a half-dozen forgettable films, perhaps he was feeling the pressure of trying to regain that initial success.[8] For the first time McQueen's name appeared above the title of the film. While Brynner feared decline McQueen was, from this point on, either star or co-star in all his films, the first star to make the transition from television to movie.[9] Or maybe Brynner resented Steve's attempts to expand a part with limited dialogue by attracting attention in the background with bits of "business."

John Sturges, who had directed *Bad Day at Black Rock* (1954), *The Old Man and the Sea* (1958), and *Gunfight at the OK Corral* (1957), got the most out of his actors. They worked in the remote Cuernavaca, Mexico, where Steve celebrated his thirtieth birthday with a big party highlighted by tossing Robert Vaughn in the pool. Vaughn almost made it doubly memorable; he couldn't swim!

Freed from television obligations after the end of *Wanted: Dead or Alive*, McQueen threw himself into his movie roles. *The Great Escape* (1963), *Love with a Proper Stranger* (1963), *The Cincinnati Kid* (1965): after six years and eight feature films, McQueen returned to the Western genre which had made him a star. In all of the above films McQueen dominated with that innocent charm, latent sexuality, and, what one of his biographers has called an easygoing quality "on the surface but inside a charge of dynamite waiting to be detonated."[10]

Nevada Smith (1966) would seem to have everything going for it. The director was Henry Hathaway, a veteran of fifty-four films, half of them Westerns. The cast, as strong as that of *The Magnificent Seven*, included Karl Malden, Brian Keith, Paul Fix, Pat Hingle, Arthur Kennedy, Raf Vallone, Martin Landau, Howard De Silva and Suzanne Pleshette. There was a difference, however. The earlier film had included many budding stars, but the cast of *Nevada Smith* contained only competent supporting players. This left it to the star and script to carry the weight. Both failed. The film had no zip. It meandered. From the opening sequence when three men murder the hero's father and torture, rape, and kill his Indian mother, the direction of the film is obvious.[11] McQueen's character will track down each man and carry out his revenge at whatever the cost. The audience understands and sympathizes with Max (McQueen), but his base motivation, revenge, allows no room for the kind of elevating sentiments and actions that redeemed the gunmen of *The Magnificent Seven*.

As Max (McQueen's character is called Nevada only briefly and near the end of the film) trails the men, the audience sees beautiful natural vistas. These are the mountains that, in a later film, McQueen will long to ride again as Tom Horn. Max is befriended by a solitary peddler, Jonas Cord (played by Brian Keith), a gun salesman who teaches him to shoot. When they part, Cord leaves Max with the advice to plan his moves, never walk away from a fight but pick his place for it, and "don't even trust a friend."

Max first tracks down Jesse Coe, played by Martin Landau. Max kills Jesse in a gunfight. The action sequence is as unexciting as is the love interest, a Kiowa Indian girl. He then takes up pursuit of the second man, Bowdre (played by Arthur Kennedy) and deliberately allows himself to be captured following a robbery to get into prison with Bowdre. Suspicious of Max, Bowdre is won over when Max saves his life. They plan an escape together, and during a fight Max kills Bowdre. Pleshette plays the romantic interest here. But she sends Max away, even as she dies of snakebite, bitter that he has used her to kill Bowdre. "You are a dirty low animal."

In the final section, Max tracks Tom Fitch (Karl Malden) to the California gold fields. After several inconclusive and interminable diversions, Max gains the confidence of his final victim. In the course of a gold shipment robbery, Max stalks Fitch. Wounded several times, Fitch begs Max to finish him off. Inexplicably, Max refuses, drops his gun, and rides off, saying only, "You're just not worth killin'!" Max has never shown any remorse or hesitation before, even in the face of the pleas of a Catholic priest, to change his ways. Max is obsessed with revenge, but fails to fulfill it in the end. As Max rides off the audience is left to wonder what will become of him, and why he has acted so contrary to his history and personality.

Nevada Smith is not an important Western. It is disappointing because it squanders an excellent cast and does not fit well into any of the major themes evidenced in other films of the 1960s. It does not fit into the "professional" mold as did *The Magnificent Seven* (1960), nor does it evidence the increasingly important "end of the frontier" theme of *Ride the High Country* (1962) or *Lonely Are the Brave* (1962). There is a good deal of graphic violence but this is not as pronounced as that in *The Wild Bunch* (1968). It is hard to determine why this film fails. The cast is strong, but there is no fire, not even in McQueen. Certainly there is no passion between McQueen and Suzanne Pleshette. Maybe this was because they knew each other so well. McQueen had known Suzanne since he was a struggling actor in New York. They met when she was fourteen and a student at the High School for the Performing Arts. McQueen saw through her tough exterior and acted as a kind of older brother. She took on the task of teaching etiquette to the orphaned reform schooler.[12]

With their long friendship it is not surprising that they had a hard time pretending to be passionate in their love scenes. "That's the worst kissing I ever had in my life," Pleshette teased after one scene. The only fire connected with the film took place after the production was finished and flames swept the Hollywood sets at the farewell cast party.

McQueen's most successful years came after filming *Nevada Smith*. He formed his own production company, Solar Productions, and made a lucrative six-picture deal with Warner Bros. in 1967. *The Sand Pebbles* (1966), *The Thomas Crown Affair* (1968), and *Bullitt* (1968) were all commercial and artistic successes. He was at the peak. Then came a disappointing Faulkner venture, *The Reivers* (1969), and his long-anticipated car racing film, *Le Mans* (1971). The latter was a disaster and reflected the chaos in his own life. His long and stormy marriage foundered on the rocks of ego, and an insatiable appetite for alcohol, drugs, and women.

Of all the star's films, "the one closest to his heart was *Junior Bonner*, the story of a former rodeo champion who lived, much as did McQueen, out of step with the times."[13] The end of the West and the hero who has outlived his time was a favorite theme of director Sam Peckinpah. As early as 1962 he had directed a classic Western on this theme, *Ride the High Country*, with two of Hollywood's greatest Western film stars, Joel McCrea and Randolph Scott. His *The Wild Bunch* (1969), *The Ballad of Cable Hogue* (1970), and *Pat Garrett and Billy the Kid* (1973) also emphasized this theme.

Like all good Westerns, it is not the story of *Junior Bonner* that matters, it is how the story is told. Set in the contemporary Southwest, this is one of the best of many Westerns of the 1960s and 1970s that focused on the cowboy hero who has outlived his time. Both Junior Bonner and his father are anachronisms. The title sequence shows Junior competing and losing in a rodeo. It is apparent that he has seen better days, and the title song confirms our surmise. "You've been a rounder and a rambler much too long, comin' home, wishin' I could stay...." Junior cares for and feeds his horse before taking care of himself. Rounder or not, we know he is an honorable man who still subscribes to the code of the West.

Junior drives to the next town on the rodeo circuit, but this one is different—it is his hometown. Pulling his horse trailer behind his beat-up and dirty Cadillac convertible, he drives up to an old shack. Bulldozers roar around him; the noise is deafening. This is the house where his parents had lived, where he was raised, and now is deserted. We watch it destroyed to make way for a trailer park developed by Junior's younger brother, Curley Bonner.

Junior seeks out his father and finds him at the local hospital where he has been taken after a drunken accident. Ace, played by Robert Preston, is a lovable dreamer and a drunk who has sold his land to Curley and now lives on an allowance. Junior leaves and makes arrangements with the man who provides the stock for the rodeo, Ben Johnson. He will rig the draw so that Junior can once again ride Sunshine, the prize bull. Junior talks to his long-suffering mother (Ida Lupino) and goes to dinner at his brother's house. Curley (Joe Don Baker) is a successful businessman but he has sold his soul for money. He tries to buy Junior's soul as well. Junior does nothing when Curley calls him "some sort of motel cowboy," but when he also insults their father, Junior sends him flying through the window with one punch.

Before the rodeo, Junior and Ace Bonner, now escaped from the hospital, share a bottle, do some dancing and flirting, ride in a parade, and start a barroom brawl. Ace confides that he wants to go to Australia to prospect for gold. He still has a dream, but he needs a grubstake that Junior cannot provide. The end of the film is no surprise. Junior rides the prize bull, buys his father an airplane ticket to Australia with the winnings, then hooks his horse trailer behind his tattered Caddy and rides out of town to the next rodeo. The end for Junior is near, but not just yet.

Peckinpah and McQueen confounded expectations while making *Junior Bonner* by getting along famously. The location shooting in Prescott, Arizona, used many local people but was built on the fine character acting of Ben Johnson, Joe Don Baker, and Ida Lupino. Peckinpah made the audience feel the dust and sweat in a distinctly unglamorous contemporary West just as he had done in *The Wild Bunch*. Ace Bonner was played believably by Robert Preston in a part unlike his usual dapper, urbane types. It was a mark of McQueen's skill that he easily dominated such a consummate scene stealer as Preston. McQueen made it look so easy. The audience has no difficulty accepting him as a broken-down, rodeo cowboy. A man who (in real life) loved machinery and did not get along with horses, rode easily in the saddle and did most of the rodeo stunts himself. His superior athletic abilities are convincing. The ability to make the viewer forget that he is Steve McQueen, the "star" and accept him as Junior Bonner is an achievement often beyond even the "greatest" actors. McQueen did not have the broad range of some, but he was almost always natural and believable. He dominated every scene, yet his art did not get in the way. Whether this was technique or presence, it was certainly "star quality."

McQueen's next film, *The Getaway* (1972), was not a critical success but it did bring him Ali MacGraw, who became his second wife. *Papillon* (1973), with Dustin Hoffman, was his biggest financial success, and in *The Towering Inferno* (1974) McQueen finally got top billing over his long-time acting rival, Paul Newman. For two decades McQueen had struggled upward always with his early Actors Studio competitor, Newman, ahead of him. Now he was on the top, a celebrity, an international super-star who reportedly made over $12 million on just one film. Steve McQueen did not make another film for four years and in six years he was dead.

Tom Horn was Steve McQueen's film. From the start of filming near Tucson, Arizona, in February 1979, he took charge of the film. Always difficult to work with, McQueen changed his mind, first delegating authority then taking it away. "Doing a 360," he called it, a car racing term. The Screen Actor's

Firing away—Steve McQueen as Tom Horn, one of the last great heroes of the American West—gets ready to battle it out with a group of cattle rustlers in this action-filled scene from the outdoor adventure drama, *Tom Horn*, a First Artists Presentation for Warner Bros. release.

Guild insisted that the film have a registered director. Four directors worked on the film before it was finished with final credit going to William Wiard. But McQueen was the real director and producer of the film. To that can be attributed the film's strengths and weaknesses. He was fascinated by the story and saw it as a metaphor for his own life. "The idea was one I could connect with today's high-powered business world. He (Tom Horn) is totally used by his employers and is eventually framed for murder. It's very applicable of the way some people, especially in the film business and in politics, use people they feel are lower than they are. It happens every day."[14]

The story of *Tom Horn* is again the story of the end of the frontier. The audience sees Tom first, through the titles, in the context of the landscape where he and his horse seem perfectly at home. The look is like a Western painting by Charles Russell, a rich, colorful, loving image emphasizing accuracy of detail. The audience is told that Tom Horn was a real person, a cavalry scout who had fought in the Apache wars and rode with Teddy Roosevelt and the Rough Riders. But it is now 1900 and Tom rides into a town on the frontier's end. After stabling his horse, Tom enters a hotel bar where he comes into jarring contact with the new urban America in the person of Gentleman

Jim Corbett. Corbett is traveling with a group of syncophants who toast his greatness and mock Tom by calling him "Tex." Tom responds by raising his glass to "Geronimo, a man so great that Jim Corbett there would have to stand on his mother's shoulders to kiss Geronimo's ass." Of course, there is a fight and Tom gets the worse of it. But he shows no fear and keeps his pride.

The next day a rancher, John Coble (Richard Farnsworth) searches out Tom as he sleeps off the beating. He finds Tom with his horse at the stable. "Are you, in fact, Tom Horn?" he asks. Coble calls him a "hero of the frontier." "Here in jerkville, where men are busy flicking dandruff off their mail order suits, they forget that it was men such as you who allow them to live out their dull little lives," he says. Coble wants Tom to take on the job of ridding the area of petty rustlers. Tom can use "any means" he sees fit. The big ranchers pledge total support. Tom says he will take their word on it.

Tom is introduced to the local ranchers at a big barbecue. "Welcome a vestige of that heroic era that we've just about lost," says John Coble. This makes Tom uncomfortable. He is further discomfited by the Maine lobsters they are served. Having earlier shown his skill with rope and rifle, Tom talks of the "high side of shooting and the low side of the law." What's the difference between a U.S. marshal and an assassin," he asks the local marshal, who without blinking an eye retorts, "Marshal's checks come in on time." Things are truly not like they were in the old West. Tom meets the local schoolteacher, playing by an as yet unknown Linda Evans. "I guess I've had a romance with the West since I was old enough to read," says the schoolmarm. "What was it like out in Indian territory?" "Lonely as hell," answers Tom.

Tom then begins to earn his pay, $200 for every rustler who "leaves." Singly or in small groups, Tom tracks them down, scares them off, or kills them. McQueen does a fine job with the action sequences. Our aging hero takes a horse to the schoolhouse and rides with the teacher, Glendolene. They romance gently. She falls in love with Horn whom she calls "a man of the old West trying to live in the new." Tom makes fun of her romantic conceptions: "Do you know how raggedy-assed the old West really was?" As they gaze at the mountains, she gently asks, "You love it out here don't you?" "Yes I do." Tom's feeling for the land is central to the film. It is ever-present.[15]

Tom is too good at his job and the numerous killings become embarrassing to the local ranchers. "It's time to divest ourselves," they conclude in private. Without the audience clearly knowing who did it, an innocent boy is shot from a great distance. Tom's sign, a rock under the victim's head, implicates him. Tom could not have done it, but he is blamed and fears the consequences. "What are you thinking?" Glendolene asks. "Thinking I want to run," he answers, but he does not run. The local corrupt sheriff invites Tom to his office and engages him in conversation, all of which is taken down by a hidden scribe, who has been told, "What I need is for Tom Horn to talk himself in a terrible tangle and for you to get it down on paper."

"The world is changing fast; a man had better get with it," begins the sheriff. "What is the best shot you ever made, Tom?" After some verbal fencing, Tom concedes noncommittally, "Well, if I killed that kid it's been the best shot I ever made—and the dirtiest trick I ever done." Tom is arrested and put into jail. His worst fear is realized; he has lost his freedom. Chill Wills, who plays the jailer, says, "I know how you love those hills. You can see a little bit of 'em from here" [through the window]. It is not enough; he tells John Coble, "I've been free all my life, John. I can see those hills over there but I can't touch 'em." At a public trial with a tent and vendors, Tom offers little defense. "You're goin' to do what you have to do." He has only one question, "Did anybody see me kill that kid?"

Tom is convicted and, after a futile escape attempt, brought to the gallows on November 20, 1903. A special automatic water-opened gallows is constructed, fittingly technological and "new-fangled." Tom will activate it by stepping on the trap door himself. "Makes me feel like I'll be committing suicide. Do you suppose that's what I've been doin' all these years, Sam?" he asks. The film ends when the trap door springs. Tom's Indian charms break and scatter, and on the screen the audience sees a statement swearing to Tom Horn's innocence signed by John C. Coble.

The Westerns of Steve McQueen amount to only four of his twenty-eight films. When *Wanted: Dead or Alive* is added, this is still insufficient to identity him with the genre in the way of John Wayne or Randolph Scott. Only one film, *The Magnificent Seven*, is considered in the top rank of Western movies. Yet each illustrated the themes popular with filmmakers of the day.

For those who love them, it is sad to have to admit that the Western is dead. But there can no longer be any doubt. The cause of death of the Western is problematical. The injection of graphic violence and steamy sex, along with the emphasis on "realistic" sweat and grime, deflowered the medium and stole its innocence and romance. By overemphasizing the "end of the frontier" and the aging Western hero who had outlived his time, the filmmakers of the 1960s and 1970s ran a good horse until its heart burst.

Immediately following his last Western, McQueen went to Chicago for the filming of a police thriller, *The Hunter*. Weakness, a chronic cough, and a constant low-grade temperature notwithstanding, he insisted, as he always had, on doing dangerous out-of-doors stunts. The strenuous filming was completed in early December 1979, and McQueen checked into Cedars-Sinai hospital for tests. He had been ill the year before but tests had shown nothing. This time X-rays indicated a problem in his right lung and surgery followed within days. The cancer they found was extensive and inoperable. Mesothelioma is a relatively rare type and was probably brought on by smoking and the inhaling of asbestos fibers from the fire-retardant clothing he wore through years of amateur race car driving.

His final year was a sad combination of fence-mending with old friends he had offended over the years and a desperate quest for a cure where none existed. In January 1980, he married Barbara Minty, his third wife. All three would be close to him at the end despite ill treatment by him over the years. Never giving up, he traveled to Mexico trying ever more extreme cures. The tabloid press followed him and exploited his agonized final months and days. Steve McQueen's heart stopped beating at his home in Santa Paula, California, on November 7th, 1980, the year of *Tom Horn*'s release.[16]

Today we debate when the moment of death takes place, when the heart stops beating or when the brain ceases all activity. To use the analogy with the Western, the brain, or the imagination and creativity of the Western, ossified over a long period. It was surely dead by the time of the release of *Heaven's Gate* (1980). The heart of the Western also weakened gradually, perhaps first noticeably so by *The Wild Bunch* (1968). The heart beat more slowly too, as fewer Westerns were made in the 1970s. The last strong beat came in 1976 with *The Shootist*. The final, faint beat of the Western's heart was Steve McQueen's *Tom Horn*.

Notes

1. Malachy McCoy, *Steve McQueen: The Unauthorized Biography* (Chicago, 1984), p. 79.

2. Curiously, also on the list was the name of the last Western role played by McQueen more than two decades later, *Tom Horn*.

3. Neile McQueen Toffel, *My Husband, My Friend* (New York, 1986), pp. 83–84; McCoy, pp. 49–51.

4. McCoy, pp. 94–95.

5. McCoy, pp. 52–53; Toffel, p. 87.

6. Gary Yoggy, "When Television Wore Six-Guns: Cowboy Heroes on TV," *Shooting Stars: Heroes and Heroines of Western Film*, Archie McDonald, ed. (Bloomingtom, 1987), pp. 242–243. Special thanks go to Gary Yoggy for his generous help in providing the author with taped episodes of *Wanted: Dead or Alive*.

7. McCoy, p. 86.

8. Ironically, the closest he would again come to that success was when he reprised the character of Chris, this time as a robot, in *Westworld* (1973).

9. Toffel, pp. 100–104; McCoy, p. 88; Penina Spiegel, *McQueen: The Untold Story of a Bad Boy in Hollywood* (Garden City, 1986), pp. 113–14. Mention should be made of the theme music in *The Magnificent Seven*, composed by Elmer Bernstein. It enhanced the drama of the film and enjoyed a life of its own as the background music for the Marlboro cigarette ads.

10. McCoy, p. 88.

11. The bodies are found by a farmer and his wife. The wife is played, in an uncredited role, by the great silent film star Lilian Gish. Strother Martin and Bob Steele appear later in the film, also uncredited.

12. When she and McQueen went off location in Louisiana to eat a fancy dinner in New Orleans, Suzanne whispered under her breath to her partner which fork to use. She was as astonished as his wife had been and many others were to be in his life when Steve ordered two steaks at once. "Why are you doing that?" she asked. "Because they might run out in the kitchen and there wouldn't be enough," he replied. Steve could never get enough of anything. Spiegel, pp. 173–76.

13. Grady Ragsdale, *Steve McQueen: The Final Chapter* (Ventura, CA, 1983), p. 93.

14. Toffel, pp. 289–90; Ragsdale, p. 98.

15. In one gunbattle Tom's horse is shot. He reacts with vengeful outrage by shooting the murderer dead, then plugging his body four more times. "You killed my horse, you son-of-a-bitch," he says as he pets the horse's body lovingly.

16. Toffel, pp. 288–325; Spiegel, pp. 319–343; Ragsdale, pp. 97–196.

James Arness:
Television's Quintessential
Western Hero

by Gary A. Yoggy

James Arness has been described as "the Virginian, Wyatt Earp, Gary Cooper, Shane and John Wayne all lumped into a single, definitive, towering good guy."[1] For more than four decades James Arness has personified the Western hero, towering head and shoulders—both physically and charismatically—over a multitude of television cowboy stars. First as Matt Dillon, the stoic and courageous marshal of Dodge City in *Gunsmoke* (1955–1975), and later as Zeb Macahan, the tough, free-spirited mountain man in *How the West Was Won* (1977–1979), Arness became the most filmed actor in the history of cinema and television. His recent appearances have been limited to made-for-television movies such as *The Alamo: 13 Days to Glory* (1987) and a remake of *Red River* (1988), but his visage can be seen somewhere in the world at virtually any hour of the day in reruns of the popular *Gunsmoke*.

Of Norwegian descent, Arness was born James King Aurness on May 26, 1923, in Minneapolis, Minnesota. His ancestry was distinguished. His paternal grandfather, Dr. Peter Andrew Aurness, studied medicine at the University of Ohio and later moved to Minnesota, where he was not only a surgeon but an inventor and sculptor of some renown. Fittingly, Arness' great-great-grandfather, William Pierce King, was a United States marshal during the 1840s in Wisconsin. Franklin Pierce, fourteenth president of the United States, was a relative.[2] Peter Graves, Arness' younger brother, was the star of the television adventures series *Mission: Impossible*.

Described by his mother as "a magnificent, sensitive primitive,"[3] Arness was a shy and withdrawn child. Self-conscious about his height, he was a loner in high school. Shunning team sports, he preferred hunting, fishing, and sailing to football or basketball. His only social activities involved singing in church and school choral groups, although he did appear in a supporting role in a school play, *The Gift of the Magi*.

Drafted into the Army during his freshman year (1942-1943) at Beloit (Wisconsin) College, Arness was wounded in the leg on the Anzio beachhead in 1944. As a result, that leg was an inch shorter than the other and caused Arness to limp noticeably when tired. Receiving a medical discharge in 1945, he returned to Minneapolis, where he attended the University of Minnesota and became a substitute announcer at radio station WLOL.

Restless and uneasy, Arness drifted to Hollywood where he appeared in several amateur theatrical productions. This led to an unsuccessful screen test at Warner Bros. An agent named Leo Lance introduced Arness to film producer Dore Schary, who gave him a role as one of Loretta Young's three brothers in *The Farmer's Daughter* (1947). Although the film was successful, earning an Oscar for Young, it did not advance Arness' career. Discouraged, he beachcombed in Mexico and worked at various jobs while collecting veteran's benefits and unemployment insurance until Schary gave him the role of a corporal in MGM's blockbuster war film, *Battleground* (1949). Amanda Blake, who later played Kitty on *Gunsmoke*, also had a minor role in the film.

Battleground helped establish Arness as an actor. In the next three years he appeared in more than twenty films. His first Western role was in *Wagonmaster* (1950), an RKO production, in which he played the "fourth moronic brother in a family of killers." Although he did not have a line of dialogue, Arness effectively utilized all of his six-foot, six-inch frame to convey the menace and evil of his character. It also gave Arness a chance to work with master film director, John Ford.

Other Westerns followed in which the hulking Arness usually was cast in a supporting role as an outlaw. He gained valuable experience by appearing with such established actors as Joel McCrea (*Stars in My Crown*, 1950; *The Lone Hand*, 1953), Rod Cameron (*Cavalry Scout*, 1951), Stephen McNally (*The Wyoming Mail*, 1950) and Robert Ryan (*Horizons West*, 1952).

It was a non–Western role, however, that earned Arness his first critical attention. Playing the unjustly accused title character in *The People Against O'Hara* for MGM in 1951, he was described by *New York Herald-Tribune* film critic James S. Barstow, Jr., as displaying "an authoritative blend of belligerence and fear surprising for a relative newcomer."[4] Because of the drawing power of stars, Spencer Tracy and Pat O'Brien, the film did well at the box office and gave Arness valuable screen exposure. Still, time after time, he would be considered for a role but would lose the part when the film's star refused to work with him because, according to Arness, "I was just too damned big."[5]

Ironically Arness got his most publicized role of this period because of his size—as the giant vegetable-monster in Howard Hawks' science-fiction classic, *The Thing* (1951). Unfortunately, Arness was unrecognizable in a jumpsuit and puttied forehead, and had no dialogue whatever. Arness later appeared to better advantage in another science-fiction classic, *Them!* (1954), in which he played an FBI agent.

Arness now could get work, but his roles offered little challenge or hope of stardom. Discouraged, Arness decided to return to the stage. He appeared as the warrior Ajax in the Greek play *Penelope*, at a small, but well-known little theater called the Player's Ring. Taking the part was a gamble. His salary had steadily risen to nearly $1,000 a week, but every casting director in Hollywood knew that actors who worked in the Player's Ring did so for nothing. Taking the stage role could jeopardize his future in films.

Once again, luck was with Arness. Talent scouts from the newly-formed Wayne-Fellows Company, a partnership formed by actor John Wayne and writer/producer Robert M. Fellows, which later became the Batjac Company when Wayne bought out his partner's interest in 1954, came to the play on opening night. Impressed with Arness' potential, they took him to meet Wayne's associates and within three weeks he was offered a contract. Wayne already was acquainted with Arness. They had met through Arness' agent and Wayne liked the younger man's size, his walk, and physical stature. They also shared May 26 as their birthday.

Wayne assisted Arness in obtaining his best role so far in his first film for Wayne-Fellows, *Big Jim McLain* (1952). In the title role, Wayne played an investigator who worked for the Committee on Un-American Activities of the House of Representatives to expose a Communist spy ring in Hawaii. Arness played Mal Baxter, a Korean–war hero who worked with McLain for HUAC. An integral part of the first half of the film, Arness appears in a number of important scenes before his character is killed. While Arness did well in his role, the film was considered by most critics to be no more than "a shallow propaganda piece against the evils of Communism."[6] But the public liked it and it was much more commercially successful than most anti–Communist films of the 1950s, grossing close to $3 million in the United States alone.

Arness was given roles in three more of Wayne's films. In *Island in the Sky* (1953) he plays a pilot who helps rescue Wayne and the crew of his transport plane after it crashed in a frozen area north of Labrador during World War II. The part gave Arness the chance to display a broad Southern accent and much more personality than any of his previous roles. He considered it the best role he had in pictures so far and credited Wayne with giving him the opportunity to expand his acting abilities. His was to have been a smaller part, but Wayne said, "Doggone it, Jim's been around a while and we owe him a good role. Let's let him play this part."[7]

Arness was not as fortunate in the other two Wayne films. In *Hondo* (1953), considered by most critics to be one of the better Wayne Westerns, Arness only appeared in the final ten minutes of the film as Lennie, a rather unlikeable Army scout. Although given only a few lines of dialogue, he did get to redeem himself by saving Wayne's life.

The Sea Chase (1955), an adventure film set during World War II, provided Arness with another minor supporting role as a seaman loyal to Wayne, who played an anti–Nazi German captain. With his blond locks cropped short, he was hardly distinguishable from half a dozen other supporting actors.

Meanwhile, Arness had married and now had a wife and three children to support. In 1948, while appearing at the Pasadena Playhouse in *Candida*, he had fallen in love with a brown-eyed, black-haired actress named Virginia Chapman. They had a daughter, Jenny Lee, and a son, Rolf, in addition to Craig, Virginia's son by a previous marriage, whom Arness adopted.

When *Gunsmoke* entered Arness' life, television was still a relatively new medium. His experience in that field had been limited to a supporting role in an episode of the popular juvenile Western, *The Lone Ranger* ("Matter of Courage," April 28, 1950), and a few minor parts on dramatic anthologies such as *Lux Video Theater*.

Considered television's first "adult" Western, *Gunsmoke* originally was developed for CBS radio in 1952 by director Norman Macdonnell and writer John Meston. The series was brought to television three years later by its creators and writer/director Charles Marquis Warren. John Wayne was their first choice to play the lead as Matt Dillon, marshal of Dodge City, Kansas, but considering himself a "*movie*" actor and not wanting to be tied down to a weekly show, Wayne rejected the offer and recommended Arness instead.[8]

At Wayne's suggestion, *Them* was screened by Warren, Macdonnell, Hubbell Robinson, vice president of television programming for CBS in New York, and William Dozier, programming vice president in Hollywood. Following the screening, according to Macdonnell, Dozier said, "That's it," and there was no further discussion of the matter: Arness would be asked to test for the role.[9] Warren had worked previously with Arness in the film *Hellgate*, which he had directed for Lippert in 1952.

Fearing that people "would get sick of seeing" his face so often and that he would be "typed," Arness initially refused to test for the role. Meanwhile, CBS began thinking of older men for the part—Randolph Scott and Van Heflin, among others. Eventually twenty-six actors tested for the role, including radio's Matt Dillon, William Conrad, and Raymond Burr, television's eventual Perry Mason, but none of them fit the Dillon image and Arness was approached again.

This time Arness decided to discuss his doubts with Wayne. "The show is mine if I want it," he told him, "but I'm still dreaming of pictures." Wayne replied,

> Look, it's rough trying to compete in this movie business with guys like me or Gary Cooper or Greg Peck. We've been at it a long time and our names mean something at the box office. But your name doesn't mean a thing—anyway not yet. Besides you're a tall galoot, and Coop's not going to play opposite you in a film unless you're the heavy. This means you're going to wind up playing character parts. Don't be a fool, Jim. Take the TV series.[10]

Convinced by this sensible advice, Arness accepted the role that earned him television stardom.

Wayne believed so strongly in Arness that he agreed to introduce the first episode of *Gunsmoke* on the air despite the objections of a cigarette company with whom he had an endorsement contract because the program was sponsored by a competing tobacco company. Viewers who tuned to CBS on Saturday evening, September 10, 1955, saw the Duke make a prophesy, the truth of which even Wayne could not have realized:

> I'm here to tell you about a Western, a new television show called *Gunsmoke*.... I think it's the best thing of its kind that's come along. I hope you'll agree with me. It's honest, it's adult, it's realistic. When I first heard about the show *Gunsmoke*, I knew there was only one man to play in it—James Arness. He's a young fella and maybe new to some of you, but I've worked with him and I predict he'll be a big star. So you might as well get used to him like you've had to get used to me....

Wayne's image gave way to that of a tall, lean cowboy, silhouetted against the sky, as he strode up a hill lined with tombstones. In calm, thoughtful, but forceful tones, the deep voice that was to become so familiar to television viewers introduced the first *Gunsmoke* story:

> If some of these men had argued a little, they might not be here. Arguing doesn't fill any graves. Take me, I'm a U.S. marshal. How many times I'd rather have argued than gone for guns. Take Dodge City over there. "Gomorrah of the plains," they call it ... jump off spot. People coming and going all the time, good, bad and worse. Tempers high. A man'll draw his gun quicker to prove his point than he'll draw on his logic. That's where I come in, whether they like it or not. When they draw their gun, somebody's gotta be around—somebody on the law's side....

Western buffs settled back to watch what most thought would be just another thirty-minute version of the routine "shoot 'em up" Westerns they had seen for years. They expected the marshal to be tough—and he was. They expected him to be a man of few words—and he was. They expected him to be tall—and he definitely was. The show seemed to follow the tried and true formula. Within the first few minutes, Marshal Dillon has a confrontation with a vicious killer named Dan Gratt. They face off on the main street of Dodge City in Kansas Territory—one of the wildest and wickedest prairie towns of the 1870s.

"Ah'm bad," the killer announces as he steps over the body of a lawman he has just gunned down. "You want me, Marshal, you got to come git me...." Dillon brushes aside the beautiful saloon girl Kitty, who tries to stop him, steps off the plank sidewalk and reaches for his trusty Colt. Then, violating every rule of the Western genre, the bad guy outdraws and outshoots the hero, leaving him writhing in the dust.

In homes throughout America, men and women blinked in disbelief and pulled their chairs a little closer to the TV set. Here was something unique: a Western hero not invincible, a Western story not predictable.

In the end Dillon recovered and got his man. Not, however, because he was faster or stronger or even braver, but because he was smarter: he figured out that Gratt maneuvered his adversaries into coming so close that he could fire without aiming and still not miss. From across a hotel lobby, Gratt fires first, but misses. The slower but more accurate Dillon does not.

Viewers were intrigued. Dillon was clearly a hero—but he did not perform heroic acts in the conventional way. He seemed genuinely disturbed when he had to kill a man. In the words of a British journalist, "He appeared more trigger sorry than trigger happy."[11]

Each week more people tuned in to see this Western that broke all the traditional rules of the genre. There were few chases and even fewer barroom brawls. The hero did not go around warbling songs to beautiful damsels in distress. He did not even ride a white steed that could fly like the wind and rescue his master when evildoers had gotten the best of him. Indeed, Arness wrote a press release for CBS in 1958 entitled "No Trick Horses for Me," in which he explained,

> When the occasion demands, I ride a big buckskin gelding named Buck, chosen not because of his intellect, nor his fidelity, but because he is very large and only a very large horse will fit me ... in the real old West, horses were cheap and a cowboy—or a U.S. marshal seldom had a favorite. He didn't keep a horse that long. He'd swap him off on a long trip for a fresh horse, or sell him between jobs knowing he could buy another when he needed it to avoid stable bills.[12]

Dillon did not always wear a white hat; sometimes it was black, as in "Kite's Reward," (November 12, 1955). And Dillon's permanently lame assistant, Chester, superbly played by Dennis Weaver, and the crusty, but dependable Doc Adams, a tour de force for Milburn Stone, were not traditional comedy sidekicks, though one might chuckle occasionally at their good-natured banter.

Gunsmoke also took the Western heroine down from her pedestal and brought her into the real world in the form of saloon "hostess" Kitty Russell, who could be both tough and tender with equal conviction. There was even the hint of an off-screen relationship between Matt and Kitty. Still, when Kitty accused him early in the series of not knowing much about women, he responded that "he hadn't made it his life's work." As Arness explained it,

> The man and woman relationship must be subtle. It has to be. As a hero, I represent law and order—authority. People look up to me ... I must be respected. I can't go too far in romancing Kitty. But I think on *Gunsmoke* we have shown that a frontier hero can sit with a girl and even kiss her—and get away with it.[13]

Jim Arness (standing, left), Milburn Stone (right) as Doc Adams, and Dennis Weaver (seated) as Chester in *Gunsmoke*.

Amanda Blake had this to say about their relationship in an interview in 1958: "Kitty is in love with Matt although she knows they will never marry. He faces death every day. He can't marry her because he doesn't want to leave her a widow."[14]

In less subtle ways Dillon differed from television's more traditional Western heroes. Almost every time he went to the Long Branch, he had a beer or whiskey, but never enough to impair his capacity for sound reasoning or straight shooting.

Most unorthodox of all, Dillon frequently violated the unwritten "code of the West" that had governed the actions of virtually all previous cowboy heroes: he did not always let his adversaries draw first. Sometimes he shot them from ambush or even in the back. Yet he retained his heroic image because, in the words of Arness, "Matt is very human and has all the failings and drives common to anyone who is trying to do a difficult job the best he knows how."[15]

According to Norman Macdonnell, all of the killing and violence was justifiable because "it arose out of the situation and was not employed for its own sake."[16] For example, in "Kittycaught" (January 18, 1958), Matt and Chester are forced to ambush two bank robbers who have taken Kitty hostage and sworn to kill her should anyone follow them. When Chester questions the fact that they are going to shoot these men in cold blood, the marshal's only response is, "Can you think of any other way?" In "No Indians" (December 8, 1956), Chester and Matt ambush a gang of rustlers who have been murdering and scalping the families they have robbed so Indians will be blamed. Again, the lawmen seem justified in gunning down these brutal killers.

In yet another departure from conventional heroics, Dillon goads a cowardly gunman who will only draw on men he knows he can beat in a gunfight so he can eliminate this brutal killer ("The Killer," May 26, 1956). Of course, when the man tries to shoot Matt in the back, the marshal is justified in killing him.

Still, Dillon was not a violent man by nature and he sometimes even wondered if he was the right man to fill a marshal's job. Most other lawmen took a simple view of their work. They represented "good," while all lawbreakers represented "bad." For them, there was nothing in between.

To Matt Dillon, however, there was an in-between, and it was a sizable one. He had jailed many men whom he did not consider a threat to society. Some had just gotten off to a bad start; others preferred to take the easy way rather than try to earn an honest living; still others probably liked the danger and excitement of a life outside the law. Most of these men were not basically vicious. To Dillon, just a few men were totally "bad," and not many were wholely "good." A man was considered "good" if he was reasonably honest and kept his word with others most of the time. If he slipped once in a while, no one would blame him—if he did not slip too badly. If he did make a serious mistake, Christian standards dictated that he should be forgiven. Thus was the moral side of Matt Dillon's world filled with not black and white but with various shades of gray.

James Arness' Matt Dillon was a lawman more concerned with the whys of men's actions, more aware of the limitations that governed human beings, more attuned to his moral than his legal responsibilities. All in all, he was more thoughtful and introspective than most Western men of action.

In "Hot Spell" (September 17, 1955), Matt protects a cruel and arrogant gunfighter who has just been released from jail from a mob of righteous townsmen who want to lynch him. Siding with a potentially dangerous stranger against his friends and neighbors, while the stranger mocks him, is a real test for Dillon's conscience. He is able to hold his head high in the face of scorn and abuse because he knows he is protecting his fellow townsmen *from themselves* and, more importantly, he is defending the law against the onslaught of those who stand to lose the most if it is ignored.

On another occasion ("Gone Straight," February 9, 1957), Dillon considers quitting rather than having to arrest a former outlaw with a questionable past who has reformed. After the man is killed in a gunfight protecting yet another reformed outlaw, Matt tells his widow that if he had decided to take her husband in "…it would have been my last official act." Here he dispensed justice tempered with mercy, showing a greater concern for the spirit than for the letter of the law.

In "Cow Doctor" (November 5, 1955), Matt is incensed when Doc is stabbed and seriously wounded by a farmer. He tells the man that if Doc dies, so will he—"…if Doc doesn't come out of this all right—I'll quit being a marshal—I'll come after you as a plain man—looking for revenge." Dillon is more than just a cold upholder of the law—he is a human being with real emotions.

There is also a gentle side to Matt Dillon. On several occasions he becomes so sick and tired of the killing that he resigns from his job. In "Bloody Hands" (February 16, 1957), Matt kills three outlaws. The fourth, whom he captures alive, accuses him of being a "butcher." Matt suddenly feels disgust and shame for the blood that he has been forced to shed in carrying out his duties as a U.S. marshal and turns in his badge.

Seeking peace, quiet, and escape from the responsibilities he has carried, Matt takes Kitty fishing. It is there that Chester tracks him down and begs him to take back his badge. Dodge City is again threatened with violence and there is no one else who can prevent the impending chaos and anarchy:

CHESTER:	I been thinkin' lately a whole lot about all this and there's just somethin' that you been forgettin'!
DILLON:	That so?
CHESTER:	Yeah, that's so. It's men like Stangler and Brand. Cause

> they gotta be stopped! That's all! They gotta be! I'd do
> it if I could, but I can't. I just ain't good enough. Most
> men ain't, but you are. It's kinda too bad for ya that ya
> are, but that's the way it is and there ain't a thing in the
> world ya can do about it.

The episode ends as Matt reluctantly, but decisively, straps on the gun Chester has brought for him.

In a much later episode, "Snap Decision" (September 17, 1966), Matt again questions the purpose of his office. He has killed a horse thief, who was once his friend, when he mistakenly thought the man was about to shoot him. Actually, he was trying to save Matt from a bounty hunter who was about to shoot him in the back. Matt ultimately has second thoughts about resigning when he disagrees with the peace-keeping methods of his successor.

Not all the stories on *Gunsmoke* conclude with conventional "happy endings." In "Kite's Reward" (November 12, 1955), Matt tries to help a former outlaw reform by persuading him to stop wearing a gun. Later a bounty hunter shows up in Dodge looking for the young man, who forgets he has taken the gun off. When he instinctively reaches for it, the bounty hunter kills him. Rightly or wrongly, the marshal feels responsible for the young man's death.

Perhaps Dillon's attitude toward death is best articulated in the Boot Hill opening to "How to Die for Nothing" (June 23, 1956), written by Sam Peckinpah:

MATT'S VOICE: Men die for a lot of reasons. I've even heard of worthy
                ones—like a man who's willing to face it for the good
                that might come after. But he's a far different breed
                than most of this Boot Hill trash. These people die for
                fool's reasons—a spilt drink ... a wrong card ... an
                imagined insult. But the worst is a man who dies for
                nothing ... for no reason at all.

Gunsmoke's basic premise was simple: a U.S. marshal trying to maintain law and order in Dodge City, Kansas, during the 1870s. Within this framework a wide variety of characters and situations evolved over a twenty-year period.

The series passed through three different stages: the first six years of thirty-minute programs, which were based mostly upon the radio scripts of John Meston; the early hour-long episodes, which permitted characters to display several aspects of their personalities and move through a series of action/reactions; and, finally the anthology format, which was instituted after the network demanded that the level of violence be reduced drastically. Since *Gunsmoke* always had relied more on characterization than action, the shift to more nonviolent story resolutions was possible. Furthermore, the introduction of guest stars to play featured roles moved responsibility away from the more action-oriented continuing characters such as Dillon.

Through all the changes Dillon remained the focal point, backbone, and protector of the community. Dodge City would revert to anarchy and chaos were it not for its lawman. The town had no security in laws; its only security was its lawman, for laws could be subverted but lawmen could not. This is the continuing message of *Gunsmoke*.[17]

It is apparent just how much Matt Dillon means to the town in an episode entitled, "Dead Man's Law" (January 8, 1968). Here we see why people have put their faith in a lawman instead of "laws." When Matt is shot and left for dead by an outlaw, the town is left to police itself. Festus and Newly, the deputies, try to maintain order, but their authority is challenged by two men who organize a cattlemen's association and proceed to raise the ugly spector of vigilante justice.

When Festus leaves to find Matt, the town falls into anarchy. The cattlemen convince the townspeople to hire a shotgun-toting killer as their acting marshal. Doc urges them to wait until Festus returns,

> For twelve years, you've had law and order in Dodge City because one man enforced the law. Now that he's not here you're willing to give the town away to the first incompetent that comes along with a shotgun and is anxious to use it.

Unfortunately, that is just what happens as the killer is given full authority to enforce the law with his shotgun. Suspected lawbreakers are shot down, Doc is beaten, and Kitty is harassed for objecting to these strong-arm tactics. Eventually Matt, who has been nursed back to health by an Indian, returns, and regains control of the town. Once again law and order prevail.

It is clear that the limits and enforcement of the law lie with a man and not with the people who seem impotent without their lawman. What makes Matt Dillon unique is that he knows the people of his town, understands them, and is willing, in extenuating circumstances, to bend the law for them.

The people need to be reminded of their marshal's importance to them. In "The Wreckers" (September 11, 1967), Matt is injured and taken prisoner by a gang of outlaws who demand a sizable ransom from the citizens of Dodge City. Doc and Kitty try to raise the money, even though they suspect that the outlaws will kill the marshal anyway. At a heated meeting held in the Long Branch, Doc describes what Matt has meant to the town:

> There's not a single person in this room that doesn't owe him a debt of some kind ... not one of ya! Now there's not enough money in the whole state of Kansas to pay another man to do what Matt's done, even if they could, and they couldn't. Now we built this town and we've seen it grow because Matt gave us the security of knowing that Tate Crocker and a hundred others like him can't come in here and burn it to the ground every time they think about it.... It may be his job, but who else would do it or who could? And what about the other debts you owe him? ...

Doc goes on to cite the debts individual citizens owe Matt. When Kitty delivers the money to the outlaws, she explains to Matt, "If you think they don't care, there's ten dollars on that table for every man, woman and child in Dodge City...." Matt, of course, eventually escapes and reaffirms the townspeople's confidence in him. But now they have been required to provide tangible proof of his value to them.

Except for a few more lines on his craggy face and the slight trace of a gray hair here and there, Matt Dillon changed little over the years. There is, perhaps, some discernible modification in his relationship toward women. In "Sarah" (October 16, 1972), viewers learn about a girl that Dillon almost married long before coming to Dodge City when he was a young deputy in San Antonio. He even pretends to be her husband in a futile effort to protect her from the advances of several outlaws.

On September 24, 1973, an unprecedented situation occurred on *Gunsmoke*. In "Matt's Love Story," Matt falls in love—but not with Kitty. While suffering from amnesia after being ambushed by a gunman he is trailing, he is rescued by a widow who nurses him back to health. Their attraction to each other is shown, first through a series of looks and then with a passionate kiss. Finally, the inevitable happens—albeit offscreen during a commercial break. All is back to normal by the end of the episode, for when Matt regains his memory he realizes he must return to his responsibilities in Dodge City, and to Kitty, of course. But another aspect of Dillon's character—perhaps the only one still hidden after eighteen seasons—has been revealed.

As time went on, Arness the actor became more absorbed by and more protective of the character with whom he had become so closely identified. In an interview in 1957, he explained,

> There's a real sense of satisfaction in this. I wouldn't trade roles with anybody on TV. It has quality. It has something to say. The man is somebody I can believe in. Dillon is a tragic figure. All those guys were. They died in the most ignominious ways. They had nothing.... That's what makes Dillon interesting.[18]

In 1959, Arness expanded his analysis of Dillon:

> Matt Dillon is a valid human being. On camera he shows the two sides of his personality that every human being has: his "on stage" character and his "off stage" side. When Dillon is working, he's stern and businesslike, as befits his job. When he's relaxing, taking a drink or eyeing Kitty, he's another kind of person....[19]

By 1971, interviewers were making reference to the obvious similarities between Arness and Dillon, to which Arness responded,

> Well, you know you can't live with a thing like this as closely as you have to over the years without it becoming part of the same thing.... Not

entirely, obviously, but I mean the two have to blend together to a large extent....[20]

One of the key reasons for *Gunsmoke*'s popularity and consequent longevity was Arness. Through the years he received an increasingly favorable appraisal from the critics. Vernon Scott, United Press International correspondent, observed, "Arness is to television what William S. Hart, Tom Mix, and Ken Maynard were to the movies."[21] *TV Guide* writer Dwight Whitney described Arness as "...capable of great toughness and tenderness...."[22] Gerald Nachman wrote in the *New York Daily News* that "Arness' slab-like face and massive outline merges all our memories of frontier lawmen... [He] is still the all-time, all-star marshal, pure, square-shouldered square shooter...."[23]

Perhaps the most detailed analysis of Arness' acting style came from *New York Times* columnist Wallace Markfield in a loving tribute to *Gunsmoke* published after the series had left the air in 1975.

> None ... ever dominated a scene as easily and absolutely as James Arness.... The camera really loved his face, and with good reason: it was a face that would carry intimations of waste, loss and futility.... An enormous man—wearing a Stetson, he is said to stand 7 feet—Arness used every last ungainly line of his body to anchor an archetype in flesh and blood. If he looked good drawing his gun faster and shooting it straighter than anyone else, he looked even better when he did some humdrum piece of physical business—when he tried to shake sleep out of his eyes or trail-dust from his clothes; when he flinched, shuddered and tried to diminish himself under the full blast of sunlight, joint by joint, into a chair; when he battled out of a chair at the sound of a shot or scream. In these and other small ways, we were made to understand, for twenty years, that Matt Dillon's life was mostly labor and exhaustion, but that it was the only life possible to him....[24]

As a Saturday-night television institution, *Gunsmoke* ranked in the Nielsen top-twenty shows from its second season until 1965, and occupied first place from 1957 through 1961. After moving to Monday evenings in 1967, the series returned to the top twenty and remained there until its final season on the air. It was an achievement unmatched by any other television program. Television historians Tim Brooks and Earle Marsh rank *Gunsmoke* the number one series of all time by a wide margin,[25] even though the show was canceled at the end of the 1966-67 season and only revived at the last minute through the personal intervention of CBS chief William Paley.

Arness did not have much time to lament the actual cancellation of *Gunsmoke* in 1975. A few days after the news became public, MGM contacted him about doing a telefilm called *The Macahans*. He fell in love with the script saying, "Forget about Matt Dillon. This Macahan guy's more colorful."[26] Arness was also pleased that John Mantley, who had produced *Gunsmoke* for its last eleven years, and as many from the old crew as were interested and available, would join the new show.

The Macahans was dedicated to "the courage of the simple people who pushed their wagons westward into the wilderness, a breed of people we'll never see again." Frontier scout Zeb Macahan decides after ten years that it is time to visit his family in Bull Run, Virginia. It is 1861 and the Civil War is about to begin. When Zeb reaches home, he sleeps out in the yard because he feels "closed in" by a roof over his head. He finds his brother Tim (Richard Kiley) and Tim's wife, Kate (Eva Marie Saint), yearning to go West and avoid the inevitable clash between North and South.

Shortly after Zeb and Tim leave for Oregon, the war breaks out and their elderly parents perish in the shelling of Bull Run. Tim, concerned for their safety, returns and finds their graves before he is captured by the Union Army and forced into the service. Tim's son Seth (Bruce Boxleitner) turns back to look for his father and finds him dying at Shiloh.

The rest of the Macahans reach Nebraska where they await Tim and Seth's return before pushing on to Oregon. Eventually Seth does join the family, but along the way he has been conscripted into the Army, fought in a bloody campaign, fled the battlefield, been branded a deserter, wounded a lawman, and stolen two horses. The stage has been set for the development of a full-fledged series.

How the West Was Won, the most watched program of the week, premiered to high ratings, as a six-hour miniseries in February 1979. Happy that the television Western was being revived, a *New York Times* critic wrote:

> For many of us, James Arness has been the American West for years...
> Two decades of *Gunsmoke* on television ... tanned the hide of fiction into
> the leather of myth. We wore it, like a pair of boots, in a slow walk toward
> *High Noon*... All right: imagine six hours of *Gunsmoke*. At the same
> time, imagine a James Arness, who wants to ride the high country and
> find places no white man has ever seen before ... in a permanent rage of
> impatience, Arness is just about perfect....[27]

The story of the Macahans resumed with Jeb responsible for his dead brother's widow Kate and her four children: Luke (the eldest—the fugitive who had been called Seth in the original film), Laura, Josh (who had been called Jeb), and Jessie. After the six-hour miniseries, Kate dies and is replaced as the family's mother-figure by Aunt Milly from Boston, played by Fionnula Flanagan. Together and separately they face the dangers and hardships caused at various times by Indians, land barons, bigots, outlaws, nature, and the other perils of an untamed frontier.

The series returned to the ABC schedule in September 1978, billed as "the longest motion picture ever made." More accurately it was the longest single-story television program produced to that time, surpassing *Roots* and *Washington: Behind Closed Doors* from the previous year.

During the 1978-79 season MGM presented twenty hours of connected plot beginning with two three-hour segments produced on a budget of $12 million. Filmed in Colorado, Utah, Arizona, and California, *How the West Was Won* utilized three Indian villages (one Sioux, one Arapaho and one renegade), a Mexican town, a complete frontier town, an Army encampment, a robbers' hideout, a cave, a mine, and Bent's Fort, a historical monument located in La Junta, Colorado. Over 1,700 animals were needed, including over 400 buffalo, a herd of cattle, oxen, mules, burros, pigs, goats, dogs, and cats, and the standard quota of horses. It was truly an ambitious undertaking even by Hollywood standards.

All the expenses and attention to detail paid off. During its first season, *How the West Was Won* earned higher ratings than any recent television Western, finishing the year in seventeenth place on the Nielsen list. It was renewed for another season in a slightly altered format. Each story was completed in a two-hour weekly episode.

Arness insisted that only a Western could have lured him back to series television. "I like what Westerns mean," he explained in an interview. "It's more pleasant, looking back at a simpler time in our history. I even liked it better back in the thirties when I was growing up."[28]

Regarding the character of Zeb Macahan, Arness claimed that he enjoyed portraying the freedom-loving mountain man even more than the straight-laced lawman of *Gunsmoke*:

> Zeb is an old-time frontier character who, I figure, came out to the West in the fur-trapping business in the early 1800s and saw the West when it was truly primitive. He's lived by his wits and experience and skill and that molded the man's character; he's pretty much of a free-spirit kind of guy, doing what he wants, as opposed to living within the law, which is what Matt Dillon has to do. If there's a problem someplace, Zeb's tendency is to jump in and take over and resolve it by whatever means are available, without trying to work it through the law.... Matt was locked into a tighter framework. This guy has a broader scope of activity.[29]

As the critics had noted, Arness seemed "perfectly" cast. The series' creators obviously had him in mind when they developed this description of the series lead character:

> Zeb Macahan was big. Had he been in the habit of standing straight, he'd have stood nearly seven feet tall in his boots. He seldom bothered to try. Thirty-odd years of survival west of the Big Muddy had left Zeb bent out of shape, and too many men, red, and white, had taken a shot at that massive gray head for Zeb to be all that interested in carrying it any higher than he had to.... Not many men who'd tried to kill him were still around these days. The big man moved, when he had to, with the deceptive clumsy grace of a grizzly. When he didn't have to, Zeb moved slow....[30]

Arness' naturally blond hair had been darkened and closely cropped for *Gunsmoke*. For the role of Zeb Macahan of the 1860s, his silver-gray hair hung long and he grew a shaggy mustache. But Arness embodied the mountain man in far more than physical appearance. As the Macahan character, Arness was able to express the less restrained side of his nature—the outdoorsman who delighted in high surf and high slopes, fast cars, and wanderlust. Not many television heroes have possessed the raw strength of a Zeb Macahan, who once killed a trapper crony rather than allow him to be tortured by the Indians. Unlike Matt Dillon, his creed was "what's right is right and wrong is wrong; there are no grays." In his virtues—loyalty, honesty, humor—and in his protective, almost reclusive, nature—Zeb Macahan and James Arness were one and the same person.

Although the plots switched back and forth between the major characters, with one usually focusing on Zeb, one on Luke, and one on Aunt Molly and the other Macahan siblings, occasionally two or all three of the story lines would come together. The focal character, however, was always Zeb Macahan. Whether negotiating with the Indians for the release of a visiting Russian count, helping a mountain man rescue his son from the Indians, or trying to prevent a bloody war between the Army and the Indians, Arness dominated every scene in which he appeared.

An appreciation of the dignity and worth of the Indians the white man slaughtered when settling the West was a recurring theme on *How the West Was Won*. Zeb felt a genuine respect for Indian life and culture. He once had taken an Indian maiden for his bride and she had given him a son. With both now dead, Zeb simply tried to keep the peace between the white and red men.

Early in the series Zeb brought the dead body of his blood brother, Satangkoi, a Dakota chief, to General Philip Sheridan. Satangkoi had committed suicide rather than bring a war on his people that he knew they could not win. Later Zeb led a band of Arapaho braves on a long and dangerous cattle drive over the barren plains so their tribesmen would not starve. And always, when the need arose, Zeb pled the cause of the Indians.

Zeb Macahan had a more open attitude toward women than Matt Dillon. When Zeb found by accident the woman (Vera Miles) whom he had loved twenty years earlier, he had no reservations about bedding down with her. Here Arness had to overcome a natural shyness around women that was more typical of Dillon.

In every other respect, Arness fit as comfortably into the role of Zeb Macahan, a man who was a law unto himself, as he had Matt Dillon, a man who not only had to see that the laws were carried out but live by them himself. As Dillon, he had to hold his own personal feelings or desires in restraint; as Macahan (for the most part), he could do what he felt like doing. There was, however, one overriding similarity between the two characters: each always governed his actions by doing what he felt was right.

In the spring of 1979 *How the West Was Won* dropped to forty-sixth place in the Nielsen ratings and was canceled.[31] Arness was out of work for the first time in nearly twenty-five years.

Arness' unemployment lasted but two years. In November 1981 he was back on the screen again—in his only non–Western role to date—as Jim McClain, a detective on the San Pedro, California, police department. Forced to retire from the force thirteen years earlier due to a leg injury, McClain returned to duty when his friend and fishing partner was robbed and murdered. Convinced that only he could find the killer, he fought to have himself reinstated. McClain preferred the old-fashioned physical methods of combating crime, and he frequently came into conflict with his new boss and his younger partner who had been trained in the modern high-tech methods of crime fighting.

Although the "new" Arness, like the "old," was engaged in preserving law and order, he did not look comfortable driving a car and wearing a suit and tie. Viewers must have agreed; the series was canceled after only sixteen episodes.

Westerns brought Arness out of retirement again in 1987. Between January 1987 and April 1988, Arness appeared in three made-for-television films, all Westerns.

The first was a modified, three-hour remake of John Wayne's historical saga, *The Alamo*. When casting the original film in 1960, Wayne had tried to lure Arness away from *Gunsmoke* long enough to play Jim Bowie. Finally succumbing twenty-seven years later to the urge to "play a role that counts for something," Arness appeared as the famous knife-wielding frontiersman in *The Alamo: 13 Days to Glory*.

Showing a few more wrinkles, Arness' Bowie was a mixture of Matt Dillon and Zeb Macahan. Putting duty and honor above personal safety, he fought with every means at his disposal until the inevitable end. Critics assessed the film, shot in Bracketville, Texas, on the same set that Wayne had used, as "a respectable addition to the Alamo repertory" full of "sweep and color." They found Arness "credible" but "forever stamped" as Marshal Dillon.[32] The role, while not stretching Arness' acting, did bring him back to television.

Arness' second appearance was a *Gunsmoke* reunion film, which had been rumored for some time. It aired on Saturday, September 26, 1987, as *Gunsmoke: Return to Dodge*. Featuring plenty of action, a lot of plotting, some colorful new characters, and beautiful locations, it was a typical *Gunsmoke* story.

In addition to Arness, his hair dark brown again, but longer, Amanda Blake, and Buck Taylor (who had appeared as Newly O'Brien from 1967–75) returned from the original series. Missing were Doc Adams (Milburn Stone died in 1980), Chester (Dennis Weaver was busy filming a new series) and Festus (problems of money and billing caused Ken Curtis' absence).

Dillon had long since retired as marshal and become a trapper. Kitty had left Dodge City earlier for New Orleans, despairing that Matt would ever put aside his badge and six-guns. Newly was now marshal of the apparently larger and more civilized Kansas community.

The choicest role went, however, to Steve Forrest, reprising his role as Mannon, one of the evilest screen "baddies" to come along since Jack Palance had menaced Alan Ladd in *Shane*. Actually, Dillon had killed Mannon in an episode telecast on January 20, 1969. According to the new version, however, Mannon had only been sent to territorial prison. Now he is being released and is out to gain revenge on the ex-lawman and Kitty who had spurned him.

Flashbacks feature clips from old episodes to fill in background and provide viewers with the chance to again see Doc and Festus. Early in the story, Matt is knifed and, after a friendly trapper has brought him to Dodge, Kitty returns to nurse him ("old habits die hard"). The first scene between Matt and Kitty is electric:

MATT: Glad ya came. Yer lookin' great.

KITTY: You cut that out.

MATT: What?

KITTY: You listen ta me cowboy. I've got you out from underneath my fingernails and yer gonna stay out. Do ya hear me?

MATT: Yes, ma'am... Kitty, I understand the rules and all, but it doesn't mean we can't still be friends does it?

KITTY: Friends? Friends? I'm staying at the Long Branch while I'm in town, so when and if you feel up to it, I might even buy you a beer.

The spark is still there.

Later, when Matt leaves to find and save an old friend, he lets Kitty know that "it's really been good" seeing her again and "when all this is over and I get back...," Kitty answers, "I'll be here." After the door closes and he has gone, she poses the rhetorical question, "Aren't I always?" In the only other scene they play together, Matt and Kitty exchange meaningful glances after he has vanquished the brutal Mannon. Then Dillon walks alone down Front Street.

While the relationship between Kitty and Matt seems not to have changed in the least, Dillon appears to be less bound by the moral and legal restraints he faced as a lawman. He taunts Mannon as "fit only to beat up women" and goads him into a gunfight. Then he shoots the outlaw three times. There obviously is more than a bit of Zeb Macahan in the older Matt Dillon.

Viewers apparently enjoyed seeing the *Gunsmoke* gang again because the film ranked in the top ten shows for the week. This lead to four subsequent *Gunsmoke* television films, *Gunsmoke II: The Last Apache* (1990), *Gunsmoke III: To the Last Man* (1992), *Gunsmoke IV: The Long Ride* (1993), and *Gunsmoke V: One Man's Justice* (1994). In each, Arness was featured as Matt Dillon, but without any other cast members from the original series.

All three films, however, did feature guest stars who had appeared in a number of *Gunsmoke* episodes. In *Gunsmoke II*, Michael Learned, reprising her role as Mike Yardner in "Matt's Love Story," writes to Matt asking him to come to her ranch. In a flashback to the earlier show, Matt and Mike are shown kissing, while he is suffering from amnesia. Out of this brief romance came a child—a daughter, Beth, whom neither the television audience nor the marshal knew existed. She has been captured by Apaches, and Mike asks Matt to help rescue her.

With the assistance of an Army scout named Chalk Brighton, who is in love with Mike, they are successful in freeing Beth from the Indian warrior, Wolf, who has taken her for his bride. Richard Kiley, another *Gunsmoke* veteran, appears as Chalk, while Hugh O'Brian (television's Wyatt Earp) plays an Army general.

In the third *Gunsmoke* television movie, Matt finds himself swept up in a bloody feud in Arizona Territory during the 1880s when one of his young drovers is murdered and his cattle rustled. With the help of a veteran lawman named Abel Rose, Matt tracks down and (in a bloody climactic gunfight) kills every member of the gang responsible. Morgan Woodward, who had appeared in eighteen different roles during the twenty-year run of the original series, plays Abel. Pat Hingle (who had been Doc's replacement during the season he missed because of heart surgery) is cast as the chief villain—a retired Army colonel and the tyrannical head of a family of rustlers and killers. In the film's only acknowledgment to *Gunsmoke II*, Amy Stock-Poynton again appears as Matt's daughter, Beth.

To the Last Man did not draw the high ratings (or favorable reviews) that the first two television films did. This may be due to an excessive amount of bloodshed and violence. In *Gunsmoke IV: The Long Ride* (shown on CBS, May 8, 1993), only Amy Stock-Poynton (again as Beth) returns with Arness from earlier *Gunsmokes*. This time Dillon is framed for robbery and murder, and sets out, with the help of an itinerant preacher named John Parsley (likably played by television veteran James Brolin), to clear his name. He must apprehend the trio of baddies responsible before a posse of bounty hunters catches up with him. Ali MacGraw appears as a reformed prostitute-with-a-heart-of-gold. Shot partly on location in Santa Fe, New Mexico, the film is scenic—and violent.

Although *The Long Ride* did not pull in the high ratings that most of the earlier *Gunsmoke* made-for-television films had, it did win its time slot by a large margin, while pleasing most fans and critics. Jeff Jarvis of *TV Guide* wrote:

Thirty-eight years after he first rode out as Matt Dillon, James Arness returns in another movie, and that's a feat worth watching. He has a voice like a dusty old trail and a face that shows 20,000 sunsets; as an admiring sheriff says, "You got a lot of bark on you." Arness makes Jack Palance look like a pup.... The script features more burial plots than plotlines—but who cares? Matt Dillon's back! My score [0 to 10]: 8.[33]

One Man's Justice (which aired on February 10, 1994) again earned respectable ratings. This time Bruce Boxleitner costars with Arness as a traveling salesman who joins Dillon on a search for a 15-year-old boy chasing the robbers who killed his mother. Stock-Poynton reprises her role as Beth and Christopher Bradley returns as her husband Josh. Although the body count was high once again, most critics were pleased. Janette and Bob Anderson of *Trail Dust* (Spring 1994), especially noted Boxleitner's contribution: "Bruce *literally* stole the show with as fine a performance as you're likely to see on a TV Western."

Arness' third 1988 telefilm was a remake of Howard Hawks' classic Western, *Red River* (1948). The film dramatically recreated the first long drive from the plains of southern Texas to the railhead in Abilene, Kansas. It is also the story of the relationship between two strong-willed men—Tom Dunson, a tough old rancher, and his equally stubborn adopted son, Matthew Garth.

Rated by many critics as the best Western ever made, the original *Red River* starred John Wayne and Montgomery Clift. Without any doubt Arness was the best replacement for Wayne the producers could hope to get. The film had been one of Arness' favorites and he was eager to take on a role against type. The arrogant and tyrannical Dunson was basically an unsympathetic character.

While the role had won plaudits for Wayne twenty years earlier ("the best performance of his career to date"),[34] the best Arness could get from critics was "competent" and many felt that Bruce Boxleitner, Arness' capable costar in *How the West Was Won*, was miscast as the neurotic Matt. As John J. O'Connor of the *New York Times* wrote,

> Why not just do a brand new adventure about a cattle drive along the Chisholm Trail and leave *Red River* alone? ... Television is being forced to enter a new stage of awareness when it comes to tinkering with material that has already been produced with skill and imagination. Shabby imitations are likely to be increasingly rejected as more viewers are able— for prices that get lower and lower—to turn to the originals on video cassettes....[35]

The producers of the television version of *Red River* added a unique twist. Trying to make it a paean to television Westerns, they cast Robert Horton (*Wagon Train*), John Lupton (*Broken Arrow*), Guy Madison (*Wild Bill Hickok*), and Ty Hardin (*Bronco*) in small featured roles. The ratings indi-

cated that many viewers did tune in to see that increasingly rare phenome-
non—old-fashioned television Western adventure—and it was good to see
James Arness in a role that differed from his previous roles.

In assessing the career of an actor who has won numerous honors, including an Emmy nomination, and great popularity, including countless fan magazine Western TV star-of-the-year awards, as well as being named "Man of
the Year" by the Hollywood Radio and Television Society in 1973, one must
still deal with the inevitable comparisons to John Wayne. To say that James
Arness has been to the television Western what John Wayne was to the film
Western in no way belittles his accomplishments. From his imposing physical presence and his deliberate manner of speaking to his careful selection of
roles, Arness has emulated Wayne more than any other television actor.

Arness' Western hero was a man of action, so too was Wayne's; Arness'
Western hero was committed obsessively to a cause, so too was Wayne's;
Arness' Western hero was a loner, so too was Wayne's; Arness' Western hero
was a towering source of physical and moral courage, so too was Wayne's;
Arness' Western hero was inner-directed, so too was Wayne's; Arness' Western hero was a charismatic leader, so too was Wayne's; Arness' Western hero
was a sociological father figure and role model, so too was Wayne's; Arness'
Western hero, especially in his later incarnations did not hesitate to choose
"illegitimate" means if he thought it would help him to right a wrong or correct an injustice; so too did Wayne's.[36]

Where the two differed most was in their relationship toward women.
Arness' Western hero was more reserved and respectful than Wayne's, perhaps reflecting Arness' own shy nature.

Arness, always conscious of the similarities between Wayne and himself, "worked mighty hard not to develop any Duke Wayne mannerisms." In
an interview in 1977 he explained, "As great as I consider Duke Wayne, and
I know he could have played the hell out of the part, I had to find my own
style."[37]

Arness has been even more protective of his private life than was Wayne.
He has refused to discuss his failed fifteen-year marriage and the tragic death
of his daughter. His second marriage, to attractive dress-shop owner Janet Sur-
tees in December 1978, was strictly a family affair. His son Rolf served as
best man and his adopted son Craig was the wedding photographer. No one
outside the family was invited.[38]

There was another difference between Arness and his benefactor—Arness
was "determinedly apolitical" except for being a self-proclaimed "radical
environmentalist" who wanted "to save the land and keep it the way it was."[39]
Still Arness was the perfect choice to host and narrate a PBS special on his
friend, *John Wayne Standing Tall*, which aired in March 1989.

More significantly, Arness has created the most enduring Western hero
in the history of television. Surely Matt Dillon is the standard against which

all television cowboy heroes must be judged. And none—not Hopalong Cassidy, nor the Lone Ranger, nor Ben Cartwright, nor Palladin—has had a greater influence on the development of the genre. James Arness has deservedly earned immortality as television's quintessential Western hero.

Notes

1. Gerald Nachman, *New York Daily News* (March 27, 1978).
2. Favius Friedman, "The Case of the Runaway Giant," *Motion Picture Magazine* (Spring 1958), p. 62.
3. *Current Biography* (November 1978), p. 3.
4. Quoted in *Current Biography*, p. 4.
5. Quoted in Friedman, *Motion Picture*, p. 67.
6. Allen Eyles, *John Wayne* (New York 1979), p. 134–135.
7. Quoted in Friedman, *Motion Picture*, p. 67.
8. Friedman, *Motion Picture*, p. 67; *TV Guide*, December 2, 1961, p. 24–25; Robert deRoos, "Private Life of *Gunsmoke* Star," *Saturday Evening Post* (April 12, 1958), p. 108. Dave Gelman, *New York Post* (December 3, 1957), p. M2.
9. Jack Ross Stanley, *A History of the Radio and Television Western Dramatic Series "Gunsmoke"* (unpublished doctoral dissertation, University of Michigan), p. 100.
10. Quoted in Friedman, *Motion Picture*, p. 68.
11. Quoted in deRoos, *Saturday Evening Post*, p. 33.
12. James Arness, "No Trick Horses for Me," *CBS Television Feature* (September 29, 1958), p. 2.
13. Quoted in Friedman, *Motion Picture*, p. 58.
14. Quoted in deRoos, *Saturday Evening Post*, pp. 108, 110.
15. Quoted in Friedman, *Motion Picture,* p. 68.
16. Quoted in Gelman, *New York Post.*
17. Ralph Brauer, *The Horse, the Gun and the Piece of Property* (Bowling Green, 1975), pp. 166–169. Consult SuzAnne and Gabor Barabas, *Gunsmoke: A Complete History* (Jefferson, NC, 1990), for a definitive study of that landmark series.
18. Quoted in Gelman, *New York Post.*
19. James Arness, "Arness Likes *Gunsmoke* Role," *New York Journal-American* (September 28, 1959).
20. Quoted in Ross, *A History of... "Gunsmoke,"* p. 129.
21. Quoted in Ross, *A History of... "Gunsmoke,"* p. 129.
22. Quoted in Ross, *A History of... "Gunsmoke,"* p. 129.
23. Nachman, *New York Daily News* (March 27, 1978).
24. Wallace Markfield, "A Fond Farewell to Matt Dillon, Dodge City and 'Gunsmoke,'" *New York Times* (July 13, 1975), Sec. 2, p. 1. See Gary A. Yoggy, *Riding the Video Range, the Rise and Fall of the Western on Television* (Jefferson, NC, 1995), Ch. IV, for a fuller discussion of the impact of *Gunsmoke* on adult TV Westerns.
25. Tim Brooks and Earle Marsh, *The Complete Directory to Prime Time Network TV Shows*, 4th Ed. (New York, 1988), p. 979.
26. Don Freeman, "Back in the Saddle Again," *TV Guide* (February 5, 1977), p. 14.
27. *New York Times*, February 4, 1977.
28. Quoted in Freeman, *TV Guide*, p. 14.
29. Robert Lindsey, "Zeb Macahan Is More Fun Than Matt Dillon," *New York Times* (September 12, 1978), p. D32.
30. Lou Cameron, *How the West Was Won*, a novel based on the teleplays (New York, 1977), p. 1.

31. J. Fred Macdonald, *Who Shot the Sheriff?* (New York, 1987), p. 123.

32. John Corry, "*'Alamo: 13 Days to Glory,'* on NBC," *New York Times* (April 10, 1988).

33. Jeff Jarvis, "James Arness Rides Again..." *TV Guide* (May 8, 1993), p. 49.

34. Brian Garfield, *Western Films* (New York, 1982), p. 266.

35. John J. O'Connor, "Why Bother Watching a Woeful Remake?" *New York Times* (April 10, 1988).

36. Emanual Levy, *John Wayne: Prophet of the American Way of Life* (Metuchen, NJ, 1988), Chapters 3 and 4.

37. Quoted in Freeman, *TV Guide*, p. 16.

38. Dick Russell, *TV Guide* (February 24, 1979), p. 22.

39. Quoted in Freeman, *TV Guide*, p. 16.

About the Contributors

Jim Collins was born and raised in the state of Wisconsin. At the age of ten he read his first paperback Western—*Top Hand* by Luke Short—and hardcover Western—*The U.P. Trail* by Zane Grey—and immediately fell in love with American History and the Old West. He spent thirteen years in the United States Army and is a veteran of the Vietnam War, where he was twice wounded in action. Collins, under the pen name Jim Miller, is the author of more than thirty traditional Westerns and has written eight nonfiction children's books about the Old West. He is currently working on a new novel of the West.

James Drury is an actor who has adapted successfully to the stage, screen, television and the business world. His film career began in 1954 when he signed a contract with MGM, where he made seven pictures, debuting in *The Blackboard Jungle* as a one day–one line actor. Later, he was featured in *The Last Wagon, Love Me Tender*, and *Bernadine* at 20th Century–Fox. Following a long line of television roles, he was signed for four Disney features: *Elfego Baca, Toby Tyler, Pollyanna*, and *Ten Who Dared*. Shortly before he was chosen to bring to life the archetype of Western heroes in his long running series *The Virginian* he made the award winning Sam Peckinpah film *Ride the High Country* with Joel McCrea and Randolph Scott. During his nine years as *The Virginian* (296 ninety-minute films), Mr. Drury starred in Universal's film *The Young Warriors* and *Breakout* for NBC. He later starred in a television movie of the week, *The Devil and Miss Sarah*. Since moving to Houston, he has been active in business and his interests include real estate, insurance, oil and gas, and finance. His responsibilities include public appearances, instructional and promotion video productions, speaking engagements and extensive travel throughout Texas and the United States.

Jacqueline K. Greb. After traveling and working all over the world (Morocco, Sultanate of Oman, etc.) Jacqueline came back to the United States to pursue a Ph.D. in Western American History at the University of New Mexico. While working on a dissertation about the life and times of Erna Fergusson she took a job with the Smithsonian-Kellogg Project writing museum education programs for Native American museums. This involved working directly with Chief Wilma Mankiller of the Cherokee Nation and the Cherokee Heritage Center. The dissertation is still in the works while Jacqueline works as technology systems manager for Fruita Middle School in western Colorado and a professor of educational technology for Adams State College.

Tom W. Hoffer is professor of communications at Florida State University. He has written extensively on film, especially the Western genre.

Gary Kramer is director of employee relations at Ball State University in Muncie, Indiana. His interest in Western movies, particularly the films of the B Western genre, began at an early age, and was renewed with the advent of the various Western film festivals that began in the early 1970s. Along with his friend Ray White, he organized the East Central Indiana Western Film Club that has met monthly for many years. Although career commitments limit his time, he hopes to do additional writing about Western films in the future.

R. Philip Loy is professor of political science, chairperson of the Political Science Department and associate dean of the Division of Social Sciences at Taylor University, Upland, Indiana. He has presented papers on Western films at the Popular Culture Association annual meetings. Mr. Loy is also a member of the Politics and Film section of the American Political Science Association. His articles on Western films and personalities have appeared in both popular and academic publications. He is the author of a forthcoming volume, *Hoofprints in the Dust: Western Films and American Life, 1930–1954*.

Archie P. McDonald is a regent's professor of history at Stephen F. Austin State University, executive director of the East Texas Historical Association, editor of the *East Texas Historical Journal*, and past president of the Texas State Historical Association. He is the editor of *Make Me a Map of the Valley: The Journal of Stonewall Jackson's Topographer* (1973), judged by *Civil War Times Illustrated* and *The Civil War Magazine* as one of the 100 best books on the Civil War; and *Shooting Stars: Heroes and Heroines of Western Film* (1987). He published *Historic Texas* in 1996.

Richard Robertson has taught history at the University of Mississippi and Auburn University in Montgomery, Alabama, where he was director of the Humanities Resource Center. He contributed "Just Dreamin' Out Loud: The Westerns of Burt Lancaster" for *Shooting Stars* (1987). He presently resides in St. Louis, Missouri.

Lane Roth, associate professor of communications at Lamar College in Beaumont, Texas, is author of *Film Semiotics, Metz, and Leone's Trilogy* (1983), the first volume to analyze the work of Italian director Sergio Leone. He is now working on *The Power of Imagination: Archetypal Images in Science Fiction Films* for Greenwood Press, applying Jungian analytical psychology. His interdisciplinary research has been published in refereed journals of the humanities, philosophy, English, cinema, and communication.

Sandra Schackel, a University of New Mexico graduate, is associate professor of history at Boise State University where she teaches women's history and history of the American West. She is author of *Social Housekeepers: Women Shaping Policy in New Mexico 1920–1940* published by University of New Mexico Press in 1992. She has written about the roles of women in Western films, in *Shooting Stars: Heroes and Heroines of Western Film* (Indiana University Press, 1987). Her current popular culture project is an examination of the impact of Elvis Presley on teenage girls in the 1950s.

Michael K. Schoenecke teaches film and popular culture in the English Department at Texas Tech University. He has published chapters and articles on such diverse subjects as film, architecture, sports, and popular music. He is presently editing a book on sport and culture as well as writing a book on golf's "holy books," and he serves as associate editor of *Reviews in Popular Culture and American Culture*.

William E. Tydeman III is currently the associate dean of libraries for Special Collections at Texas Tech University. He holds a Ph.D in American Studies from the University of New Mexico where he studied with the late historian of photography Beaumont Newhall. Tydeman's research interests and publications concentrate on the cultural history of the American West. He is co-editor of *Reading into Photography* and is completing a study of Route 66 in the Southwest.

Ray White is professor of history emeritus at Ball State University in Muncie, Indiana, where he developed and taught a course on the low-budget Western. He has presented papers at meetings of the Western History and Popular Culture associations and published in *The Indiana Media Journal, The History Teacher, Under Western Skies* and *Favorite Westerns*. He authored "Ken Maynard: Devil on Horseback" for *Shooting Stars* (1987) and is in the process of finishing *Roy Rogers and Dale Evans: A Bio-Bibliography*.

Gary A. Yoggy is a professor of history at Corning Community College, Corning, New York, where he has taught since 1963. In 1981 he developed a course on the history and culture of the American West. He presented the first in a series of papers on television Westerns at the annual meeting of the Popular Culture Association in 1984. Among his published writings on this subject are *Riding the Video Range: The Rise and Fall of the Western on Television* (McFarland, 1995), "When Television Wore Six-guns: Cowboy Heroes on TV" in *Shooting Stars* (1987), "Prime Time Bonanza! The Television Western" in *Wanted, Dead or Alive: The American West in Popular Culture* (1996), and fifteen entries on various television Westerns for *The Encyclopedia of Popular Culture*. Professor Yoggy has been an active member of the PCA since 1984 and has served as vice president and area chair of the West and Westerns section.

Index